the CELTS

the CELTS

Bronze Age to New Age

John Haywood

PEARSON
Longman

Harlow, England • London • New York • Boston • San Francisco • Toronto
Sydney • Tokyo • Singapore • Hong Kong • Seoul • Taipei • New Delhi
Cape Town • Madrid • Mexico City • Amsterdam • Munich • Paris • Milan

PEARSON EDUCATION LIMITED

Edinburgh Gate
Harlow CM20 2JE
United Kingdom
Tel: +44 (0)1279 623623
Fax: +44 (0)1279 431059
Website: www.pearsoned.co.uk

First edition published in Great Britain in 2004

© Pearson Education Limited 2004

The right of John Haywood to be identified as author
of this work has been asserted by him in accordance
with the Copyright, Designs and Patents Act 1988.

ISBN 0 582 50578 X

British Library Cataloguing-in-Publication Data
A CIP catalogue record for this book can be obtained from the British Library

Library of Congress Cataloging-in-Publication Data
Haywood, John, 1956–
    The Celts: from Bronze Age to New Age/John Haywood.—1st ed.
        p. cm.
    Includes bibliographical references and index.
    ISBN 0–582–50578–X
    1. Celts. I. Title.

    D70.H39 2004
    909′.04916—dc22

                                                2004040141

10 9 8 7 6 5 4 3 2 1
08 07 06 05 04

Set by 35 in 10.5/12pt Bembo
Printed and bound in China
PPLC/01
The Publishers' policy is to use paper manufactured from sustainable forests.

Contents

List of plates

Acknowledgements

We are grateful to the following for permission to reproduce copyright material:

Plates 1, 4, 5, 10, 12, 15, 17, 19, 24, 28 and 33 Bridgeman Art Library, www.bridgeman.co.uk; Plate 2 The British Museum; Plate 7 Werner Forman Archive; Plate 8 Humber Archaeology Partnership and BM Photographic Services; Plate 13 English Heritage Photographic Library; Plate 20 Ffotograff; Plates 21 and 23 © Crown Copyright reproduced courtesy of Historic Scotland; Plates 30 and 35 Getty Images/Hulton Archive; Plate 37 PA Photos.

In some instances we have been unable to trace the owners of copyright material, and we would appreciate any information that would enable us to do so.

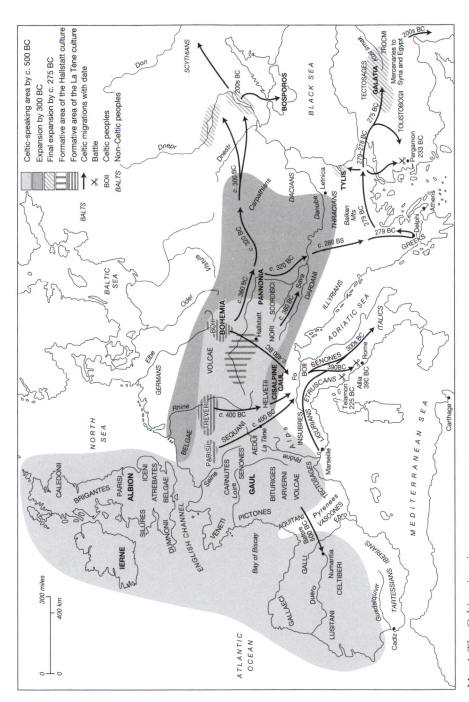

Map 1 The Celtic migrations

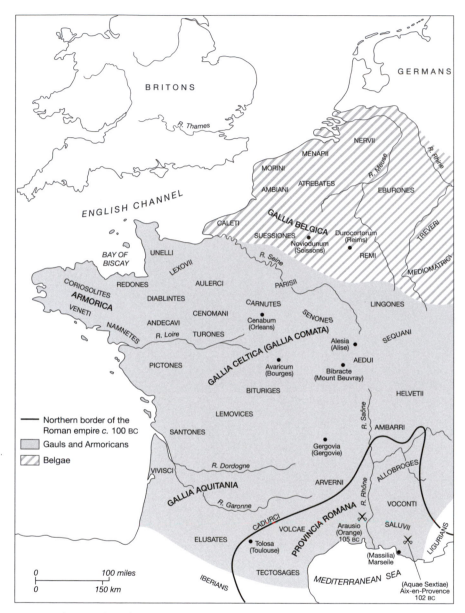

Map 2 The peoples of Gaul in the late Iron Age

— Northern limit of Roman conquest AD84

CORNOVII

SMERTAE

CAERENI

CARNONACAE

CREONES

DECANTAE

TAEXALI

VACOMAGI

CALEDONES

VERTURIONES

VENICONES

Firth of Forth

NORTH SEA

EPDII

DAMNONI

Antonine
Wall

VOTADINI

Firth of
Clyde

SELGOVAE

VENNICONII

ROBOGDI
(DÁL RIATA)

NOVANTAE

Hadrian's Wall

R. Tyne

ERNAEI

Navan

DARINI

Solway Firth

CARVETII

BRIGANTES

NAGNATAE

VOLUNTI
(ULAID)

PARISI

EBDANI

IRISH
SEA

ANGLESEY

SETANTII

Tara

Drumanagh

CAUCI

DECEANGLI

R. Trent

CORITANI

AUTEINI

MANAPII

GANGANI

R. Shannon

USDIAE

ORDOVICES

R. Severn

ICENI

GANGANI

CORIONDI

CORNOVII

TRINOVANTES

VELLABORI

BRIGANTES

DOBUNNI

CATUVELLAUNI

IVERNI

DEMETAE

St Albans
(Verulamium)

Colchester

SILURES

R. Thames

(Camulodunum)

London
(Londinium)

BELGAE

ATREBATES

CANTIACI

REGNI

DUROTRIGES

Fishbourne

DUMONII

Maiden
Castle

ENGLISH CHANNEL

0   150 miles

0   200 km

Map 3 The peoples of Britain and Ireland in the late Iron Age

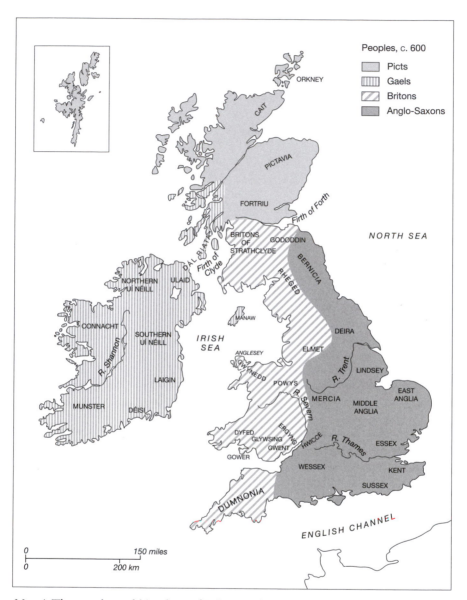

Map 4 The peoples and kingdom of Britain and Ireland *c.* AD 600

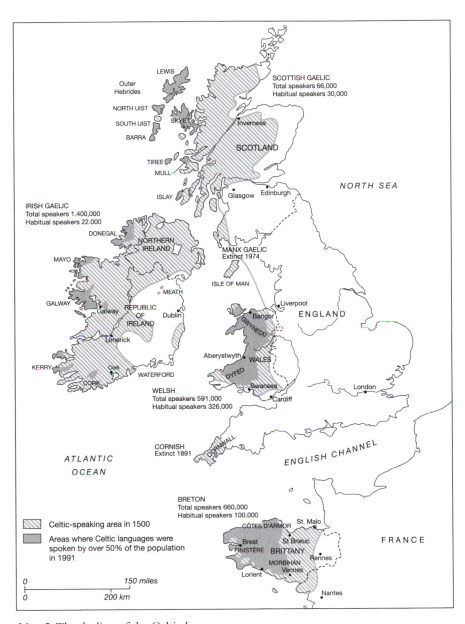

Map 5 The decline of the Celtic languages

INTRODUCTION

Few European peoples have proved quite as durable as the Celts. From obscure beginnings in the Bronze Age, the Celts came to dominate the European continent in the Iron Age before their neighbours, the Germans, Dacians and Romans, forced them into a fighting retreat. By the first century AD the Celts were confined to Europe's Atlantic fringe, yet they outlasted the Romans and the Dacians and survived to play an influential role in the cultural life of early medieval Europe. By the later Middle Ages, Europe's last autonomous Celtic societies were under constant pressure from the English, Lowland Scots and the French and all had been suppressed by the middle of the eighteenth century. At this point, when their extinction seemed inevitable, European intellectuals began to take a serious interest in Celtic history, language and culture. Romanticised by poets, artists and nationalists, the Celts fired the popular imagination and began a remarkable revival of Celtic identity, which continues to this day.

Much recent academic writing about the Celts has focused on the nature of the Celtic identity: did the ancient Celts really exist, or are they simply a modern construct? Are the modern Celts real Celts or just an invention of the Romantic era? With some reservations, which I explain in the book, I am satisfied that both are real. For those people who do not believe in the ancient Celts, their survival into the modern age is not an issue (the modern Celts are simply an interesting cultural phenomenon). Those people who do believe in the ancient Celts rather take their survival into the modern world for granted, or, if they are romantically or nationalistically inclined, explain it in terms of heroic struggle against the odds. But, when you think about it, the fact that there were still people around in the Romantic era who could rediscover themselves (or reinvent themselves, if you are a sceptic) as Celts is really rather remarkable. After all, where are most of the other peoples of Iron Age Europe? The Etruscans, Iberians, Illyrians, Thracians, Dacians, even the Romans, have all vanished. Rather than looking at Celtic history as a two-millennia-long decline, there is a real story of survival there.

The survival of the Celts over more than 2,500 years requires a proper consistent and systematic explanation. Historians of the Celts have generally been more interested in explaining why they were conquered and assimilated, rather than why they resisted conquest and assimilation so successfully for so long, and their conclusions are often mutually contradictory. For example, the Gauls' decentralised tribal society is supposed to have allowed the Romans to divide and conquer but early medieval Ireland's similarly decentralised tribal society is supposed to have made it impossible for the Vikings to conquer and hold territory, bar a few fortified enclaves. Then when we come to later medieval and early modern Ireland, we are back to Irish disunity as the reason for the English conquest.

As an early medievalist, I have always been struck by the way that it was the well-run kingdoms that got conquered most easily. Charlemagne conquered the outwardly powerful Lombard kingdom of Italy in a single campaign, yet it took him 25 years to conquer the pagan and still tribal Saxons. England in 1066 was arguably the best-run kingdom in western Europe and the Normans conquered it after just one battle. But when the Normans tried to repeat the feat in Wales and Ireland, their success was quite limited, despite enjoying a clear superiority both on the battlefield and in the art of fortification building. What was going on was this. In a centralised kingdom, where power and leadership are concentrated in few hands, 'all' an invader has to do is knock out that elite and step into its shoes to take over completely. This is what happened to England in 1066. Where power and authority are decentralised this cannot be done. Early medieval Ireland is a perfect example. Not only was it divided up into dozens of sub-kingdoms and over-kingdoms but all of these kingdoms had very extended royal lineages. There was no way that the Irish were going to unite to fight off an invader and that makes early medieval Ireland look weak, and in a way it was. The lack of unity meant that the Vikings and Normans could raid and plunder at will, but actually holding, controlling and settling land with your own people is quite another matter. Who was there to negotiate a lasting peace with? What institutions of government were there to be taken over and used to control the natives? How do you wipe out the elite to deprive discontented natives of leadership? Kill an Irish king in battle, together with his sons and even their sons too, and that was hardly a beginning. In early medieval Ireland there was an almost infinite supply of credible royal claimants to lead resistance. Though they both won most of the battles they fought, the Vikings stayed cooped up in their walled towns on the coast, while the Normans did conquer territory but were similarly dependent on fortifications. Once the Irish had learned to avoid fighting them on their own terms, the Anglo-Normans could rule wherever they had an army or a castle and that was it. Had power and authority been as centralised in Ireland in 1170 as it was in England in 1066 it would surely have been conquered just as easily.

Decentralisation was a hidden strength for the Irish, and if so in the early Middle Ages, why not at other times too?

The Romans had an incredibly effective battle-winning army but, just as the Normans did, they found it a lot easier to conquer centralised, hierarchical urbanised societies than decentralised tribal societies. Egypt, with a 3,000-year-long tradition of centralised government, was taken over without even a fight. What a contrast to their conquest of Celtic Spain. For nearly 200 years the Romans had an average 20,000–25,000 troops engaged against the Spanish Celts every year. In the same amount of time the Romans conquered the entire eastern Mediterranean. And Celtic Spain never came close to uniting against the Romans. And where did the Roman war machine finally run out of steam in western Europe? Northern Britain, Ireland and Germany: all areas where very decentralised, tribal societies prevailed. The significance of this is emphasised by a consideration of Caesar's conquest of Gaul. By 58 BC Gaul was actually becoming a very civilised place; it was still tribal but state institutions were emerging and society was narrowly hierarchical. For six years Gallic resistance was uncoordinated and Caesar had to race from one end of Gaul to the other putting down uprisings with no end in sight. Then in 52 BC Vercingetorix united the Gauls and concentrated almost all their armed strength at Alesia, where the Roman army smashed it in a few weeks. The Gallic war was almost over. The Gauls would have done much better without Vercingetorix.

The nature of Roman and medieval English colonialism adds weight to the conclusion that disunity was not a decisive weakness for the Celts. The Roman empire depended on the cooperation of the provincials; it simply could not afford to impose direct coercive military government on its provinces. Once they were conquered, the local elites had to be persuaded to take on the task of local government. The more authority had been concentrated in these elites before the conquest, the easier the task was. It also helped if the area had an intensive agricultural system (arable rather than pastoral) with a settled peasantry that was already being efficiently exploited by the elite. Gaul in 58 BC and southern Britain in AD 43 satisfied these requirements: it was both practical and profitable for the Romans to conquer them. Northern Britain, Ireland and Germany did not and this made them difficult and expensive to conquer. It follows from this that, had Gaul been more united, that is more centralised, than it was in 58 BC, it would have been even easier for the Romans to conquer it. Only if the Gauls had developed a more efficient military system than the Romans could the outcome have been any different. Like the Romans, the English found it hard to conquer and hold places where they could not impose an English social and economic system. Like the Romans, the English expected their conquests to pay for themselves, as they simply could not afford prolonged military occupations. The more fertile parts of South Wales and south-eastern Ireland were well suited to the imposition of the manorial system and so were attractive to English settlement. North Wales and western and northern Ireland were not. Of course, all of Wales and Ireland were eventually conquered by the English, but the cost was enormous, and by the end of the sixteenth century the English had simply given up on the idea that the Irish could ever be assimilated, so they resorted, with limited success, to ethnic cleansing.

So, these are the interacting themes that run consistently through Celtic history for nearly 2,000 years. One is the way their decentralised social structures made them difficult to conquer, even when faced by an enemy with a vastly superior military system. The other is the limitations of their enemies' colonial systems, which could not easily assimilate decentralised societies even after they had been beaten in battle. These are the reasons why the Celts survived that this book sets out to explore.

1

ORIGINS OF THE CELTS

The Danube has its source in the country of the Celts, near the city of Pyrêné, and runs through the middle of Europe, dividing it into two portions. The Celts live beyond the Pillars of Hercules, and border on the Cynesians, who dwell at the extreme west of Europe.

Herodotus, *Histories* (c. 444 BC)

The Celts have proved an amazingly durable group of peoples. In ancient times the Celts were contemporaries of the Romans, Iberians, Illyrians, Thracians, Dacians, Etruscans, Ligurians, Scythians, Greeks and Germans among many others. Only the Celts, Greeks and Germans are still with us. Defining the Celts through their long existence is not easy. There have been such enormous cultural, technological and social changes that the modern Celts would be completely unrecognisable to their ancient forebears. Little survives of the culture of the ancient Celts and there was even a long period – well over a thousand years – when the name 'Celt' fell out of use completely before being revived in the eighteenth century. The strongest and most widely accepted definition is based on language, which is the one sure thread of continuity linking the ancient Celts with their modern descendants: the Celts are people who speak Celtic languages. In ancient times these peoples included the Gauls, Belgae, Celtiberians, Lusitanians and Galatians, and the ancient Britons and Irish.

The Celtic identity

The word 'Celt' (Greek *Keltoi*, Latin *Celtae*) was first used by Greek authors about 2,500 years ago to describe the barbarian tribes that lived inland from the Greek colony of Massalia (Marseille). The Greeks soon expanded their use of the word to describe all the barbarian peoples of Europe north of the Alps, including some, like the Franks, who are not now considered to be Celts. The Greeks also used another name,

'Galatians' (Galatoi), interchangeably with 'Celt' specifically to describe those Celtic-speaking peoples of central Europe who invaded Greece and Anatolia in the third century BC. The Romans used a similar word, 'Gaul' (Galli) to describe the continental Celtic-speaking peoples. The origins of all three words are unknown but all are likely to be Celtic as they appear as elements in tribal names (Gallaeci, Celtici, Celtiberi), personal names (Celtius), and even place names (Celti). Julius Caesar tells us that 'Celt' was also used as a collective name by some of the Gaulish tribes. These were the original Celts encountered by the Greeks of Massalia. However, it was never the case that all of the peoples we now regard as being Celtic ever described themselves as such. Although they are now regarded as Celts, the ancient Britons never described themselves as being either Celtic or Gaulish but saw themselves as a quite separate people, as the Romans too saw them, despite recognising great similarities of language and custom. As for the ancient Irish, they did not even have a common identity for themselves until the early Middle Ages, when they adopted the name *Gaidel* (in modern Gaelic *Gaedheal*) from *Guoidel* ('savages'), the Britons' name for the people of Ireland. The custom of describing all the Celtic-speaking peoples collectively as 'Celts' is actually quite recent, dating only to the eighteenth century. Because it was not used historically by the Celtic-speaking peoples to describe themselves collectively, some modern historians and archaeologists argue that the idea of the Celts as a people is simply a modern construct. Historians and archaeologists have imposed an artificial unity on what was really a diverse group of peoples with no sense of common identity. If the politically correct position is taken, that the only name which can justifiably be used to describe a people is the one they use themselves, then we would have to agree with the archaeologist Simon James that there is no justification for describing the ancient Britons and Irish as Celts and that the term is fairly meaningless even when applied to Iron Age continental Europe. This is a position that understandably infuriates modern Celts, most of whom hail from Britain and Ireland, as they see it as an attempt to deny their ancient roots and write the people they regard as their ancestors out of history. The view taken here is that the sceptics are being overly pedantic. There objectively was a major group of peoples in Iron Age Europe who spoke closely related languages and who shared much the same religious beliefs, art styles, fashions in dress and weapons, social structures and values. This accumulation of shared characteristics does make it meaningful to use a common name to describe these peoples, as well as those modern peoples who are descended from them.

When the Celts first emerged from prehistoric obscurity in the fifth century BC they were already a widespread group of peoples. Celtic was the language spoken across most of western Europe, from Austria and Bohemia, across southern Germany and France, to Britain, Ireland and the Iberian Peninsula. How the Celts came to be there and where they originated is far from clear. The ancient Greek writers, such as the geographer Hecateus and the historian Herodotus, who wrote the earliest accounts of the Celtic lands, have nothing to say on the subject and, as they never developed a fully literate culture, the Celts were never able to record their own origin myths and legends and they are now irretrievably lost. In the centuries that followed, the Greeks traded with the Celts, fought with them and employed them as mercenaries and slaves, but if they ever asked them about their origins, they certainly did not think the answers worth recording. After all, what could a Celt know? They could not even speak properly – in Greek of course – but simply made incomprehensible bar-bar noises, from which we have inherited the habit of describing those we perceive to be uncivilised as 'barbarians'. The Greeks preferred to explain the genesis of the Celts by inventing colourful etymological myths. According to one of these myths, recorded by the historian Appian of Alexandria, Polyphemus, the infamous Sicilian Cyclops, and his wife Galatea had three sons, Celtus, Galas and Illyrius, who all emigrated from Sicily and ruled over peoples who came to be named after them, Celts, Galatians and Illyrians (the ancestors of the Albanians). Another story, recorded by Parthenius (first century BC), is that Keltine, the beautiful daughter of King Bretannos, fell in love with Hercules while he was herding the cattle of Geryon from Erythreia. Keltine hid the cattle and refused to tell Hercules where they were unless he made love to her. Hercules did not take much persuading and from their union a son was born. He was named Keltos and it was from him that the Celts descended. The Romans were not much better than the Greeks. According to Caesar, the Gauls claimed to be descended from an underworld god to whom he gives the Roman name Dis Pater (Pluto). What his Celtic name was Caesar does not say, because the idea of doing so would not have occurred to him. Romans believed that their gods were universal but that other peoples knew them by different names that would have meant nothing to his audience. The historian Tacitus confirmed this indifference when he wrote that it was only to be expected that nobody bothered to enquire into the origins of barbarous peoples.

The archaeological record shows that at the time the Greeks first became aware of their existence the Celts already possessed a sophisticated aristocratic culture characterised by advanced iron and bronze working skills and a distinctive style of decorative art. This earliest recognisable Celtic culture was the Hallstatt culture, named for an Iron Age cemetery in the Austrian Alps excavated in the nineteenth century. The graves, over 2,000 of them, contained a wealth of offerings for the dead that revealed an aristocratic warrior society with far-flung trading connections that reached as far as the Baltic and North Africa. It was through these connections that the existence of the Celts had become known to the Greeks. The Iron Age Hallstatt culture did not spring into existence fully formed: it was the product of a long cultural tradition, which can be traced back through several phases to around 1200 BC when it began to develop as a central European variant of the widespread middle Bronze Age Urnfield culture. Back beyond that, the Celts become archaeologically invisible. Yet Celts, or at least Celtic-speaking people, must already have existed for over 1,000 years by this time.

The Celtic languages

The Celtic languages are a branch of the Indo-European family of languages, which includes Greek, Latin, Iranian, Urdu, Hindi and the modern Romance, Germanic and Slavic languages. Today, Celtic has the smallest number of speakers of any of the Indo-European language groups but around 300 BC it was probably the most widespread language group in Europe, being spoken from the river Dnepr to the Atlantic Ocean. Celtic exists in two forms, which both originated in prehistoric times, p-Celtic and q-Celtic. In ancient times q-Celtic was spoken in Iberia and Ireland, spreading to Scotland and the Isle of Man in the early Middle Ages. P-Celtic, which was the more widespread, was spoken in Britain, Gaul, northern Italy, central Europe and Anatolia. The ancient forms of q-Celtic included Hispano-Celtic and Goidelic (the ancestor of modern Irish, Scottish and Manx Gaelic), while p-Celtic included Gaulish, Lepontic and Brithonic (the ancestor of modern Welsh, Breton and Cornish). The division into p- and q-Celtic is based on phonological differences, as seen, for instance, between Welsh *map* ('son') and its Gaelic equivalent *mac*.

The Indo-European languages were not originally indigenous to Europe. The earliest known languages of Europe were all completely unrelated to the Indo-European languages. Some, such as Minoan, Etruscan and Iberian, are known from inscriptions; the existence of others can be inferred from place names or words in later languages. Probably the only survivor of these early languages is Euskara, the language of the Basques: Indo-European languages had displaced all the others by the early first millennium AD. The modern Indo-European languages are all descended from a common ancestor that is known to linguists as Proto-Indo-European. Though other homelands have been proposed, notably Anatolia, most linguists believe that the original Indo-European speakers were a nomadic pastoralist people who lived on the steppes of western Central Asia around 4000 BC. The language was subsequently spread by migrations into India, the Middle East and Europe, where it began to diversify into its modern daughter languages as different groups settled down and lost contact with one another. As it is known that Indo-European languages were being spoken in Europe soon after 2000 BC, linguists argue that these migrations must have taken place some time in the third or fourth millennium BC. Many attempts have been made to identify a specific archaeological culture with the early Indo-Europeans. The best candidate is the Yamnaya culture, which flourished *c.* 3500–2500 BC on the steppes north of the Caspian Sea. The Yamnaya people were the earliest to combine pastoralism (sheep, cattle and horses) with wheeled vehicles. This mobility allowed them to adopt a migratory lifestyle, moving their flocks and herds long distances across the steppes in search of fresh pastures. By 2500 BC groups of Yamnaya people had spread east of the Urals onto the Asian steppes and west across the Ukrainian steppes into south-east Europe, which is compatible with the linguistic evidence for the arrival of Indo-European speakers in Europe. Recently discovered mummies from the Tarim Basin in Chinese Turkestan show that tall, fair-skinned, light-haired people who tattooed their skin and wore tartan were living on the steppes 4,000 years ago. Though their appearance fits closely with descriptions of the ancient Celts, these people were not Celts but Tocharians, a now extinct Indo-European-speaking nomad people. Through contacts with these people the early Chinese learned of bronze, wheeled vehicles and domesticated horses.

Exactly when and where the Celtic languages developed from Proto-Indo-European is a matter of dispute. Most linguists believe that the Celtic languages probably emerged in approximately the area of central Europe that the Hallstatt culture developed in and that they were subsequently spread to western Europe by migrants who displaced or, more likely, assimilated the indigenous population. The spread of ornamental metalwork styles, such as the Hallstatt style, is seen as material evidence of these migrations. Critics of this view argue that the evidence of prehistoric Celtic migrations is far from conclusive. Ornamental metalwork styles, religious beliefs and burial customs could just as easily have been spread as a result of trade and social contacts as by migrating peoples. It was once believed, for example, that widespread cultural changes that marked the beginning of the Iron Age in Britain were the result of Celtic immigration. Now it is known, from excavations of sites that span the transition from the Bronze Age to the Iron Age, such as Runnymede Bridge on the river Thames, that these changes were entirely indigenous developments. It may or may not be significant in this respect that the ancient Britons regarded themselves as the aboriginal population of Britain. There is also a growing appreciation of the way that ethnic groups expand as much by recruitment and assimilation as by biological reproduction. This is supported by an increasing body of evidence for a high degree of genetic continuity in European populations between the end of the Ice Age and the Migration Period at the beginning of the Middle Ages. This seems to rule out the possibility of large-scale prehistoric Celtic migrations to Britain and Ireland, for example (though not smaller-scale folk movements, which certainly did take place). Archaeologists, especially in Britain, are now gripped by a doctrine of immobilism that virtually denies any important role to migrations as agents of cultural change. But if there were no migrations of Celtic-speaking peoples, how did Gaul, Spain, Britain and Ireland become Celtic-speaking?

The archaeologist Colin Renfrew has proposed an alternative theory that explains the spread of Celtic languages without recourse to migrations. Renfrew proposes that the original Indo-European home-land was not in Central Asia but in Anatolia, which before the arrival of the Turks in the Middle Ages was an Indo-European-speaking area. Proto-Indo-European was introduced to south-east Europe from Anatolia by the first farmers who arrived there around 7000 BC, and was subsequently spread, along with the farming way of life, to most of Europe by 4000 BC. Proto-Indo-European's European daughter lan-guages, including the Celtic languages, then developed across much the same areas that they were spoken in at the beginning of historical times. In other words, Gaulish could have developed from Proto-Indo-European in Gaul, Brithonic in Britain, Hispano-Celtic in Iberia and so on. Although it has an elegant simplicity, and fits the archaeological evidence, Renfrew's theory is not acceptable to linguists on the grounds that they believe that Proto-Indo-European could not have been spoken as early as 7000 BC. The question of prehistoric Celtic migrations there-fore remains open. However, while there can be little doubt that the culture of the Celts spread more widely than their DNA, we should be wary of ruling out prehistoric Celtic migrations when their propensity to migrate in historical times is so well attested.

Bronze Age Europe

Hierarchical, aristocratic societies, like those of the earliest historical Celts, began to develop in northern Europe during the Bronze Age (c. 2500 BC–750 BC), the period in which the use of metal tools and weapons first became common. The earliest use of metals in Europe dates back to as long ago as around 6000 BC. At first only those metals, such as gold and copper, were used which occur naturally in their native form (i.e. as pure metal, not as ore). The technique of extracting metal from copper ore by smelting was first used in Europe in the Balkans c. 4500 BC. The technique may have been invented quite independently in Poland, southern Spain and south-west Ireland, where copper smelt-ing began a few centuries later. Copper and gold are both too soft to make useful tools and they were used mainly to make personal orna-ments. Metal tools only began to replace stone tools in everyday use with the invention of bronze, a hard alloy made by adding small amounts of arsenic or tin to copper during the smelting process. Bronze was first made in the Middle East in the fourth millennium BC but it seems to have been invented independently in central Europe c. 2400 BC. Within a thousand years, bronze metallurgy had spread throughout Europe. This new technology must have seemed almost magical to Bronze Age Europeans, a precious gift from the gods. Enormous quan-tities of weapons, tools and other artefacts were given back to the gods, deposited as thank offerings in pits or bogs by a grateful people.

The adoption of bronze led to a great increase in long-distance trade within Europe. While most places have supplies of stone suitable for tool making, copper ore is much less widespread and cassiterite (tin ore) is quite rare. Formerly self-sufficient communities had to trade if they wished to obtain supplies of metals. The increase in trade created ideal circumstances for the easy exchange of ideas. Metals, if they were not traded as ingots, were traded as finished artefacts, so knowledge of new types of tools or new decorative styles spread quickly, promoting considerable uniformity of material culture across much of Europe. By around 1000 BC the many different cultures of early Bronze Age times had been replaced in most of central and western continental Europe by the Urnfield complex of cultures, which is named for its distinctive burial practices. Bodies were cremated and the ashes placed in pottery funerary urns for burial in huge flat grave cemeteries containing hundreds or even thousands of graves. One of the largest Urnfield cemeteries, at Kelheim in southern Germany, contained over 10,000 graves. Urnfields first appeared c. 1350 BC in Hungary, spreading from there into Poland, Germany, Austria, Switzerland, Belgium, France, Italy and Spain. The spread of the Urnfield cultures across western Europe is seen by some as evidence of Celtic migrations from their hypothetical central European homeland, but it has proved impossible to assign the Urnfield cultures to any particular ethnic group. These cultures represent an ethnically and linguistically varied group of peoples, which probably numbered early Celtic-speaking peoples among them. The European Bronze Age began to come to an end around 1200 BC with the introduction of ironworking to Greece from Anatolia, where it had been invented about 300 years earlier. Iron keeps an edge better than bronze, and it was much less costly because iron ore is very common indeed, especially bog iron ore, easily extractable rusty deposits found in bogs, which were widely exploited in ancient and medieval times. From Greece ironworking spread north through the Balkans and west along the Mediterranean trade routes to reach central Europe and Spain by around 750 BC. By 500 BC ironworking was practised throughout Europe.

While the early farming societies of the Neolithic Age had been relatively egalitarian, that is lacking in great disparities of wealth and status, Bronze Age societies developed dominant social elites. These developments are most clear in changing burial practices. Burial in the megalithic tombs of the Neolithic was communal, but in the Bronze Age burials reflected the status of the individual. Members of the social elite were interred with rich offerings of jewellery, weapons and armour, while the common folk were buried with few or no offerings: a member of the elite might have his or her grave marked by an earth barrow, while the graves of the common folk were unmarked. These important social changes were probably a consequence of the increase in trade. Whoever could take control over the trade, production and use of metal tools and weapons could secure for themselves and their families a position of considerable power and authority in their community. As societies became more hierarchical, warrior elites and ruling chieftains appeared. The emergence of social elites was a great stimulus to craftsmanship. Fine weapons and armour, jewellery, religious cult objects and luxury tableware made of gold, silver and bronze were produced so that the elite could display – and so reinforce – their superior wealth and status. The later Bronze Age saw increasing militarisation in western Europe, with the appearance of hillforts and defended lake settlements, and the introduction of new types of weapon, like the bronze slashing sword. Possession of one of these highly specialised and costly weapons made the owner instantly recognisable as a member of the social elite. Anthropologists describe this kind of hierarchical aristocratic society as a 'chiefdom' and it was typical of the Celts through much of their recorded history: the Celtic chiefdoms of the Scottish Highlands survived into the eighteenth century AD. Most of the peoples described by Classical Mediterranean writers as 'barbarians', such as the Germans, Dacians, Huns and many others, also had this type of social structure.

The Hallstatt Celts

The earliest material culture that is generally recognised as belonging to the Celts is the Hallstatt culture, which spans the late Bronze and early Iron Ages. The culture takes its name from the cemetery of an ancient salt-mining community in the Austrian Alps, which was excavated between 1846 and 1863. Hallstatt became wealthy from the salt trade, and the graves of its inhabitants contained rich offerings, including long slashing swords that the excavators immediately recognised from descriptions of Celtic weaponry in ancient Greek sources. Appropriately, although Hallstatt sounds very Germanic, it is actually a Celtic place name, meaning 'salt place'. The Hallstatt culture is divided into four phases, Hallstatt A (1200–1000), B (1000–800), both of the late Bronze Age, and C (800–600) and D (600–450), of the early Iron Age. The culture first developed along the Danube in Austria and southern Germany and in Bohemia as part of the Urnfield complex and it was only in its Iron Age phases that it developed a truly distinctive character. The Iron Age Hallstatt culture became enormously influential, spreading to much of Germany and the Low Countries, Switzerland, France, Spain, Portugal and south-eastern Britain by 500 BC. Although, thanks to the evidence of ancient Greek writers, we can be confident that the people of the Hallstatt heartland were Celts, the Hallstatt culture itself is not identical with them, that is, the emergence of the culture does not mark the emergence of the Celtic-speaking peoples themselves. The spread of the culture was more likely the result of trade and social contact between peoples who already spoke Celtic languages and shared similar values, than of migrations out of the Hallstatt heartland. Even when the Hallstatt culture was at its peak, there were Celtic-speaking peoples who did not come under its influence; Celtic Spain adopted it select-ively, Ireland not at all.

There is little to distinguish the earliest phase of the Hallstatt culture from the rest of the Urnfield complex. Urnfield influence declined in the Hallstatt B period, when distinctive styles of weapons, including a long slender sword, appeared. More dramatic change followed the introduction of ironworking to central Europe in the eighth century. Hillforts increasingly began to dominate the landscape in the Hallstatt heartland in Austria, southern Germany and Bohemia. Around the forts were clustered cemeteries of luxuriously furnished barrow burials, the richest of which often contained horse gear and four-wheeled funer-ary wagons. The practice of placing vehicles in elite burials became a long-lived characteristic of the Celts, though war chariots later replaced wagons. These developments are evidence of the emergence of a markedly hierarchical and centralised society of powerful and wealthy chiefdoms. A change from the cremation burials of Urnfield times to inhumation points to wider changes in belief systems accompanying the social changes. The cause of this transformation of Hallstatt society is not at all clear. One possibility is that the availability of more effect-ive iron weapons allowed the warrior elite to achieve a stronger hold on power. The obvious importance of the horse in the Hallstatt C cul-ture, and the appearance of a long slashing sword suited to cavalry war-fare, has led to suggestions that the changes may be connected to the arrival of horse-mounted Indo-Iranian nomads, called the Cimmerians, who dominated the western Eurasian steppes at this time. Cimmerian immigrants may have become assimilated with the warrior elite and introduced the new burial customs, inhumation being the normal way to dispose of the dead among the Indo-Iranian nomads. Alternatively, the indigenous elite may simply have borrowed these alien and exotic customs from the Cimmerians as a means of displaying and reinforcing their status. Another likely factor in the emergence of Hallstatt C cul-ture was probably nothing more complicated than a rising population. In all pre-industrial societies agricultural production was by far the most important source of wealth. The level of agricultural production was directly related to the amount of effort, human and animal, that was applied to the land, so the greater the population, the greater the workforce, the greater the production and the greater the surplus for the elite to cream off for themselves from the toiling peasantry. (This was why the first civilisations all emerged on fertile flood plains, such as Mesopotamia, which could easily support very dense populations even using simple farming techniques.)

In the final phase of the Hallstatt culture (Hallstatt D), the centre of the culture shifted west, to the upper reaches of the Danube, the Rhine, the Neckar, the Moselle, the Saône and the Seine rivers. Powerful centralising forces were at work in this area. A host of small hillforts were abandoned during the sixth century to be replaced by a relatively limited number of large hillforts, which emerged as pre-eminent power centres. These were the strongholds of the powerful chieftains whose burials have been found in the surrounding countryside. These so-called 'princely' burials were far more splendidly furnished than earlier Hallstatt burials. Possibly the most magnificent of these burials, of a six-foot (1.8 metres) tall male aged 30 to 40 discovered near Hochdorf in Germany, included a funerary wagon, a bronze couch, gold-covered shoes, drinking horns and other feasting gear and imported luxury metal-work, including a Greek bronze cauldron. These late Hallstatt chieftains clearly lived in some splendour. The Hochdorf burial was covered with an enormous barrow, 100 feet (30.5 metres) high. If a vast barrow was not sufficient to emphasise the high status of its occupant, some were also topped with monumental stone sculptures, such as the rough sandstone warrior from Hirschlanden in Germany. This warrior is naked apart from a neck torc and a sword, both of which were symbols of power in the Hallstatt world, and a conical helmet. Later Classical writers would often comment on this Celtic practice of going into battle naked. The great barrows often served as a focus for later burials, as other family members sought to associate themselves in death with these symbols of dynastic power. One huge barrow built around 600 BC at Magdalenenburg bei Vlissingen in Germany remained in use for 200 years and eventually contained 120 secondary burials. The frequency of elite burials declined in the course of the sixth century, reflecting the decline in the number of major power centres. Power was becoming centralised not only in fewer places but also in fewer hands.

The refocusing of the Hallstatt culture to the west was connected to the founding of a Greek colony at Massalia (Marseille) c. 600 BC. Beginning in the eighth century, Greek city-states had seen founding overseas colonies as a useful way of defusing social tensions caused by rising populations. Although these colonies were independent from the outset, they created greatly increased commercial opportunities for their mother cities and also helped to diffuse Greek influences around the Black Sea and most of the Mediterranean. Greek colonies founded in Italy in the eighth century, for instance, played a formative role in the emergence of the Etruscan civilisation in Tuscany, which was in turn the major influence on the civilisation of early Rome. The Greeks had bitter commercial rivals in the Phoenicians, whose homeland was in modern Lebanon. Stimulated by the demands of the powerful Assyrian empire in Mesopotamia, the Phoenicians had pioneered trade routes through the Mediterranean and the Pillars of Hercules to establish a monopoly of trade with Europe's Atlantic coastal zone, which was the source of valuable metals, especially tin. Gades (Cadiz) became their main trading post in the region. The Phoenicians regarded geographical knowledge as a valuable commercial secret, not to be shared, so it is not at all certain how far they sailed north along the Atlantic coast. Possibly they were the first representatives of the Mediterranean civilisations to make contact with the Celts of Britain. The competitive

Greeks actively sought to open alternative trade routes. With its fine natural harbour and easy access to north-western and central Europe via the valley of the Rhône and its tributary the Saône, Massalia was a very promising location: it prospered and has never ceased to be a major port.

The new trade route opened by the foundation of Massalia enriched the west Hallstatt chiefdoms and gave them access to exotic Mediterranean luxuries, such as wine and the fine tableware associated with wine drinking. Control over the consumption and distribution of these luxuries, probably at feasts, became an important way for the Hallstatt elite to display and reinforce their status: it must have been rare indeed for the common people to have access to them, as Mediterranean imports have rarely been found outside hillforts and princely burials. It is unclear how these luxuries were paid for. They may have been diplomatic gifts designed to facilitate trade in more mundane commodities such as grain, hides and slaves. Along with the luxuries came other forms of Mediterranean influence. Hallstatt craftsmen borrowed and adapted decorative elements from Mediterranean metalwork and incorporated them into a rich mix of native and Scythian influences to create their own distinctive geometrical, vegetal and animal ornaments that mark the emergence of Celtic art. Another important Greek influence was the introduction of the potter's wheel.

Most long-distance trade in the Iron Age was conducted through a chain of intermediaries – the goods getting more expensive every time they changed hands – with the final recipient probably having little idea of an object's ultimate source. Valuable commodities could travel very long distances this way: for example, Chinese silk has been found in the grave of a Hallstatt 'princess' at Heuneburg in Germany. Greek traders may usually have gone no further than Bragny-sur-Saône, near the confluence of the Saône, Doubs and Dheune rivers. Large quantities of Massaliot wine amphorae and Mediterranean pottery and glass found here suggest that Bragny was the major centre for the onward distribution of Mediterranean imports in the sixth century. Despite this, it is likely that some Greeks found their way to the Hallstatt heartlands, as c. 580 BC the hillfort at Heuneburg was equipped with mud-brick walls and bastion towers identical to those used in contemporary Greek military architecture but quite alien to local traditions. The walls were unsuited to local climatic conditions and they were soon replaced: unlike baked brick, mud-brick dissolves in rainwater. It is also likely that a Greek craftsman from Sparta or Taranto visited the hillfort of Mont Lassois in eastern France and while there cast (or at least assembled) the magnificent bronze krater (a wine vessel) which was discovered in a 'princess's' burial nearby at Vix. The krater's huge size – it was 1.64 metres high and weighed 208 kilogrammes – would have made transporting it over a long distance impractical. Stories told by these traders and travellers made the Mediterranean world aware of the peoples called *Keltoi* for the first time. The Hallstatt Celts could probably see

Plate 1 Krater, from the tomb of a Princess Vix (bronze). Greek school (sixth century BC)

Source: Musée Archéologique, Châtillon Sur Seine, France/Bridgeman Art Library, www.bridgeman.co.uk

nothing but advantages in the new links being forged with the Mediterranean civilisations, but they were to have fatal consequences for their descendants. By beginning the integration of the Celtic world into the Mediterranean economy and spurring the process of political centralisation, they ultimately also made it more vulnerable to conquest and political and cultural assimilation by the Romans.

The opulent world of the Hallstatt chieftains came to an abrupt end around 450 BC with the abandonment of all the main power centres, at least one of which, the Heuneburg, was violently destroyed. The reason for the decline of the Hallstatt chiefdoms is unclear. The Massaliotes' increasing interest in subjugating the Celtic and Ligurian tribes of Provence, and competition from the Etruscans, who had opened new routes over the Alps, may have led to a decline of the Rhône trade routes. This may have cost the Hallstatt chieftains their monopoly on the distribution of Mediterranean imports and deprived them of the prestige goods they needed to underpin their status. Another factor in the decline of the Hallstatt chiefdoms seems to have been the rise of new centres of chieftainly power to the north. Associated with the rise of these chiefdoms was an astonishingly inventive new culture, the La Tène culture.

The La Tène Celts

The La Tène culture is characterised by its instantly recognisable art style based on captivatingly complex swirling geometrical patterns. For many people the La Tène style *is* Celtic art. Celtic art was not merely ornamental, however; it had symbolic religious and magical functions, so the change in style probably also represents a major change in belief systems accompanying the rise of the La Tène chiefdoms. On the continent the influence of the La Tène style continued for over 400 years, until the Roman conquests in the first century BC. In Britain and Ireland, where the style was adopted *c.* 200 BC, La Tène influence continued right through the Roman period into the early Middle Ages, being transformed in the process from a pagan into a Christian art form. The La Tène style was not homogeneous. Early examples of the style are clearly imitations and adaptations of Greek and Etruscan

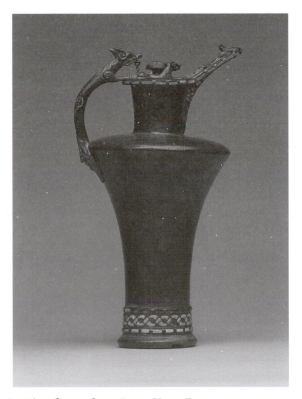

Plate 2 Early La Tène flagon from Basse-Yutz, France
Source: © The British Museum

decorative motifs, but as it developed distinct regional styles appeared. For instance, vegetation motifs predominated in France and Germany, while in Britain and Ireland the style was more abstract and geometrical. The Greeks and Romans were pathologically incapable of recognising that barbarian art could be good art (they would have seen it as a contradiction in terms) and the dominating influence of Classicism on European art meant that it was not until the later nineteenth century that the La Tène style was recognised for the great artistic achievement that it was. The abstract style of La Tène art appeals to modern tastes and has been successfully revived by modern jewellers.

The La Tène culture is named for a site on Lake Neuchâtel in Switzerland but its early centres lay far to the north, the most important being in the valley of the river Moselle and a second, smaller and poorer centre in the valley of the Marne. A third centre later developed in Bohemia, and by 400 BC La Tène influence had spread across most of Austria, Switzerland, southern Germany and France. About 150 years later the La Tène culture had spread to south-eastern Britain and had begun to spread slowly north and west to Ireland. The La Tène culture was also adopted in Celtic Iberia but only in a very selective way. The striking feature of early La Tène society was its martial character. While elite Hallstatt burials did contain weapons, these were suited mainly for hunting or for show. When the early La Tène elite went to their graves, they went fully prepared for battle. There was an increase in the number of weapons placed in elite graves and, when vehicles were placed in burials, they were not the four-wheeled funerary wagons of Hallstatt times but an altogether more martial form of transport, the two-wheeled chariot. This innovation may have been adopted as a result of contacts with the Etruscans. Just as in Hallstatt times, elite burials were also accompanied by drinking sets, including Greek and, now, Etruscan vessels. As later Greek and Roman writers confirm, feasting was of central importance to the La Tène warrior elite as an opportunity to display wealth and boast of one's prowess in battle. The appearance of this warlike culture marked the beginning of a long period of instability in northern and central Europe.

2

THE GREAT MIGRATIONS

The Celts, who make up one of the three peoples of Gaul, were dominated by the Bituriges and this tribe, therefore, supplied the Celtic people with a king. At that time, the king was Ambigatus, who, by his abilities, and good fortune . . . had achieved great power. Under his rule Gaul grew so wealthy and populous that it became a matter of great difficulty to control such a multitude. The king, who was an old man, wishing to rid his kingdom of the burden of its excess population, announced his intention to send his two nephews, Bellovesus and Segovesus, two adventurous young men, out into the world to find such homes as the gods might direct them to by augury.

Livy, *History of Rome*, V.34 (*c.* 27 BC)

If the question of prehistoric Celtic migrations remains undecided, Celtic migrations in historical times are well attested and dramatic in their scale and impact. Between the fifth and third centuries BC, migrations carried the Celts from central Europe across the Alps into Italy and, following the Danube, they spread east to the Carpathian Mountains and beyond onto the Ukrainian steppes and south-east to the Balkans, Greece and Anatolia. Small groups even finished up in Egypt. In the process the Celts earned themselves a terrifying reputation for savagery in war. As a result of their migrations, the Celts became the most widespread group of peoples in Europe. But their vast domain was in no sense a Celtic empire. There was no central direction to the migrations, no imperial master plan. Tribes allied with one another when it suited them but remained each an independent chiefdom.

The Celtic migrations were probably a means to relieve social tensions caused by rising population or shortage of resources. Julius Caesar tells us that when the Helvetii, a tribe of Gauls, decided to migrate in the first century BC they did so because they were hemmed in between the Alps and the river Rhine and thus restricted in their opportunities for making war on neighbouring tribes. The Helvetii liked fighting and resented these restrictions on their freedom of action and felt that their own territory was too small for their population. Celtic society was dominated by a warrior elite. For them warfare was essential, both as a theatre in which to perform status-enhancing acts of valour, and for the spoils, which when distributed enhanced the status of a leader, attracted more warriors into his retinue, and so made even larger-scale and wide-ranging raids possible. Ambitious leaders had also to compete with one another for status and followers, reinforcing the warlike tendency of Celtic society. If the opportunities for raiding were restricted for some reason, the competitive nature of warrior society might turn inwards. In these circumstances, migration offered a way out. It is clear that Celtic migrations could involve part of a tribe, a whole tribe or even a coalition of tribes. Migrations were evidently well-planned affairs. The Helvetii spent two years preparing for their migration, building up their food supplies, purchasing draught animals and wagons and negotiating with neighbouring tribes whose territories they needed to pass through to reach their intended new homeland on the Atlantic coast of Gaul. When they were finally ready to leave, they burned their *oppida* and villages, so that return would not be an option. Caesar, who may have been exaggerating to magnify his own achievements, claimed that there were 368,000 migrants altogether, 263,000 Helvetii and 105,000 from four allied tribes. Of these 92,000 were warriors – a very considerable force by ancient standards. In the sixth and seventh centuries BC the Greek city-states had experienced similar problems of overpopulation to the Celts, and they too had sent out waves of emigrants, who had founded colonies all around the Mediterranean and the Black Sea coasts. Massalia, which had had such a great influence on the Hallstatt chiefdoms, was one of these. The Greek colonists were chosen by drawing lots but it is not known how the Celts decided who should go or if the emigrants had any choice in the matter.

The earliest historically attested Celtic migration was across the Alps into Italy. According to the fullest account of these migrations, by the Roman historian Livy, the first Celts migrated into Italy during the reign of Tarquinius Priscus (r. *c.* 616–579 BC), the fifth king of Rome. Livy tells us that the 'Celts', which he describes as one of the three main peoples of Gaul, were at this time dominated by the Bituriges. In Livy's day, the Bituriges lived in central Gaul, the heart of the area that the Romans knew as Gallia Celtica. Ambigatus, the king of the Bituriges, saw that his kingdom was becoming overpopulated and decided to send his two nephews Bellovesus and Segovesus out with as many followers as they could muster to find new homelands. The gods were duly consulted and Segovesus was sent to southern Germany, Bellovesus 'on the fair road to Italy'. Bellovesus' followers came from many tribes, the Bituriges, Senones, Aedui, Arverni, Carnutes, Aulerci and the Ambarri. Classical writers firmly believed that Italy's wine, olive oil and warm climate were a great attraction for the Celts. According to a tradition recorded by the naturalist Pliny, it was a Gallic craftsman called Helico who introduced his countrymen to the delights of Italy, when he returned home from a trip to Rome with dried figs and grapes and containers of wine and olive oil. The migrating Gallic horde at first had difficulty finding a route over the Alps and they travelled as far south as the Mediterranean, where they helped a group of Greek settlers found the colony of Massalia. Encouraged by this success, which they took as a good omen for their own plans, the Celts redoubled their efforts, finally finding a route across the Alps, probably by the Col de Mont Genèvre, and descending into the upper reaches of the valley of the river Po. The Etruscans had already laid claim to this extensive fertile area, but the Gauls defeated them near the river Ticino. The Gauls subsequently settled north of the Po in Piedmont and Lombardy, founding Milan as their main centre. This mixed bag of Gauls became known as the Insubres, after the name of the territory they had settled.

Livy's account of the origin of the Insubres was written some 600 years after the events it describes and some, or quite probably all, of it may be legendary. Other Classical writers make no mention of Celtic migrations into Italy before *c*. 400 BC. Yet a number of inscriptions of an extinct Celtic language known as Lepontic, found in the foothills of the Alps, prove that Celtic speakers were certainly established in Piedmont and Lombardy by the sixth century BC. Richly furnished warrior graves of the Golasecca culture found in this area show that it was inhabited by an aristocratic warrior society that had much in common with the Hallstatt chiefdoms then flourishing north of the Alps. However, the roots of the Golasecca culture can be traced back to around 900 BC, long before the migration described by Livy. Were the Golaseccans Celtic-speaking from the beginning or did they become so as a result of trans-Alpine trade contacts or migrations such as Livy describes? There is insufficient evidence to tell, but it does seem likely that, if the Golaseccans were not Insubres, they were at least their ancestors.

In later years other groups of Gauls followed Bellovesus across the Alps into Italy. First came the Cenomani who settled around Brescia and Verona. According to Livy, this was during the lifetime of Bellovesus, but there is no archaeological evidence of Celtic settlement in Italy at this time outside the area of the Golasecca culture. As the earliest Celtic artefacts known from this area belong to the La Tène culture, they cannot have arrived before *c*. 450 at the very earliest. Some time later, the Libui and Saluvii followed, so that by the time the Boii and Lingones arrived there was no territory left for settlement north of the Po. They had no choice but to build rafts and invade the Etruscan and Umbrian territory between the river and the Apennines. Scenes of fighting with Celtic warriors are a prominent theme of a group of fifth-century BC Etruscan burial stelae from Bologna, so it is certain that their invasion was resisted. Roman sources also mention conflict between the Etruscans and the Celts, or Gauls, as they usually called them. The last major Celtic migration into Italy was by a tribe called the Senones and this must have taken place close to 400 BC. They moved further south still and occupied a strip of the Adriatic coast extending roughly from Rimini as far south as the river Aso, an area that became known as the Ager Gallicus ('the country of the Gauls'). The

Romans knew the whole area of Celtic settlement in Italy as Cisalpine Gaul ('Gaul-this-side-of-the-Alps').

The tribal names of the La Tène period migrants probably give some indication as to their origin. In later historical times, the Senones, Cenomani and Lingones all lived in central or eastern Gaul, the Saluvii in Provence, and the Boii in Bohemia (from *Boihaemum*, 'the home of the Boii'). Of course, we have no way of knowing for certain if they all lived in those areas as early as the fifth century BC, but archaeological evidence from Bohemia, at least, does point to a decline in the population around the time of the migrations as many cemeteries went out of use and elite burials disappear. Comparable evidence of population decline has also been found in the other early La Tène heartland of the Marne–Moselle region. It would seem reasonable to conclude that the reason for this depopulation was migration to Italy. There are also striking similarities between items of jewellery found in Celtic graves near Bologna and from Bohemia. Even the burial rites themselves are similar. Graves from the areas settled by the Senones and the Cenomani reflect burial customs of the Marne region of France. The Celtic settlers north of the Po retained a typical La Tène material culture, or, in the case of the Insubres (if they are to be identified with the Golasecca culture), they adopted it from the newcomers. South of the Po, the Boii, Lingones and Senones adopted some of the material culture of the peoples they had conquered, for example, living in the same kind of stone and timber two-storey houses that the Etruscans built, quite unlike those they would have been used to north of the Alps. The Celts built hill-forts but also settled in Etruscan villages and towns, such as Felsina, which became the chief centre of the Boii and which derives its modern name – Bologna – from them. In cemeteries near Bologna and elsewhere Etruscan burials are found side by side with typical La Tène warrior burials. The natives were clearly not wiped out, but the Celts probably formed the new social elite. There was a gradual Celticisation of the local population, with La Tène objects appearing in Etruscan graves. By the fourth century BC the natives had become assimilated to Celtic culture.

The Gauls brought with them to Italy not only their material culture but also their social structure. For La Tène warrior society war – or at least raiding – was essential if the elite were to maintain their status. This made it all but inevitable that they would begin raiding the prosperous Etruscan territory on the other side of the Apennines. These raids led to the fateful first contacts between Celts and Romans. At this time no one could have guessed at Rome's future greatness. It was just one prosperous city-state among many, but it was already trying to increase its influence in Italy. In 391 BC (or possibly 387) the Romans sent three ambassadors to mediate in a territorial dispute between the Etruscan city of Clusium (modern Chiusi) and the Senones. When negotiations failed and fighting broke out, the Roman envoys joined in on the side of the Etruscans, quite against all the rules of diplomacy, killing one of the Gallic chieftains. Such an offence demanded retaliation and, after the Romans stubbornly refused to hand over the guilty men for punishment, an army of Gauls crossed the Apennines in

July 390 (or 386) and headed with terrifying speed down the valley of the river Tiber towards Rome. Brennus, the leader of the Gauls, was an able general and he easily routed the Roman army sent to stop him at the river Allia a few miles from Rome.

Undefended and abandoned by all but the sick and the old, Rome fell the next day and was comprehensively sacked. According to Roman tradition a token garrison of diehards who held out on the Capitoline Hill were saved from a surprise night attack only when alerted at the last minute by the cackling of the sacred geese in Juno's temple. It was fortunate that the hungry soldiers had not dared to eat the geese for fear of incurring the wrath of the notoriously testy queen of the gods. The Gauls were finally persuaded to leave Rome after seven months when the Romans agreed to pay them the huge ransom of a thousand pounds of gold. The Gauls had it in mind to fleece the Romans of even more of their gold by using weights that were loaded in their favour. When the Romans complained of this, Brennus is said to have added his sword to the scales on the side of the suspect weights, saying simply '*vae victis*' – woe to the vanquished!

The subsequent history of the world would have been very different had the Gauls been able to occupy Rome permanently, but their withdrawal was probably inevitable: they were a long way from home, isolated in hostile territory and short of supplies. The departure of the Gauls may also have been hastened by news of an attack on their own lands by the Veneti, an Italic tribe of north-east Italy. A late Roman tradition has it that the Gauls were pursued and defeated on their way home but this is probably nothing more than a face-saving invention. The experience of defeat was highly traumatic for the small republic, which had not long emerged from the shadow of its Etruscan neighbours. Fortunately for Rome, the Etruscans were far more exposed to Gaulish raiding so they were in no position to take advantage of the situation. By weakening the Etruscans, the Gauls may unintentionally even have helped Rome on its road to achieving dominance in Italy.

The Romans were a people with an unrivalled ability to bear grudges (think of Carthage), and it mattered not that they recognised that the disaster of 390 had been largely of their own making. Brennus' words haunted the Roman imagination, and long after they had ceased to pose any realistic threat, self-serving politicians like Julius Caesar would find it easy to persuade the Roman people that hordes of Gauls were poised to descend on Rome and sack it a second time. Although it could not have been clear to anyone at the time, the sack of Rome represented the high tide of Celtic expansion in western Europe. Rome clashed with raiding Gauls several more times in the fourth century. Though there was no repeat of the disaster of 390 – Rome had been given a city wall in 378 to defend it against Gaulish attacks – one raiding party got within a few miles of Rome in 367 before it was defeated in the Alban Hills. Another raid in 361 got even closer, being stopped at the river Anio, only three miles from the city. The same raiding party returned later in the year and was fought off within sight of the Colline Gate. The cities of Latium, which Rome was trying to dominate, often gave provisions and other support to the Gauls. Gradually, the Romans got the measure of the Cisalpine Gauls, with each attack being defeated more easily than the last, and eventually, in 334, the two agreed a peace treaty.

The Gauls did not settle anywhere south of the Apennine mountains but some groups did travel as far south as Apulia, where they served as mercenaries for Greek rulers such as Dionysius I of Syracuse (r. 405–367 BC). Dionysius was an expansionist ruler who spent the greater part of his reign at war with either the Carthaginians or the Etruscans. In the 380s Dionysius captured the Etruscan port of Adria, near the mouth of the Po, and founded a colony at Ancona in the Ager Gallicus. In 385 he struck up a formal alliance with the Senones and began to recruit mercenaries, some of whom took part in a naval expedition against the Etruscan port of Pyrgos (Santa Severa) in 384. Dionysius and his son, Dionysius II, continued to recruit mercenaries through Ancona for 30 years. One of their mercenaries was buried in some splendour in a rock-cut tomb at Canosa di Puglia (Apulia) later in the fourth century. Among the grave goods was a truly splendid iron helmet, covered with bronze sheets decorated with vegetal patterns and coral inlay: originally, the helmet would also have been decorated with feathers. Whether or not it was with the encouragement of their Greek employers, Apulia became a base for the Gauls to raid Roman territory, for example in 367 and again in 348.

Only two years before the Gallic–Roman peace treaty, another group of Celts had a memorable meeting with the young Alexander the Great of Macedon. Alexander was planning the spectacular conquest of the vast Persian Empire that would make him a legend in his own, short, lifetime, but he first had to secure the frontiers of his kingdom with a campaign against the Illyrian and Thracian tribes. Alexander's campaign reached as far north as the middle Danube, where he met representatives from several Celtic tribes, some probably from as far away as Italy. Alexander asked the envoys what they were most afraid of, egotistically hoping, of course, that they would say that it was him. When they answered that they were most afraid that the sky might fall on them, Alexander was heard to mutter under his breath that these Celts had too high an opinion of themselves. Despite this, the Celts were evidently impressed by Alexander, for they went to the trouble of sending an embassy all the way to Babylon to meet him in 323.

Celtic migrations into eastern Europe began early in the fourth century BC and continued up to its end. This region was as yet beyond the horizons of literate Mediterranean observers but the general direction and chronology of the migration is made clear by the spread of the La Tène culture. By the end of the fourth century populations using the La Tène material culture had spread along the Middle Danube, settling in Slovakia, Hungary and Serbia, and in pockets in Transylvania and even north of the Carpathian mountains themselves around Kraków in southern Poland. Evidence from cemeteries suggests that there were probably two main waves of Celtic migration, but it is likely that some of the observable changes in material culture are the result of indigenous peoples adopting the La Tène culture. A scatter of Celtic weapons and other artefacts from across Moldova and the Ukraine provide evidence for a Celtic presence on the European steppes. As most of these are stray finds or come from the graves of the local Scythian steppe nomads, this presence may have been nothing more than roving war bands. Only one Celtic grave has been found, near Chernobyl, and a single settlement at Bovshev on the river Dniester, but place names such as Gallitsyja and Galich in the western Ukraine are suggestive of more widespread settlement. The attraction may have been the Greek cities on the Black Sea coast. Coins of King Leucon II of Bosporos, a Hellenistic kingdom on the Sea of Azov, depict Celtic shields and weapons. These may commemorate a Greek victory over Celtic raiders. A third-century BC inscription from Olbia (Nikolayev, Ukraine) records that the threat of attack by the Galatians, the Greek name for the Celts, was deemed so great that Protogenes, one of the local great and good, had paid for the building of a city wall. The inscription also noted that the Galatians had forced the local Scythian nomads to seek protection in the city. Had the Scythians been at the peak of their power they could easily have prevented the Celts from penetrating the steppes, but they had recently suffered a serious defeat by another nomad people, the Sarmatians, and were in terminal decline.

Within months of meeting the Celtic ambassadors at Babylon, Alexander died, still aged only 33. He left no adult heir and his empire was quickly torn apart by his generals in a violent struggle for land and power, which lasted over 20 years. The Celts exploited this obvious weakness in the Hellenistic world to continue their expansion south-east. Around 300 BC a loose confederation of Celtic tribes moved into the Balkans and attacked the Illyrians, Triballi and Paionians. In or around 298 one Celtic leader, Cimbaules, led a raid into Macedonia itself but he was quickly chased out again. The Celts invaded again in 281 under Bolgios. The king of Macedonia at this time was Ptolemy Keraunos (the nickname means 'thunderbolt'), an unscrupulous opportunist who had won power by murdering his predecessor on the throne. Ptolemy did not lack military ability but he was also an impetuous hothead who vainly fancied himself to be a new Alexander. When Bolgios – whose name, like Ptolemy's, probably also has some association with thunder – offered to withdraw in return for a large payment, Ptolemy interpreted this not as an attempt at blackmail but as a sign of weakness and he rushed headlong into a poorly planned attack. Ptolemy's army was the larger and the better armed, but the Celts' savage appearance and reckless courage won the day. Ptolemy was killed and his severed head was paraded in triumph on the point of a spear. In the same year, another Celtic force under Cerethreus successfully invaded Macedonia's neighbour, the kingdom of Thrace, and sacked its capital Seuthopolis.

This success encouraged the Celts to launch a raid on Greece in 279 under Brennus (possibly a legendary name or a title) and Achichorios. It is difficult now to be sure of the size of the Celtic raiding force. Greek writers deliberately presented the Celtic invasion as a replay of Xerxes' massive Persian invasion of 480 BC and gave figures in the hundreds of thousands. Although these figures are very hard to believe, if they are exaggerated it is impossible to say by how much. Unity never came naturally to the Celts, however, and this huge force began to break up as a result of internal dissent even before it got to Greece: around a third of the force, led by Leonorios and Lutorios, decided to head east into Thrace instead. As it turned out, these were the lucky ones. Ptolemy's incompetence had led the Celts to believe that Greece was weaker than it really was.

Despite the departure of Leonorios and Lutorios, Brennus headed south into Greece as planned, leaving a smaller force behind to secure control of Macedonia itself. Macedonia's new king Antigonos Gonatas was a far cannier operator than Ptolemy had been. Realising that the Celts' main interest was loot, Antigonos prepared a trap for them by ordering his army to abandon its camp in a feigned retreat. As he expected, the Celts quickly fell upon the camp to plunder it, losing all cohesion in the process, upon which they were ambushed and annihilated. About a year later (in 278 or 277), Antigonos went on to defeat Cerethreus at Lysimacheia, not far from Gallipoli. Resistance to Brennus' main force was led by Athens. Brennus was moving south, following Thessaly's Aegean coast, meeting little resistance on the way. The Greeks simply fled to the safety of their walled cities, which the Celts, lacking any experience of siege warfare, could not take. The Greeks decided to try to halt the Celts at the Pass of Thermopylai, where the Spartans had made their heroic stand against the Persians in 480. The Celts tried to force a way through the pass but were beaten back with heavy losses, just as the Persians had been 200 years before. Brennus, who seems to have been a resourceful commander, now discovered the same 'secret' mountain path that the Persians had used to outflank the Spartans in 480. Now Brennus divided the Greek defence by sending Achichorios with a force west over the Pindhos Mountains into Aetolia. Here Achichorios fell unexpectedly upon the city of Callium, which was sacked with great savagery, including the mass rape of its women. This was enough to send the Aetolian contingent of the Greek army hurrying home. The depleted Greek army in the pass was then enveloped by the Celts, but it escaped the fate of its Spartan predecessor thanks to the Athenian navy, which evacuated it by sea.

Now that the Greek forces were temporarily scattered, Brennus made for the sacred city of Delphi, home of a famous oracle who spoke for the sun god Apollo, high on the slopes of Mount Athos. As no Greek would dare to attack Delphi, many Greek cities had their treasuries there for safekeeping. For the same reason Delphi was also virtually defenceless. The rough mountain terrain was not suitable for a pitched battle, and though the Greeks harried the Celts as best they could, they appeared unstoppable. What happened next is unclear as the ancient authors fall back on supernatural explanations. The most important account is that of Pausanias, a Greek travel writer of the second century AD. His *Guide to Greece* is still a useful travelling companion on a touring holiday in Greece today, despite

Plate 3 Delphi
Source: John Haywood

being nearly 2,000 years old. According to Pausanias, Apollo spoke to the terrified citizens of Delphi through his oracle, urging them not to be afraid, saying 'I will protect my own.' The situation immediately began to improve. News came that Achichorios' army had been badly mauled by the vengeful Aetolians as it withdrew from Callium and had lost all its loot. Earthquakes and unseasonable snowstorms triggered rock falls, which killed many in the Celtic army, and the Greeks saw long-dead heroes fighting in their ranks. Brennus himself was seriously wounded. Faced with so many ill omens as they approached what they knew to be the most sacred site in Greece, the Celts seem to have been filled with a superstitious dread and they began to retreat, harried continuously by the Greeks. During the night, the mood of dread turned to panic and, wrongly believing that the Greeks had entered their camp, the Celts started fighting among themselves. The Greeks believed that Apollo had made the Celts unable to understand one another's speech, though perhaps the confusion really arose because there were non-Celtic contingents in the army. After this débâcle, the retreat degenerated into a rout. Brennus, his authority surely shattered by the scale of the disaster, did the decent thing and committed suicide, thereby securing himself an honourable place in the afterlife.

Some historians believe that the Greeks exaggerated the extent of their victory – after all, they did compare it to their truly great victories over Xerxes' Persians in 480–479 – and that the Celts did actually succeed in sacking Delphi. The Romans certainly believed that they had recovered treasures originally looted from Delphi when they sacked a Celtic shrine at Tolosa (Toulouse) in 106 BC – members of a local tribe, the Tectosages, had taken part in the invasion of Greece – but apart from this, there is no other evidence to support this version of events. In one respect, at least, the Greeks did exaggerate their success: they claimed that scarcely a Celt made it out of Greece alive, but in reality the Celts remained a potent force despite the débâcle at Delphi.

The survivors of Brennus' expedition eventually settled on the Black Sea coast of Thrace in the area of modern Burgas (in Bulgaria) where they founded the kingdom of Tylis. Under its earliest known king, Commontorios, Tylis became a robber kingdom, living on tribute blackmailed from the Greek cities around the Black Sea, until the Thracians destroyed it in 212 BC. Because it was so short-lived, the Celtic presence in Thrace has left little trace, though the remains of a chariot have been found in an aristocratic tomb at Mezek in Bulgaria. It is not clear if it belonged to a Celtic or to a Thracian chieftain. If it was a Thracian chieftain, the chariot may have been a diplomatic gift or an item of plunder taken in battle with the Celts. A clearer example of interaction between Celts and Thracians is the famous Gundestrup cauldron, which was found in a Danish peat bog. This spectacular silver cauldron is decorated with images of Celtic gods and warriors but its workmanship is quite obviously Thracian, the product of a Thracian craftsman for a Celtic patron (or owner?). Another group of survivors of Brennus' expedition returned to the Balkans under the leadership of Bathanatos, where they contributed to the formation of a new Celtic tribe called the Scordisci. Singidunum – modern Belgrade – became their main centre. The Scordisci became a power to be reckoned with, occasionally raiding Macedonia and Greece and in the second century repulsing the Cimbri and Teutones, two migrating German tribes who went on to annihilate several Roman legions before they were eventually defeated.

Some Celts remained behind in Greece voluntarily, recruited into the army of Antigonos Gonatas, who had been impressed by their bravery. Though Antigonos' arch-rival, Pyrrhus of Epirus (the winner of the original pyrrhic victory), would boast of the number of these Celtic mercenaries he had slain, they must have earned their pay as it was Antigonos who eventually emerged victorious in the struggle. Around this time too – the exact date is uncertain – another band of Celts was recruited into the army of Ptolemy Philadelphos, the Greek ruler of Egypt. These mercenaries soon plotted a rebellion but they were overheard and betrayed to their employer. Ptolemy herded around 4,000 of the mercenaries onto an island in the Nile. Faced with an ignoble death by starvation, many chose suicide. Perhaps surprisingly, Egyptian rulers continued to recruit Celts for at least another century. When discharged they were given lands to settle and became cleruchs ('sleepers', i.e. reservists) who could be called back to arms in times of emergency, as happened in 217 BC, when they helped repel an invasion of Egypt. The well-preserved shield of one of these Celtic cleruchs has been found at the desert oasis of Faiyum, where many of them were settled in the third century. Another trace of the Celtic presence in Egypt is an inscription, dated to *c.* 185 BC, which commemorates a successful foxhunt by a party that included Celts. The sons and grandsons of these Celtic mercenaries continued the family tradition and also served in Egyptian armies: there were still soldiers with Celtic names in the garrison of Hermopolis in Middle Egypt even at the end of the second century BC. The lives of these desert-dwelling Celts must have been very different from those of their ancestors in central Europe, and presumably they were eventually assimilated into the local Egyptian population.

Most of the 20,000 Celts who followed Leonorios and Lutorios into Thrace belonged to three tribes, the Tectosages, Trocmi and Tolistobogii. About half of the group were women, children and old folk, suggesting that they were migrants in search of land to settle and that the reason they had broken with Brennus was because he was more interested in plunder. At the invitation of King Nicomedes of Bithynia (now north-west Turkey), Leonorios and Lutorios crossed over from Thrace to Anatolia in 278–277, the first via the Bosphorus, and the second by the Dardanelles. Nicomedes was prepared to let the Celts settle in exchange for their service in a war with the Seleucid (Syrian) king Antiochus I, who already controlled most of Anatolia and wanted the rest too. Nicomedes never had to deliver on his promise as Antiochus defeated the Celts in 275–274 at the so-called Battle of the Elephants near the now ruined city of Sardis. Antiochus earned himself the title 'Soter' (saviour) for this victory. The Celts were unbroken, however, and they subsequently forged a new alliance with King Mithridates I of Pontus (on the Black Sea coast) who granted them the right to settle in eastern Phrygia in central Anatolia. Mithridates' was a cynical offer as Phrygia actually belonged to the Seleucid kingdom. However, Antiochus was unable to dislodge the Celts and was eventually killed in battle with them in 261.

The area of Celtic settlement in Anatolia became known as Galatia, from the Greek name for the Celts. The Galatians were not very numerous in comparison with the native population they came to rule over. Yet these isolated Celts resisted assimilation for centuries. Even as late as the fourth century AD, St Jerome would remark that the Galatians spoke the same language as the Gauls. The Galatians preserved a form of government based on their original three tribal divisions. Each of the three tribes was divided into four septs or clans, each of which was ruled by a tetrarch (from Greek, *tetra*, 'four'; *arkhos*, 'chief'). Each tetrarch was assisted by a judge, a general and two deputy generals. It is not known how these governing officials were selected. The positions may have been hereditary, though in later times, at least, some Gallic tribes elected their officials. The twelve clans sent a total of 300 'senators' to an annual council, which was held at a 'national' shrine called *Drunemeton* ('oak grove'). In Gaul and Britain *nemeton* place names are associated with Druidism, though there is no other evidence for the presence of Druids among the Galatians, unless, perhaps, the judges were Druids.

Relatively few Celtic artefacts have been found in Anatolia, though this may be partly because they have not been looked for. One of the few Galatian sites that have been extensively excavated is Gordion, once the capital of the fabulous Phrygian king Midas. Archaeological evidence suggests that Gordion was occupied by the Galatians soon after 270 BC and became a prosperous *oppidum* and trade centre (*emporium*) with monumental buildings and advanced craft working. The Galatian occupation of Gordion lasted for over a century, during which time it was twice destroyed and rebuilt, first in the late third century BC by unknown attackers and again in 189 by a Roman army under Manlius Vulso. A lack of metal finds in the destruction layers indicates that the Romans looted the settlement thoroughly before firing it. Gordion was finally abandoned around the middle of the second century.

Though a few typically Celtic artefacts were found, the excavations have shown that the material culture of the Galatians quickly became Hellenised. Many of them could read Greek, which they used to inscribe some of their possessions. We also know from literary sources of Galatian parents giving their children Greek names. The Roman use of the term Gallograeci to describe the Galatians seems justified. In religious matters, however, they retained Celtic practices. A double-faced 'Janus' sculpture, similar to several found in Celtic Europe, was found as well as three pits of human and animal remains, the victims of grisly ritual killings involving strangulation, decapitation and dismemberment. One human skull showed clear signs that it had been displayed on the point of a wooden stake, a practice that is well documented in Celtic Europe. Classical writers may not have been exaggerating, therefore, when they wrote that many people preferred to

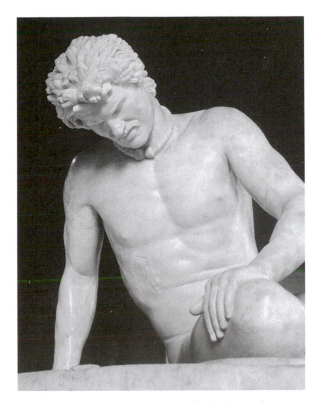

Plate 4 Dying Gaul, copy of a Greek original of 230–220 BC by Epigonos
(marble)

Source: Pinacoteca Capitolina, Palazzo Conservatori, Rome, Italy/Bridgeman Art Library,
www.bridgeman.co.uk

commit suicide rather than be taken prisoner by the Galatians, for fear of
becoming a sacrificial victim if they were not ransomed.

For nearly fifty years after their initial settlement, the Galatians lived
alternately by plundering their neighbours and hiring themselves out
to them as mercenaries. To prevent arguments among themselves, the
Galatians had agreed exclusive zones for raiding for each of the three
tribes. The Trocmi raided around the Dardanelles, the Tolistobogii the
rich Greek cities of the Ionian coast, and the Tectosages concentrated on
inland Anatolia. Special taxes were raised in the Greek cities of the coast to
ransom prisoners taken in these raids, the fate of unransomed prisoners
being only too well understood. King Eumenes I of Pergamon was one of
several rulers who kept his lands free of Galatian raids by paying protection
money. His successor Attalus I (241–197) was made of sterner stuff and he
ended the payments. When the Galatians retaliated by invading, Attalus
defeated them in battle at the Springs of Caicus in 240. The Galatians
tried to get their revenge by allying with the Seleucid king Antiochus II
against Pergamon, but Attalus won another victory, over a raiding force
of Tolistobogii, near a shrine of Aphrodite, not far from Pergamon itself.

In 232 the Galatians agreed a peace with Attalus in which they promised to stop raiding Pergamon. The peace treaty did not entirely pacify the Galatians – and they even raided Pergamon again after Attalus died in 197 – but western Anatolia was much more secure from then on. In celebration of his victories Attalus commissioned a monument for the acropolis of Pergamon. This included many sculptures portraying Celtic warriors, including the famous *Dying Gaul*, a marble copy of which can still be seen in Rome. The peace with Pergamon did not quite mark the end of the Celtic migrations to the east. In 218 Attalus recruited another Celtic tribe from Europe, called the Aigosaiges, to fight in another war with the Seleucids. After the war, he settled the Aigosaiges near the Dardanelles but they soon turned to raiding their neighbours, even besieging Ilium – ancient Troy. Their depredations were eventually ended by King Prusias of Bithynia in 217, who massacred them all, even the women and children.

By the end of the third century BC, the great period of Celtic migrations had run its course, and in Italy at least the Celts were already in retreat. Powerful neighbours restricted further advances. Migrations did continue, however, within the Celtic world. The migration of the Helvetii in 59 BC has already been mentioned, and around 100 BC there was a migration of Belgae to Britain. There were probably other, undocumented migrations from Gaul to Britain, as two other British tribes, the Atrebates and the Parisi, have continental namesakes.

Celtic expansion was certainly impressive. By the early third century BC they were probably the most widespread of the European peoples. Most of this new territory had been gained at the expense of peoples who were at a similar level of social development to the Celts themselves. This must have made it relatively easy for conquered populations to be assimilated to Celtic culture and identity. Although it is their forays into the world of the Classical Mediterranean civilisations that are, for obvious reasons, the best documented, the Celts made little headway against them. The Mediterranean civilisations generally proved militarily superior. Though they could raid, plunder and terrorise, their territorial gains were limited to a slice of Etruscan territory between the river Po and the Apennine mountains, which the Etruscans themselves had not long held, and that part of central Anatolia which became known as Galatia. Galatia was undoubtedly a successful colony, surviving as an independent entity for over 250 years. Yet there were special factors at play in Anatolia that made Galatia's survival more likely. Throughout Galatia's existence, Anatolia was a theatre of competition between great powers, and the Celts would always be welcomed as allies by someone because of their terrifying reputation. This also staved off the Galatians' assimilation with the native population because it allowed the elite to maintain their status in the traditional Celtic way by raiding and plunder. However, Galatia's eventual assimilation into the Mediterranean world was probably inevitable. Celtic culture may have proved attractive to other barbarian peoples but it was never going to win many converts in the more sophisticated Mediterranean world. It was always more likely that the Galatians would be assimilated to Mediterranean civilisation than vice versa.

3

THE LA TÈNE WORLD

> [The Celts] *lived in unwalled villages without any permanent buildings. They slept on beds of straw or leaves and fed on meat and were exclusively occupied with war and agriculture. . . . Each man's property consisted of gold and cattle, as these were the only things that they could easily carry with them as they moved from place to place, changing their dwellings as their fancy determined. They made a great point of friendship, for the man who had the largest number of clients or companions was looked upon as the most formidable and powerful member of the tribe.*
>
> Polybius, *Histories* (*c.* 150 BC)

Most of what we know about the customs and beliefs of the ancient Celts we owe to Classical Greek and Roman writers. These writers present a very consistent stereotyped picture of the Celts as a superstitious and savage people; economically backward, warlike and quarrelsome, emotional, boastful and vain, and fond of drink, feasting and song. This stereotype was not intended to flatter the Celts. Classical writers did find things to admire about the Celts, especially their courage, but, almost without exception, they regarded them as culturally inferior barbarians, who posed a deadly threat to the well-ordered, rational, urbanised Mediterranean world. Remarkably, the Classical stereotype lives on, though, thanks to the influence of the Romantic movement, it is now seen to be a rather positive one. The Celt has become the noble savage, uncorrupted and unrestrained by decadent civilisation. Under the impact of modern environmentalism and New Age beliefs, the Celts have come to represent all those virtues in which our materialistic society is most lacking, in particular spirituality and respect for nature. At their most idealised, for example, as presented at the *Celtica* visitor centre at Machynlleth in Wales, the Celts have come to resemble refugees from Middle Earth more than real people. There is also the other side of the coin. Because Western civilisation owes so much to the ancient Greeks and Romans, we tend to think of them as being much more modern in their outlook than they really were. In reality, the ancient Celts were much more like their contemporaries, the Romans, Greeks and also the Germans, than is generally recognised.

Social structure

The Celtic world was not homogeneous and its social structures depended to some extent on the environment and the resources available. In the less fertile lands along the Atlantic fringe of Britain and Ireland, for example, less hierarchical and smaller-scale forms of social organisation prevailed than in the richer farmlands of southern Britain and continental Europe. The main form of social organisation in the Celtic world at the beginning of the La Tène period was the chiefdom, a type of hierarchical society that survived in Ireland and the Scottish Highlands until after the Middle Ages. Chiefdoms were hierarchical societies where rank and status often depended on lineage and inheritance. In historical Celtic societies, chiefs usually came from the senior lineage of the community, that is the one that was believed to trace the most direct line of descent from the community's

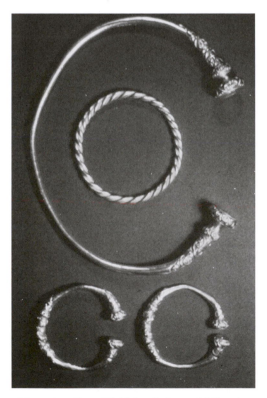

Plate 5 Necklet and bracelets from Waldalgesheim, mid fourth century (gold)

Source: Rheinisches Landesmuseum, Bonn, Germany/Bridgeman Art Library, www.bridgeman.co.uk

founder. Most chiefdoms appear to have been tribally based. In Gaul tribal territories were subdivided into *pagi* ('districts'), which were ruled by subordinate families or clans. Below the chief, the most important class in Celtic society was the warrior aristocracy. Feasting and war were the most important activities for both the chief and his warriors. The feast was an opportunity for the chief to display his wealth, indulge in lavish hospitality and distribute gifts of jewellery, weapons or cattle. There was nothing unselfish about this largesse: it was intended to attract new followers and keep existing ones loyal. Those who accepted the chief's hospitality and gifts were also put under an obligation to do something in return. The warriors fulfilled this obligation by military service. For the warriors' part, their honoured position at the feast and the chief's gifts reinforced their social status within the tribe. The feast was a competitive occasion for the status-conscious warriors: the boasting, heroic eating and drinking and occasional fights over who got the best piece of meat were not just the bad manners that Greeks and Romans thought was all that could be expected of barbarians. Below the warriors was a small class of specialist craftsmen and bards whose activities reinforced the status of the elite, either by producing spectacular jewellery, weapons and armour for them to wear or by singing their praises at feasts and other public occasions. In Britain and Gaul there was also a professional class of priests called Druids, who had a high status because of their knowledge of divination, law, tribal traditions, medicine and such like. The largest class of Celtic society was the peasantry but, as Caesar observed dismissively, they had no political influence in the tribe. Though technically free, most peasants were dependent in some way on the aristocracy. This was the price of calling on their support after crop failures or other disasters, which in pre-industrial farming societies could be expected every six years or so. The Celts also kept, and traded, slaves, but not on the scale of the Mediterranean civilisations. Women enjoyed higher status than they did in the Mediterranean world and in Britain there were even women rulers. Greek and Roman writers, whose wives spent most of their lives confined to their homes, thought the relative freedom the Celts allowed their women a sign of their barbarity. However, Celtic society was still male-dominated and there is no convincing evidence for either institutional matriarchy or matrilineal descent, as is often claimed by feminist historians.

Typically, a chieftain's residence would be in a hillfort, which also served as a refuge for the tribe and its cattle in time of war and, often, as a religious centre. The simplest form of hillfort was just a ditch backed by an earth rampart and timber palisade surrounding a suitable hilltop. It was common for extra defences to be added over time – for example, extra circuits of ramparts, and sophisticated gateways that could not be approached except under a hail of defending fire. Construction techniques varied from simple dumped earth ramparts to the complex *murus gallicus* (Gaulish wall) technique of timber lacing. In timber-laced ramparts a framework of timbers was filled with earth or rubble and faced with a vertical stone wall. Timber-laced ramparts were harder to scale than sloping earth ramparts and they

Plate 6 Mousa Broch, Shetland
Source: John Haywood

were very resistant to undermining and battering, but they could be set on fire. Several hillforts are known in Scotland where the intense heat of burning vitrified the surrounding stonework. Studies of the Iron Age settlement of the Hampshire Downs in southern England have shown how the hillfort of Danebury was the 'capital' of a territory that included several dependent villages. Hillforts were not built throughout Celtic Europe. In northern and western Scotland hundreds of small stone round forts called duns and stone towers called brochs were built. The proliferation of these family-sized fortifications is a sign that a very decentralised form of society prevailed in these regions, with no large-scale political units capable of enforcing peace over a wide area.

Chiefdoms survived in Ireland until the sixteenth century AD and in the Scottish Highlands until the eighteenth century, but in much of Celtic Europe they were beginning to develop into kingdoms and tribal republics by the last centuries BC. Trade with the Mediterranean world may have helped stimulate this process of state formation but the main causes were internal: a rising population and increasing prosperity based on efficient agriculture. The process of centralisation can be seen in changing settlement patterns. In England's South Downs the 24 hillforts that were occupied c. 500 BC had been reduced to just eight by 100 BC as power became focused on a few pre-eminent centres. The defences of those hillforts that remained in use had become more heavily fortified, reflecting their increased status. By this time, hillforts had been abandoned across much of Celtic Europe in favour of more convenient and larger sites called *oppida*. *Oppida* served the same functions as hillforts but were also centres for long-distance trade, tax gathering and craft production. Though *oppida* were often built on lower ground, the suitability of the site for defence was still an important consideration. The *oppidum* of Kelheim in Germany, for example, was built at the confluence of two rivers, giving it natural defences on two sides. *Oppida* usually also had well-built ramparts and sometimes additional defences, such as the linear earthworks which protected the approaches to the *oppidum* of Colchester in Essex. Most *oppida* have a semi-urban character, but some were fully functioning towns with densely packed populations, like the Celtiberian *oppidum* of Numantia, which was laid out on an orderly grid of streets. Such evidence of urban planning is a sign of the existence of strong centralised authority.

The institutions of these Celtic states were similar to, and may have been modelled on, those of the Mediterranean civilisations. The Gaulish Aedui were ruled by elected magistrates called vergobrets and had a constitution that prevented any one family achieving a monopoly over the office. The Belgic Nervii were ruled by a king and an advisory 'senate' of the 300 leading aristocrats of the tribe. Early Celtic states were based on the tribe and kinship groups, rather than on control of a particular territory. Because of this, a Celtic state could, if necessary, move, as the Helvetii did twice in the first century BC. Political life in Celtic states was not so very different from that of the Roman Republic. Just as ambitious Romans like Caesar and Pompey plotted to sideline the elected magistrates and the Senate and win absolute power for themselves, so too did ambitious Celtic aristocrats like Orgetorix of the Helvetii and Vercingetorix of the Arverni. The system of clientage by which Celtic chiefs and aristocrats maintained and protected dependants in return for their military or political support was not a world away, either, from that practised by Roman aristocrats under the Republic.

The process of state formation led to the adoption of literacy, using a variety of borrowed scripts. The earliest Celtic language to be written down was Lepontic, which was spoken in north-east Italy in the fifth and sixth centuries BC. About 40 inscriptions in this language are known, all using the Etruscan alphabet. The Celtiberians had adopted a version of the Iberian script (itself based on the Phoenician script) by the third century BC. The Gauls used both the Greek and Latin alphabets, and in Britain the Latin alphabet was used by the first century AD. The Celts did not become fully literate before the Roman conquest and most culture was always orally transmitted. Writing was used mainly for memorials and dedications, but on the eve of the conquest it was becoming increasingly used in administration for tribal censuses and the like. After Caesar defeated the Helvetii in 58 BC, he found documents in their camp, written in Greek characters, that named all the members of the tribe who could bear arms and listed the numbers of old men, women and children. Considering that the total, including allies, was 368,000, this was a considerable administrative achievement. The eloquence which Greek and Roman writers thought one of the distinguishing characteristics of the Celts continued to be necessary, however, as rhetoric, the skill of persuasive speech, remained the main way to win influence at tribal councils. This was one skill that the Greeks and Romans admired the Celts for, because rhetoric was an important political skill for them too.

Another sign of the increasing political and economic sophistication of the Celts was the adoption of coinage. In the second century BC the Celts in central Europe and Gaul began to use and issue gold and silver coins. The coins were usually based on Greek or Roman prototypes and were often of very high quality, with legends in Greek or Latin characters and portraits of the rulers who had issued them. Thus Celtic rulers were aware, as were Mediterranean rulers, of the propaganda value of coins. At first these coins were probably used mainly by chiefs to reward their followers, but by the time of the Roman conquest of Gaul a true cash economy was beginning to develop. Coins were also in widespread use in south-east Britain in the century before the Roman conquest.

Economy

The economy of Celtic Europe was based on subsistence farming, which occupied probably somewhat more than 90 per cent of the population. It was the surplus agricultural production of the peasantry, delivered as taxes or rents, that ultimately supported the chief, his warrior elite and the craftsmen who served them. The exact nature of farming varied according to the environment. In the wet north-west cattle rearing was the most important source of wealth; grain was important in southern Britain, northern Gaul and Spain; in southern Gaul a Mediterranean farming economy, based on grain, olives and vines, prevailed. Not surprisingly, southern Gaul was one of the first Celtic areas to be fully assimilated into the Roman system, while those areas most dependent on cattle, northern Britain and Ireland, were never conquered. Sheep were bred throughout the Celtic world for their wool and milk and pigs for their meat. Horses were bred mainly for war, cattle being the most important draught animals. The Celts' farm animals were all substantially smaller than their modern counterparts. As well as varieties of wheat, barley and oats, beans, peas and lentils were widely grown. Flax was cultivated to make linen cloth. The landscape of Celtic Europe was much more intensively farmed than is generally realised. By the late Iron Age the Celts used ploughs with iron shares and coulters which could work the heaviest soils efficiently and it is likely that rural population densities and distributions were not greatly different from that of the modern European countryside. There were few areas left that were genuinely wild and untamed. Most of the primeval forests that covered Europe after the Ice Age had been felled even before Celtic times and the woodland that survived was intensively managed to ensure a sustainable supply of building timber, fence posts and fuel. Most Celtic peasant families were self-sufficient in everyday necessities, such as food, clothing and pottery. The main stimulus to trade came from the Celtic elite because of its need to underpin its status through the display of material wealth, such as jewellery and fine weapons, and by the conspicuous consumption of exotic luxuries, especially Mediterranean wine. Trade was, therefore, not motivated by modern economic considerations; its function was essentially social. The scale of imports from the Mediterranean world was such that in Gaul, central Europe and south-east Britain, the Celtic elite had already adopted a very Romanised lifestyle even before they had been conquered. This was something even normally dismissive Roman observers noticed. What the Celts used to pay for these imports is unknown, but the likelihood is that it was mainly agricultural products such as grain, hides and salted meat.

In technological terms, the La Tène Celts lacked the Romans' building skills but in other respects they cannot be considered backward. The Celts were skilled shipbuilders and their efficient 'frame first' construction method was adopted by the Romans. Other Celtic innovations that the Romans adopted included chain mail, barrels and iron tyres for cartwheels. The Romans even copied the pattern of their legionary helmet from the Celts of central Europe. What the Celts never developed was the Romans' industrial capacity that allowed them to mass-produce weapons and armour. While the Romans could equip every soldier with an iron helmet and an iron breastplate or coat of chain mail, these remained expensive luxuries among the Celts and were out of the reach of all but a minority of warriors.

Houses and living conditions

Rich or poor, Celts lived in simple houses constructed of whatever natural materials were most readily available in the local environment. In most areas this meant timber, wattle and clay but in Spain and upland parts of Britain unmortared stone was also used. Celtic houses usually conformed to two main types. In most of Celtic Europe houses had a roughly rectangular plan but in Britain, Ireland and north-west Spain they were usually circular. In Italy Celtic houses are difficult to recognise because the Cisalpine Gauls seem quickly to have adopted the building techniques of the conquered native peoples. Monumental buildings on the scale of those common in the Mediterranean world were unknown before the Roman conquest, but the size of a house was probably a reliable indicator of the wealth and status of its owner, the larger buildings being the homes or feasting halls of the aristocracy. Preservation of Celtic houses is naturally best in those areas where there was extensive use of stone. In a few areas timber houses were built on stone foundations, which would protect them from the damp and make them last longer, but in most areas timbers were simply set directly into the ground. Houses built in this way typically last only 20 years or so before they need to be rebuilt, so all traces of their structures have long since decayed. However, archaeologists can recover the ground plans of wooden houses by plotting the patterns of post holes which are left in the ground. Long after the timbers which once stood in these holes have rotted away, they remain identifiable to archaeologists because the soil which has filled them is usually of different colour and texture to the surrounding undisturbed soil. Because of the extensive deforestation which Iron Age Europe had undergone, timber was used economically. Irrespective of their plan, most houses were built with timber frames, but non-load-bearing parts of the walls were filled with wattle-and-daub, that is a lattice of thin branches sealed with clay to make it draughtproof. Roofs were made of thatch. The interiors of Celtic houses were dark and smoky – there were no windows or smoke holes because these would have caused draughts and let rain in – but they were also well insulated and weatherproof. Celts would not have shivered round their fires on winter nights. The permanently smoky area under the roof was put to good use – being dry, deficient in oxygen and insect-free, it was ideal for hanging and preserving meat. There is little evidence of the use of furniture but written accounts say that Celts sat on furs and ate off low tables. Though the larger houses of the aristocracy might have up to four rooms, most Celtic houses had only one room so there was little privacy for the occupants. The stone wheelhouses that were built in northern Scotland had alcoves radiating from a central living area around the hearth (in plan they resemble a spoked wheel, hence the name). Some of these alcoves may have been used as bedrooms, others for storage. As well as the family dwelling house, a typical Celtic farmstead would also have a number of outbuildings, such as byres for livestock, storerooms and workshops.

Greek and Roman writers often drew attention to the striking appearance of the Celts, describing them as being very tall, fair skinned and blond or red haired. This is undoubtedly a stereotypical description as skeletal evidence from Celtic burials does not suggest that they were in general physically distinct from other Europeans. Celts apparently took great pride in their dress and personal grooming, but fashions varied in different regions. The appearance of the Gauls is best documented, not only from Greek and Roman writings and sculptures, such as the famous *Dying Gaul* from Pergamon, but also from Celtic coins and rare stone heads. Gallic men wore long sleeved tunics belted at the waist and long baggy trousers; women wore long dresses. Cloaks decorated in colourful tartan and other patterns were worn by both sexes. Most clothes were made of wool or linen cloth and could be decorated with embroidery and, for the rich, gold thread. Silk was a luxury available to the rich. Both sexes shaved or plucked their body hair – a painful business – but men wore luxuriant moustaches and sometimes beards. Men in particular seem to have paid a lot of attention to their hair, which they washed with a mixture of lime and water to whiten it and stiffen it so that it could be moulded into spikes. Although men were expected to be able to eat and drink heroically at feasts, they also had to watch their weight as pot bellies were considered to be very unattractive. This is unusual because in pre-industrial societies an ample girth was generally treated as a desirable sign of prosperity (poor people did not usually get to eat enough to put on weight). Both sexes wore much of their personal wealth in the form of jewellery. Some jewellery was practical – most brooches, for example, were used as fasteners for dresses and cloaks – while other pieces, such as bracelets, arm rings and necklaces, were purely decorative. The item of jewellery which is most closely associated with the Celts is the torc, which was a heavy metal neck ring. Representations of Celtic gods often show them wearing torcs, so they may have had a symbolic or religious meaning or perhaps were signs of rank. Tattooing or body painting seems not to have been practised by the Gauls but was distinctive to the Britons.

Life expectancy for the ancient Celts appears to have been comparable with that of other pre-industrial societies. Although child burials are rarely found – children may have been treated differently from adults in death – infant mortality was almost certainly very high. Most men, if they survived to adulthood in the first place, would die before reaching their fifties, while the risks associated with childbirth were such that a woman would be lucky to see her thirtieth birthday. Physically demanding and repetitive domestic tasks, such as grinding corn, meant that by their late twenties most women were suffering from osteoarthritis of the spine. Health care was probably rudimentary, based on a mixture of herbal medicines and magic, but some Celts possessed surgical skills as sets of surgical instruments have occasionally been found as grave goods.

Celtic religion

The popular image of Celtic pagan religion as promoted by neo-Druids and various New Age pagan groups is a simple and somewhat other-worldly nature worship. This view comes from an over-reliance on the testimony of Caesar and other Classical writers who wished to portray the Celts as irrational and superstitious barbarians. The Celts had some highly distinctive religious practices, especially their cult of the severed head, and they were unusual in ancient Europe in having a class of professional priests known as Druids. However, in most respects, the religious beliefs and prac-tices of the Celts were similar to those of contemporary Romans, Greeks and Germans. All were polytheists, all believed in the efficacy of sacrifice and divination, magic spells and witchcraft. All reverenced significant fea-tures of the landscape, such as springs and rivers. All were mortally afraid of ghosts and believed that there was no clear boundary between the natural and the supernatural. Human sacrifice and the cult of the severed head apart, there was really nothing in Celtic religion that was not com-patible with Roman beliefs.

Though they were polytheists, the Celts did not have an ordered pantheon of gods like the Greeks and Romans. The names of over 400 Celtic deities are known, the vast majority of which were associated only with a particular tribe or, like the Roman *genius loci*, with a particular place. The goddess Sequana, for instance, was worshipped only at her shrine at the source of the river Seine. Each tribe probably had its own pantheon, which overlapped to some degree with those of neighbouring tribes, as some gods are known that were worshipped more widely. A mother goddess, who was frequently portrayed as a triple entity, was worshipped almost universally. Hammer-wielding Sucellus, a god of the underworld, was worshipped across most of Gaul, Switzerland and southern Germany, while the warlike god Teutates was worshipped in Britain, Gaul and the Alpine region. The worship of a god with horns or antlers who was a lord of the beasts was also widespread: in Gaul he was called Cernunnos. One of the most widespread cults was that of the sun god Lugh, who was worshipped in Iberia, Ireland and Gaul, where his major cult centre was at Lyon (*Lugdunum*). Given their reputation for clever speech, it should be no surprise that the Celts also venerated a god of eloquence called Ogmios. These gods did not necessarily have the same attributes everywhere they were worshipped. Lugh was a musician and a war god in Ireland but he was a god of trade and technology in Gaul. The Celts did not have any concept of Heaven or Hell or the judgement of the dead. The Otherworld was con-ceived of as being essentially subterranean and they apparently believed that the afterlife would be similar to this one as they buried their dead with offerings appropriate to their rank and sex. The Hallstatt practice of barrow burial was abandoned by the La Tène Celts in favour of interment in flat grave cemeteries. From the second century BC the practice of cremation gradually spread through most of the Celtic world, though not to all parts of the British Isles. On the continent Celtic burials became scarce after 150 BC,

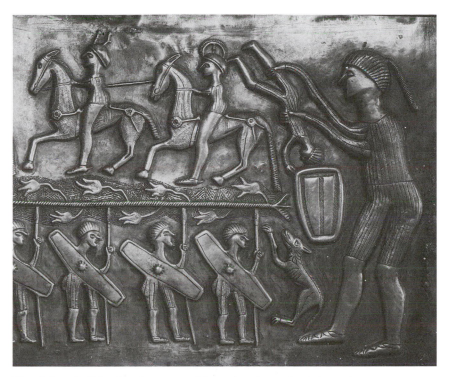

Plate 7 Panel of the Gundestrup cauldron showing a ritual drowning
Source: National Museum, Copenhagen, Werner

perhaps indicating another change in funerary customs. The dead may have been disposed of by exposure or some other method that has left no trace in the earth.

Celtic gods had to be propitiated by sacrifices, which could range from food to hoards of weapons and jewellery and human sacrifices. Sacrifices were usually buried in the ground, a sign of the importance of chthonic (underworld) deities to the Celts, or deposited under water. Though there is some suggestion that the practice was declining at the time of the Roman conquest, human sacrifice was neither rare nor unusual. Many methods are recorded. The victims of Teutates were drowned in a vat of water, those of the thunder god Taranis were burned in wicker effigies or beheaded. A feature of Celtic human sacrifice is overkill, such as the triple death (head injuries, garrotting and throat cutting) meted out to Lindow Man, who was killed and placed in a peat bog in Cheshire, England, in the first century AD. The Lusitanians sacrificed human victims for the purpose of divination, so that their entrails could be examined for signs and portents, but the exact purposes of most human sacrifices are conjectural. Late Iron Age sanctuaries at Ribemont-sur-Ancre and Gournay-sur-Aronde (France), in the territory of the warlike Belgae, provide evidence that the sacrifice of prisoners of war was common. At Gournay the bones of around a thousand people were burned in square-shaped, open-topped ossuaries. The bones had first been crushed to expose the marrow, which the Gauls, in common with the Greeks, believed to be the home of the soul on which the gods of the underworld fed. Thousands of weapons and pieces of armour were displayed, both on a platform over the gateway to the sanctuary and on poles around its perimeter. When the weather and the decay of wooden and leather parts finally brought these to the ground, they were ritually destroyed by the priests and thrown into a ditch, a common practice for ritually deposited weapons throughout the Celtic world. The sanctuary at Ribemont also provided evidence for the burning of human bones, but the most spectacular find was a deposit of 80 decapitated skeletons mingled with weapons that was found by the sanctuary's outer wall. The headless bodies and weapons had probably been heaped together as a communal trophy to celebrate a victory in war. The missing heads had probably been offered to Taranis, who was partial to severed heads, or were kept by individual warriors as personal trophies. We know from written sources that the heads of important victims could become treasured family heirlooms, to be passed from one generation to the next. To modern sensibilities, these displays of rotting dismembered corpses seem nothing short of horrifying, yet for the Celts who owned and created them they probably gave feelings of security and pride, knowing that they would intimidate their enemies and win the favour of their gods.

The practice of human sacrifice does not set the Celts so far apart from their contemporaries as it was common among the Germans too. The Greeks and Romans of Classical times did not normally perform human sacrifice, but even these most gruesome of Celtic practices have some parallels in the Mediterranean civilisations. Not only was ritual destruction of weapons practised by other European peoples, such as early Germans and pagan Vikings, but also, according to Plutarch, by the Romans. A sunken altar found at Gournay, similar to the Greek *escharon*, which was sacred to the gods of the underworld, provides evidence of links between Gallic religion and Greek chthonic cults. In Homer's *Iliad* Achilles sacrificed Trojan prisoners on the funeral pyre of his friend and lover Patroclus. Homer regarded this as a primitive practice, long since abandoned. Gladiatorial combats (adopted in Rome in 264 BC from the Etruscans) were in origin funeral games in which slaves fought to the death. The fresh blood that spilled onto the ground was thought to benefit the soul of the deceased. Later Roman scholars, such as Festus (second century AD), believed that it was a less cruel substitute for human sacrifices which had formerly been performed over the graves of the deceased. And was the Roman practice of executing prisoners during the celebration of a triumph not really a form of ritual killing?

No aspect of Celtic religion has attracted more attention than the Druids. Druids were more than just priests. They served a demanding 20-year apprenticeship during which they had to commit to memory a vast body of orally transmitted verse (a mnemonic device) comprising religious lore, magic, medicine, law, astronomy and tribal history. As well as performing religious rituals and divination, Druids also had educational and legal responsibilities. Their knowledge gave them political influence and status, though most were probably drawn from the aristocracy in the first place as no peasant could afford the luxury of such an apprenticeship. Though a single reference mentions Druids wearing white robes, there is really no reason to believe that they habitually dressed any differently from any other member of the tribal elite. It is also uncertain how widespread Druidism was as Druids are only ever mentioned by Classical writers in connection with Britain and Gaul. Druids performed ceremonies in sacred oak groves, but from the second century BC temples and sacred enclosures became increasingly common in Gaul, central Europe and south-east Britain. This seems to indicate that the process of state formation in the Celtic world was accompanied by a move to more formal forms of worship, comparable to those in the Greek and Roman world. In southern Gaul, the architecture of Celtic temples shows Classical influences, but they retained distinctive Celtic features, including skull niches. Elsewhere, an indigenous form of rectangular ditched enclosure appeared, containing a central sanctuary building and sacrificial pits. The temple at Gournay-sur-Aronde, discussed above, was of this type.

Warfare

Greek and Roman writers liked to portray the Celts' fondness for war as a sign of their irrational and hot-headed temperament. In fact the Celts liked war for the entirely rational reason that it was the surest route for the ambitious chief or warrior to increase his status. The power of a Celtic chieftain or king depended entirely on the size of his warrior following. Warriors expected to be rewarded for their service by gifts of weapons, jewellery and cattle and an honoured place at the feast. Chiefs needed to make war on their neighbours to gain the reputation and the means, by plundering, to attract and retain a warrior band. For warriors war was in some ways a continuation of the feast by other means. A warrior wanted to go to war, not only because of the material rewards, but because it was a chance to indulge in individual heroics that would increase his standing and get him a seat nearer to the chief at the feast by proving that there was more than hot air behind his drunken boasting. Because warriors were competing almost as much with one another as with the enemy, Celtic armies were not highly disciplined like the Roman legion or the Greek phalanx, or even the Germanic shield wall. The long Celtic slashing sword needed space if it was to be wielded efficiently and battles were often preceded by individual contests designed to allow champion warriors to show off. The Romans generally reckoned Celtic cavalry to be superior to their own, but most Celts fought on foot, sometimes using chariots as battlefield transport. Chariots seem to have fallen out of favour on the continent after the third century BC, but they continued in use in Britain up to the Roman conquest. The early Irish epics often refer to the use of chariots in warfare, but this is not substantiated by any archaeological evidence. Celtic chariots were

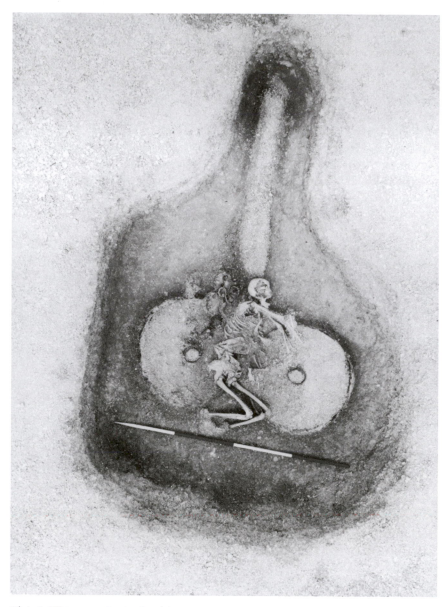

Plate 8 Wetwang chariot burial
Source: Copyright Humber Archaeology Partnership and BM Photographic Services

lightweight constructions of wood and wicker, with spoked wheels shod with iron tyres. In the famous statue on Victoria Embankment in London, 'Boadicea' (Boudica) is shown heroically charging into battle in a chariot with scythes fitted to its wheel hubs. Sadly for romantics, this is a product of the nineteenth-century sculptor's imagination and is not supported by any historical evidence. Greeks and Romans often commented on the Celtic custom of going into battle completely naked with only a shield for protection. This probably had some ritual purpose and it was not practised by all Celtic warriors. Head-hunting was another ritual practice associated with warfare and it also provided concrete evidence of a warrior's valour. The lack of formal military discipline meant that sophisticated tactics were impossible. The prelude to battle involved a great deal of shouting, boasting and the raucous blowing of long war trumpets called carnyxes to intimidate the enemy. Battle was joined by a headlong charge that was terrifying in its recklessness and dash, especially for inexperienced opponents who often turned tail and ran. However, if a confident enemy stood his ground and beat off the charge, a Celtic army could very quickly turn into a disorganised shambles that could easily be routed. The Romans formed the opinion that the Celts were fierce in the first onrush but were easily discouraged and prone to irrational despair if checked. This, of course, contrasted unfavourably with the steadiness of the legions, but was only to be expected of barbarians. Roman prejudices aside, this tactic did win a lot of battles for the Celts, the last being at Falkirk in 1746, when a rebel Highland army armed with swords routed a larger government army armed with cannons and muskets. However, against a well-armed and disciplined opponent, the Celts usually fought at a serious disadvantage. Siege warfare was not a Celtic specialism and they were rarely able to capture well-fortified sites except by surprise. During his conquest of Gaul Caesar reported that the Celts were beginning to imitate Roman siege warfare tactics and use them effectively. However, this came too late to change the course of the war.

Tactics apart, the contrast between the Roman and Celtic attitudes to war can be exaggerated. Ambitious Romans like Julius Caesar used war in exactly the same way as any Celtic warrior or chief, as a means to enrich himself, win prestige and a loyal following of legionaries, and seize power for himself. Nor were Roman commanders immune to the appeal of publicly performing acts of personal valour. In 361 BC the dictator Titus Manlius fought an enormous Gaulish warrior in single combat on the bridge over the river Anio while the two armies looked on. After dispatching the giant, Titus beheaded his corpse (a very Celtic thing to do) and removed his torc, which, though it was still covered in gore, he wore proudly as he returned to his own cheering ranks. A similar single combat was fought between another giant Gaul and the tribune Marcus Valerius in 348. The reputations of neither man suffered for indulging in this typically barbarian behaviour. Ordinary Roman soldiers, it is true, fought mainly for pay, but they too sometimes gave in to the desire to show off to their comrades. However, individual heroics were generally disapproved of, as success usually depended on group cohesion.

A people ripe for conquest

The picture that emerges of the Celts in the late Iron Age is not one of a simple otherworldly folk but of a sophisticated people moving quickly towards the development of full-blown urban civilisation. Although Greek and Roman writers, for their own reasons, emphasised the differences between the Celts and the Mediterranean civilisations, they were in reality not so very different. Unfortunately for the Celts, it was this that doomed them. Their individualistic military system, centralised political structures, well-established social hierarchy and prosperity made the conquest and assimilation of the Celts both an attractive and a practical proposition for the Romans. Neither the Celts' religion nor their values were obstacles to this. The Roman Empire was not built on military force alone; it could not have lasted as long as it did if it had been. Long-term military occupation would have been economically unsustainable. Rome's success as an imperial power was due as much to its ability to Romanise people as to its conquering legions. Though provincial governors and a few other senior officials might be centrally appointed, most government in the Roman Empire was local government and that was in the hands of the provincials themselves. Rome coopted the local aristocracies of the peoples they conquered by offering them secure status and a comfortable Romanised lifestyle, in turn exploiting their prestige in the local community and traditional ties of patronage and loyalty. Even if the peasantry was discontented under the burden of Roman taxation, it was leaderless and capable of nothing more serious than banditry. For this to be possible the societies the Romans conquered had already to have a high degree of centralisation – this was why Rome was so successful in the Mediterranean world. It was these conditions that defined the limits of conquest for the Romans. The Romans could win battles against peoples like the Caledonians of northern Britain and the Germans, who had not attained a high degree of centralisation, but they could not assimilate them, so neither could be conquered. The same factors would have pertained in Ireland had the Romans tried to conquer it. Ironically, the Celts were vulnerable to conquest not because they were too primitive but because they were too civilised.

4

THE CELTS AND THE ROMAN REPUBLIC

These [Gauls] are not the Latin or Sabine enemy you can deal with,
one who will become your ally when you have defeated them in
battle. We have drawn our swords against wild beasts whose blood
we must shed or spill our own.

Consul M. Popilius Laenas (348 BC)
(Livy, *History of Rome*, VII.24)

When it was sacked by the Cisalpine Gauls Rome was just one of dozens of Italian city-states while the Celts dominated most of central and Western Europe. That Rome would one day conquer almost the entire Celtic world (not to mention the Mediterranean world) would have seemed a vanishingly remote possibility, yet by the first century AD the only independent Celts would be those in Ireland and northern Britain. It is something of a cliché to say that history is written by the winners, but it is not the less important to say so for all that. The Celts had not developed a fully literate civilisation at the time of their conquest and so could not record their version of events. As a result, this is a story that can be told only from the Roman point of view, with all the limitations that that implies, especially as Roman perceptions of the Celts were always coloured by the memory of the sack of 390 and the generalised prejudice of the civilised towards the barbarian.

Divide and conquer?

The Roman conquest of the Celts looks much like the working out of an implacable vengeance for the sack of Rome. But Roman expansion was no more centrally planned than Celtic expansion had been – it was driven mainly by internal politics and the search for secure frontiers – and the Romans' hostility toward the Celts can be exaggerated. Although the

Romans certainly did see the Celts as inferior and potentially dangerous barbarians, their relations with them were usually far more pragmatic than their rhetoric might lead one to suppose. They formed alliances with many Celtic peoples, who welcomed Roman protection against hostile Celtic or non-Celtic neighbours. And the Romans were usually punctilious when it came to keeping their side of the bargain, as much with the Celts as with other peoples. Of course, alliances with Rome tended to lead in one direction only, that is to eventual absorption into the Roman Empire, but if the influence, status and wealth of the tribal elite were thereby secured, this would not necessarily be unwelcome. The Celts had only a very weak sense of common identity: their primary loyalty was to their tribes, or even their families. Tribes were often divided into factions based on kinship and sometimes one of these might call on Roman assistance against its rivals. Such divisions were certainly exploited by the Romans. Tribal elites usually acted in what they perceived as their individual best interests. This did not preclude cooperation between tribes, but none of them could conceive that they all had a common interest in defending the abstract notion of 'Celtic independence' against Roman imperialism because no such common interest existed. Why fight the Romans simply to carry on paying tribute to the overbearing Celtic tribe in the next valley? For good reasons, Rome simply was not seen as the common enemy by all Celts. Modern historians usually see this lack of common identity and common purpose among the Celts as the main factor in their eventual conquest by the Romans. Even the Romans saw it this way. For example, Tacitus noted how long it took the Britons to learn 'that a common danger must be repelled by union'. Disunity allowed the Romans to divide and conquer.

Or did it? Rather than simply asking why the Romans were able to conquer the Celts, it is also worth asking why it took them so long. Taking, as it did, all of 400 years, the Roman conquest of the Celts was no blitzkrieg, and it was never actually quite completed. In the same time that it took them to conquer the Celtic peoples of Iberia, that is, the last two centuries BC, the Romans conquered the entire eastern Mediterranean with its ancient and sophisticated civilisations, like those of Greece and Egypt, and well-ordered kingdoms with standing armies and strongly fortified cities. Sometimes resistance was fierce, but battles often had decisive results and, once an area had submitted to Roman rule, rebellions were rare and brief (except in Judaea). In contrast, Celtic Iberia was still a decentralised tribal society, albeit one that was moving towards urbanisation and state formation. Battles there were rarely decisive and rebellions were frequent and bloody. Yet the Iberian Celts never came close to uniting in common cause against the Romans. In contrast, the Gauls' resistance to Rome collapsed within a year of their uniting under the leadership of Vercingetorix. Clearly disunity cannot have been the disadvantage it is so often assumed to be. More than this, could disunity, or, more precisely, the decentralisation that came with it, actually have been the reason why the Celts resisted Rome for so much longer and with so much more success than anyone else bar the Germans (another decentralised society)?

The conquest of Cisalpine Gaul

The Roman conquest of the Celts began with the breakdown of the peace agreed with the Cisalpine Gauls in 334 BC. Given the nature of Celtic society and the needs of its warrior elite, this was almost inevitable, but there was also a new factor involved. By the end of the fourth century it was obvious to all that Rome was becoming a power to reckon with, and this began to make friends of old enemies among the other peoples of peninsular Italy. In 299 Etruscans joined the Gauls in raiding Roman territory and two years later the Samnites joined in with them too. In 295 the Romans faced, and defeated, an even greater alliance of the Senones, Etruscans, Umbrians and Samnites in a hard-fought battle at Sentinum in Umbria, but not before the Senones had wiped out a Roman legion at Clusium (Chiusi). Livy describes the triumphant Celts carrying severed heads hanging around their horses' necks or on the points of spears and singing victory songs. Another victory over a Roman army at Arettium (Arezzo) in 284 made the Senones overconfident and they foolishly and provocatively murdered ambassadors sent from Rome to negotiate terms for the release of prisoners. This made a Roman counterattack inevitable, and this time it was the Senones who were defeated and conquered. A Roman military colony was founded at Sena Gallica (Senigallia) in 283 to prevent any rebellions. The neighbouring Boii tried to liberate the Senones but they too were soundly defeated and negotiations were followed by a long peace.

The key to Roman success against the Gauls was a change in their military organisation and battlefield tactics. At the time of the sack of Rome, the Romans fought in the Greek style, as a phalanx of heavily armoured spearmen. Fighting in a phalanx was the antithesis of the Celtic way of war, as it required strong discipline and teamwork rather than individual heroics. But the phalanx proved to be a dangerously inflexible formation when faced with the more irregular tactics employed by the Celts and it was especially vulnerable to outflanking. The Romans, therefore, abandoned the phalanx and began to develop more flexible tactics based on smaller units of 60 heavily armed infantrymen called maniples (literally 'handfuls') supported by light infantry and cavalry. The emphasis on teamwork and discipline remained. The army was organised into legions of 3,000–4,000 men (originally legion simply meant 'levy' and applied to the whole Roman army). Of great significance, too, was the replacement of the spear as the main weapon by the javelin. Unlike the Romans, whose heavy infantry were well armoured, most Celts fought with only a shield for protection. This made them very vulnerable to attack with javelins. A Celtic warrior might successfully stop a javelin with his shield, but if the javelin stuck in the shield it became heavy and unwieldy and had to be thrown away, leaving him even more vulnerable.

Conflict between the Gauls and Romans again broke out in 225. A decision by the Romans in 232 to seize the land of the conquered Senones and divide it between the Roman poor alarmed the Boii. In alliance with the Insubres, Taurisci and the Gaesati ('spear-men': Celtic mercenaries

51

from the Alpine regions), the Boii invaded Roman territory with a huge army, claimed by later Roman writers to have included 50,000 infantry and 20,000 cavalry and charioteers. Over 50 years had passed since the last major conflict between the Cisalpine Gauls and the Romans. In that time Rome had completed the conquest of peninsular Italy and captured Sicily, Sardinia and Corsica from Carthage in the First Punic War, making it the major power of the western Mediterranean. Even without its Italian dependencies, Rome could now raise nearly four times as many troops as the Gauls (in 225 Rome had 250,000 citizens qualified to serve as infantry and another 23,000 who could serve as cavalry), and, because the state now usually provided arms and armour, they were equipped to a much higher standard than the average Celtic warrior. The invasion initially went well for the Gauls: they defeated one Roman army at Fiesole, near Florence, and captured an enormous quantity of plunder, prisoners and cattle. When only three days' march from Rome, the Gauls learned that a second Roman army was approaching from the south, so they began an orderly with-drawal north along the Mediterranean coast. Unknown to the Gauls (and, at first, to the pursuing Roman army too), another Roman army, which had been hurriedly withdrawn from Sardinia, had landed at Pisa to their north and cut off their line of retreat. At Telamon, near the coast of Etruria 100 miles (160 kilometres) north of Rome, the Celtic army was trapped between these two Roman armies and annihilated after heavy fighting. Roman javelins caused great execution among the poorly armoured Gauls, quickly breaking up their charges. The shorter Roman thrusting swords also proved more deadly in close combat than the long Celtic slashing swords. The Gaesati fought completely naked, hoping to intimidate the Romans with their fine physiques, and they suffered dreadful casualties as a consequence. The Gaulish chariots played little part in the battle and there is no further record of their use on the continent after Telamon. The dead included a Celtic king and a Roman consul, whose head was taken as a trophy by the surviving Gauls. Another king, Aneroestes, took his own life. The Romans immediately seized the initiative and began the complete subjection and annexation of Cisalpine Gaul. The Gauls were vulnerable to Roman attack, as many of them had settled in the former Etruscan cities. The conquest took only three years and was completed with the capture of Mediolanum (Milan), the main settlement of the Insubres, in 222. Even the Cenomani, who had taken no part in the battle of Telamon, were conquered. The Romans began to consolidate their conquest by found-ing military colonies at Piacenza and Cremona, but these had hardly been established when, in 218, the Second Punic War broke out with Carthage.

Recognising that Carthage could not win a long war of attrition, its leading general Hannibal decided on an invasion of Italy in the hope of persuading the Italian peoples to rebel against Rome, so depriving it of most of its manpower. Hannibal took the Romans by surprise by march-ing his army overland from Spain and crossing the Alps to descend on the valley of the river Po. Hannibal's army already included a large contingent of Celtiberians and he was immediately greeted as a liberator by the Boii and the Insubres, who joined his army in their thousands. Hannibal was one of history's great battlefield commanders, yet, despite a string of spectacular victories, culminating in the battle of Cannae in 216 in which over 30,000 Roman soldiers died, the mass defections he had hoped for never materialised. Most of Italy, including many of the Gauls even, remained loyal to Rome. After Cannae, the Romans wisely gave up trying to fight Hannibal on his own terms and avoided set-piece battles. Using irregular harassing tactics, the Romans gradually pinned Hannibal down in a strategic cul-de-sac in southern Italy while they concentrated their forces on destroying Carthage's empire in Spain, whose defence was in the hands of Hannibal's less able brother Hasdrubal. As the war dragged on with no prospect of victory in sight, the Gauls began to desert Hannibal: he had, in any case, always regarded them as disposable 'cannon fodder'. Carthage finally surrendered to Rome in 201 and the Romans returned to the business of subduing Cisalpine Gaul. Serious resistance to Roman rule ended with the surrender of the Boii in 191, though there was one last invasion from over the Alps in 186, sent back whence it came three years later. Within a few decades most of Cisalpine Gaul south of the Po had been divided up and given to settlers from peninsular Italy, but the land north of the river was left in Gaulish hands. The Alpine tribes still gave occasional trouble into the reign of the emperor Augustus (27 BC–AD 14) and many Gauls took part in the Italian slave rebellion led by the Thracian gladiator Spartacus in 73 BC. The Celtic warrior tradition of single combat made captured Gauls ideal candidates for the gladiatorial schools, and Spartacus' two most trusted lieutenants, Crixus and Oenomaus, were both Gauls. The rebellion shook Roman Italy to its core, but too many of the participants had no goals beyond plunder and vengeance: despite Spartacus' fine generalship, the revolt was crushed in 71 BC.

Spain: the hardest conquest

Rome's victory over Carthage transformed it into the unrivalled superpower of the Mediterranean world. Among the spoils of war was Spain's Mediterranean coastline, which had formerly been under Carthaginian rule. To compensate itself for its losses in the First Punic War, in the 230s Carthage had begun to build a territorial empire in Spain. The Iberian peoples of the Mediterranean coastal areas were brought under direct Carthaginian rule: the Celtiberians of the interior were ruled indirectly through alliances with important chieftains and occasional large-scale punitive expeditions. Celtiberians fought on both sides in the Second Punic War and earned a reputation for side-changing and desertion. This merely confirmed Roman prejudices about the unreliability of Celts in general, but the Celtiberians actually faced a real dilemma. They were trapped between two warring great powers: neutrality was impossible but neither side had anything very positive to offer them in return for their support – hence their indecisiveness. After they defeated the last Carthaginian army in Spain at Ilipa in 206, the Romans retained control of the coast from Gades (Cadiz) to the Pyrenees, and behind it a hinterland extending some 60 to 120 miles (96 to 192 kilometres) into the interior. This area, roughly corresponding to that occupied by the Iberians, was socially and economically the most advanced region of Spain, having been integrated into the Mediterranean–Near Eastern trading systems for five hundred years. This area the Romans divided into two provinces, but the Celtiberians resumed full independence.

It is very doubtful that the Romans had a master plan for the complete conquest of Spain but the Celtiberians and their neighbours the Lusitanians cannot have known this. Mutual suspicions soon led to conflict between the Romans and Celts. Lusitanian support for an Iberian rebellion in 197 inevitably fed the Romans' fear of barbarians, while Celtic anxieties cannot have been eased by the Roman seizure of silver mines in their territory and a bungled attempt in 195 to capture Numantia, the *oppidum* of the strongest Celtiberian tribe, the Arevaci. Thereafter, the search for secure frontiers drew the Romans more and more deeply into Spain, but it was not until 16 BC that the peninsula was completely subdued, after nearly 200 years of frequent and bitter warfare. In one campaign alone, in 179–178, the Roman general Tiberius Gracchus boasted of destroying over 300 Celtiberian settlements. The Romans suffered heavy casualties too, for example losing over 15,000 soldiers against the Lusitanians alone between 155 and 153 and another 12,000 between 147 and 141. On average, the Romans had to keep 20,000–25,000 troops stationed in Spain every year. The Spanish wars were an enormous drain on Roman manpower and wealth.

After Tiberius' scorched earth campaign, Spain was considered secure enough for Roman colonisation to begin, but arbitrary Roman demands caused a resurgence of resistance by the Lusitanians and Celtiberians in 155–153. Although the two peoples made some attempts to coordinate their efforts, theirs remained two essentially separate and independent rebellions. The initial Roman response was vigorous and they soon seemed to have the rebellion under control. The Celtiberians surrendered in 151 after the Romans laid siege to Numantia, and the following year the Lusitanians also sued for peace and agreed to a Roman proposal to resettle them on new lands. Meeting the Romans at an agreed rendezvous, the first group of Lusitanian settlers was disarmed, divided up into smaller groups and massacred. The entirely predictable result of this Roman treachery was an immediate renewal of hostilities by the Lusitanians. By 147 Viriathus – a shepherd and sometime outlaw who is still a national hero in Portugal – had emerged as the leader of the Lusitanians. His background made him a natural guerrilla fighter and for years he ran rings around the armies Rome sent against him, even briefly occupying the Roman province of Hispania Ulterior. Viriathus doubled the Romans' problems by persuading the Celtiberians to renew their resistance in 144. In 141 Viriathus enjoyed his greatest victory when he surrounded a consular army and forced it to surrender on condition that its men did not fight in Spain again. No sooner were they free than the Romans reneged on the agreement and returned to the attack. His victory made Viriathus too willing to confront the Romans on their own terms and

Plate 9 Reconstructed Celtiberian house at Numantia

Source: John Haywood

they soon had him on the defensive, beating him every time he met them in battle. But a truly decisive victory eluded the Romans: so long as Viriathus remained at large, resistance continued. Despairing of capturing him themselves, the Romans finally disposed of Viriathus by treachery, bribing one of his servants to murder him in 139. Two hundred pairs of warriors fought in single combat at the funeral games held in honour of Viriathus, but, deprived of his inspirational leadership, Lusitanian resistance finally collapsed.

The Celtiberians continued to resist, forcing the surrender of another Roman army at Numantia in 137. Once again the Romans dealt in bad faith – a clear sign of their frustration with their Spanish ulcer – and the war continued. The unfortunate Roman commander who had negotiated the surrender was stripped and bound and handed over to the Celtiberians, who decently enough released him. In 134 Scipio Aemelianus was appointed to command the Roman armies in Spain. An able but cautious commander, Scipio was a master of siegecraft – it was he who had captured and destroyed Carthage after besieging it for three years in the third and final Punic War in 146. With over 60,000 men under his command, Scipio probably enjoyed a clear numerical superiority over the Celtiberians, but their morale was low after years of indecisive warfare. Scipio decided to play to his strengths and, after he had spent several months restoring discipline to his army, he decided to lay siege to the Celtiberian 'capital' at Numantia. Numantia had already withstood several Roman sieges but none had been so determinedly prosecuted as this would be. Scipio methodically surrounded Numantia with seven forts and a 9 km/5.5 mile-long wall with watchtowers and fronted with defensive ditches. Even the local rivers were obstructed with ingenious contraptions of revolving wooden beams with sharp spikes on them. Scipio did a thorough job, for the remains of his siegeworks can still be seen. It is clear that the Celtiberians had concentrated all their forces to defend Numantia. Scipio was not expecting the arrival of a relief army because he built no outer wall to defend his positions from attack from the rear. Because of their earlier successes, the Celtiberians were probably very confident of holding out. This confidence was not entirely misplaced: in ancient and medieval times sieges usually did fail. However, Scipio had cleverly invested the stronghold before the harvest could be got in and, as a result, the supply situation in Numantia soon became critical. This forced the Celtiberians into battle on Roman terms as they made desperate attempts to break through the lines of circumvallation. Predictably enough, the Romans, fighting with the advantages of numbers and strong defensive positions, repulsed all attempts and after eight months, early in 133, Numantia surrendered. According to some accounts, the Celtiberians had resorted to cannibalism before the end and many chose to take their own lives in preference to enslavement by the Romans.

The fall of Numantia broke the back of Celtiberian resistance but rebellions continued for many years. Many of these rebellions were quite shamelessly provoked by glory-seeking Roman governors who wanted military victories to enhance their reputations and career prospects back home in Rome: Julius Caesar was one of these cynical opportunists. At the same time that they tried to wear down Celtic resistance by military campaigns, the Romans also undermined it by granting privileges, the greatest of which was citizenship, to those who proved loyal and cooperative. This process started early. The Celtiberian chieftain Thurrus, who was captured during Tiberius Gracchus' campaign in 178, went on to become a commander in the Roman army. If they did not yet feel that it was a blessing, by the early first century BC most of the Celtiberians and Lusitanians had come at least to accept Roman rule. When the Lusitanians rebelled again in 80 BC they did so in support of Sertorius, a Roman dissident who offered not independence but a reformed Roman government. All the same, it had taken over a century of warfare to reach this point.

Sertorius made good use of his Lusitanian allies' guerrilla fighting expertise but his rebellion collapsed when he was murdered in 73. Spain enjoyed a decade of relative peace, until Julius Caesar was appointed governor in 61. Caesar was eager for military glory and he immediately campaigned against the Lusitanians, who were still not under firm Roman control following Sertorius' rebellion, before leading a naval expedition against Brigantium (modern La Coruña), the capital of the Gallaeci, in 61 BC, but though it earned him a triumph back in Rome, and won him the consulship in 59, it achieved nothing permanent. The Gallaeci and their neighbours in the mountainous and mineral-rich north-west, the Astures and Cantabri, remained stubbornly independent. Not that this worried Caesar: he had a bigger prize in his sights – Gaul.

Galatia: the buffer state

At the same time that they were consolidating their hold on Spain, the Romans were also extending their power eastwards into the Greek world. King Philip V of Macedon had given ineffectual support to Carthage in the Second Punic War and in 197 the Romans set out to punish him for his unprovoked aggression. After winning an easy victory over Philip at Kynoskephalai and forcing him to free the Greek city-states, which had been under Macedonian domination since the reign of Alexander the Great's father, Philip II, the Romans withdrew. But they were soon back, drawn deeper and deeper into the quarrels of the Greek states until in 146 they imposed direct rule. Their involvement in the Greek world brought the Romans into contact with the Galatians. The Seleucid ruler Antiochus III (r. 223–187) was another Hellenistic king who liked to think of himself as a new Alexander the Great. Antiochus resented the Roman intervention in Greece, which he saw as being properly in his sphere of influence.

In 191 Antiochus took an army to Greece but was quickly driven out by the Romans. The next year, the Romans invaded Anatolia and won a decisive victory over Antiochus at the battle of Magnesia (Manisa, western Turkey). Antiochus' army included such novelties as armoured cavalry, war elephants and scythed chariots, as well as a large contingent of Galatian mercenaries, none of which made much impression on the Roman legions.

As a result of their participation in the battle of Magnesia, the Galatians became the victims of a Roman punitive expedition in 189. The Tolistobogii and Trocmi were defeated together at the battle of Olympos near Pessinus. The victorious Romans sold some 40,000 prisoners, including women and children, into slavery. The Romans then occupied the hillfort of Ancyra (modern Ankara) before defeating the Tectosages at Magaba, about 30 miles (48 kilometres) to the north-west. Roman peace terms included a ban on the Galatians raiding in western Anatolia. In the aftermath of this defeat a chieftain of the Tolistobogii, Ortiagon, tried to unite the Galatians under a Hellenistic-style monarchy but without success.

Relations between the Galatians and the Romans improved after 189. When the Galatians renewed their raids on Pergamon in 167, the Romans intervened to restrain Pergamene retaliation and helped negotiate a peace treaty two years later that appears to have left both sides believing that they had won. The Galatians celebrated the peace by sacrificing their Pergamene prisoners to the gods, the Pergamenes with a sculptured frieze on their altar of Zeus, showing heaps of captured Celtic weapons. After 133, when Pergamon was bequeathed to Rome by its last king Attalus III, the Romans came to see Galatia as a valuable buffer against invasion from the east and happily encouraged Galatian attacks on Pontus and Cappadocia. In 88 the Galatians suffered a terrible blow when most of the tetrarchs, their ruling aristocracy, were massacred by King Mithridates VI of Pontus. Mithridates was an ambitious despotic ruler with a hatred of Rome and its Celtic allies. Catching the Romans unprepared, he captured Pergamon in 88 and massacred the resident Roman population. This, perhaps, should have made the Galatians wary of accepting Mithridates' invitation to peace talks: all but one of the 60 chiefs who attended were treacherously murdered in breach of all of the laws of diplomacy and hospitality. Many of those who had not attended, as well as the families of those who had, were also hunted down and killed. Altogether, only three tetrarchs survived. By the end of the following year, the Romans had driven Mithridates back to Pontus and restored Galatia's independence, but it never really recovered from the loss of its ruling class. Mithridates continued to be a destabilising influence in Anatolia until his final defeat by the Roman general Pompey in 66. The Galatians remained loyal allies of Rome throughout.

In 64 Pompey reorganised the government of the Galatians, appointing a king (who was still called a tetrarch, however) to rule over each of the three tribes. By skilful use of diplomatic marriages, King Deiotarus of the Tolistobogii soon emerged as the dominant tetrarch and came to be regarded by the Romans as the sole ruler of Galatia. Deiotarus had been one of the three tetrarchs to survive Mithridates' terror. When civil war broke out between Caesar and Pompey in 49, Deiotarus loyally supported his old patron. He survived Pompey's defeat only because he had a good lawyer, Cicero, to argue his case before the Senate. Cicero later complained that Deiotarus proved rather mean when it came to paying for his services. Deiotarus seems to have had a knack for picking the losing side in Roman civil wars for he later supported Brutus against Mark Antony, but he still managed to die in bed of old age. The last Celtic king of Galatia was Deiotarus' son Deiotarus II, who proved himself beyond doubt his father's son by supporting Mark Antony against Octavian, the future emperor Augustus, in the last civil war of the Roman Republic. Deiotarus II was briefly succeeded by a native Anatolian, Amyntas. On his death in 25 BC Galatia was peacefully annexed and became a Roman province. In the years after Mithridates' devastating attack, the Galatians had become increasingly Romanised in their way of life. Deiotarus I had even introduced Roman practices of estate management and legionary-style training for his army. This, together with the development of a centralised single monarchy for the three tribes, made the final assimilation of the Galatians into the Roman imperial system both easy and painless for all concerned. The Galatians kept their identity for a long time under Roman rule. Even as late as the fourth century AD, St Jerome would remark that the Galatians spoke the same language as the Gauls. How long they continued to do so is unknown but it must have died out before the eighth century as the name Galatia had fallen out of use by this time.

The threat from the north

The annexation of Carthaginian Spain had the effect of focusing Roman attention more closely on Gaul. Roman officials and soldiers frequently travelled overland between Italy and Spain, following the Mediterranean coast. The route was dotted with friendly Greek cities such as Massalia, Antipolis (Antibes) and Nicea (Nice) but the roads between them were exposed to attacks by the Gauls and Ligurians (a Celtic-influenced but non-Celtic-speaking people). These attacks were not limited to simple banditry – in 189 a Roman governor was killed while travelling to Spain despite being accompanied by 7,000 troops – and they were as much of a threat to the Greek cities as to the Romans. The need to protect themselves and their allies drew the Romans into deeper and deeper military engagement in the region. Finally in 125, following an appeal for assistance by Massalia, the Romans conquered the Ligurians and two Gaulish tribes of the Rhône valley, the Saluvii and Voconti. This Roman intrusion into Gaul provoked the Arverni (from the Auvergne) and the Allobroges (from between the Rhône and the Isère) into war, but in typical Celtic fashion they did not coordinate their efforts. The Allobroges were defeated near Avignon in 121 and brought under Roman rule; the Arverni were defeated soon afterwards but escaped with their liberty. The Romans then pushed west, securing their route to Spain by completing the conquest of Gaul's Mediterranean coastline in 118. The conquered territories became the province of Gallia Transalpina or simply Provincia Romana, whence Provence. By no means all the Gauls were dismayed to find the Romans encamped on their door-step. The Aedui welcomed the Romans as allies against their traditional tribal enemies and as trading partners, an arrangement which served them well for 70 years.

Plate 10 Doorway with skulls, from a sanctuary of the Saluvii, Roquepertuse, France (third to second century BC)

Source: Musée Borély, Marseille, France/Lauros-Giraudon/Bridgeman Art Library, www.bridgeman.co.uk

The Romans had scarcely completed their conquest of southern Gaul when they received an unwelcome reminder of the threat from the north. Some years previously two German tribes, the Cimbri and Teutones, had left their homeland in Jutland and begun a seemingly aimless rampage that took them across the length and breadth of central and western Europe. The first the Romans heard of this was that the tribes had passed through the territory of the Boii in Bohemia on their way south-east to the middle Danube. There they had been defeated by the Scordisci near Belgrade before turning west into the territory of the Taurisci, a Celtic tribe of the eastern Alps who were allied to Rome. The Romans dispatched an army to protect them but it was heavily defeated at Noreia in 113.

The way to Italy now lay open, but the two tribes inexplicably turned north-west before reappearing on the frontier of Transalpine Gaul in 110 in alliance with two Gaulish tribes, the Helvetii and Tigurini. After the Germans' victory over another Roman army, sent to drive them off from the frontier in 109, they were joined by two more Gaulish tribes, the Volcae and Tectosages from the region around Toulouse. The Romans quickly conquered the Volcae and Tectosages in 107–106, plundering a hundred tons of gold and silver from their temple at Toulouse in the process, but if they thought the worst was over they were sadly mistaken. In 105 the Cimbri and Teutones caused panic in Rome when they annihilated a third Roman army at Arausio (Orange) in Transalpine Gaul. Once again the way to Italy lay open, and once again the Germans let the Romans off the hook. After the battle, the two tribes split up, the Teutones heading north into the territory of the Belgae, the Cimbri heading west into Spain. The consul Marius used the breathing space to reorganise the Roman legions as a full-time professional army. Arms drill and weapons training, adapted from the gladiatorial schools, was introduced. The maniple was abandoned in favour of the larger cohort of 480 men, subdivided into six units of 80 men called centuries. A legion was made up of 10 cohorts, one of which was double strength. Equipment was standardised. All soldiers were issued with an oblong shield, a chain mail coat, iron helmet, javelin and *gladius*, a short thrusting sword well suited to close-order fighting. Soldiers had to carry emergency supplies, cooking equipment and tools to build a fortified camp every night when on campaign. Only Roman citizens could join the legions, but auxiliary units, often of specialist troops such as archers and cavalry, were recruited from the provinces and allied states. These reforms gave Rome one of the most effective instruments of imperial expansion known to history. When the Cimbri and Teutones again returned to Roman territory they were defeated and massacred: the Teutones at Aix-en-Provence in 102, the Cimbri, having finally invaded Italy, at Vercellae a year later. The Romans heaved a collective sigh of relief but they did not forget.

5

CAESAR'S CONQUEST OF GAUL

Caesar was informed that the Helvetii intended to cross the territories of the Sequani and the Aedui and then enter the country of the Santones, which is near to that of the Tolosates, a tribe living in the Roman Province. He saw that it would be very dangerous to the Province to allow such a warlike people, hostile to Rome, to become established so close to its rich cornlands, which were without any natural defences.

Julius Caesar, *The Gallic War* (58 BC)

The extraordinary incursions of the Cimbri and Teutones led to a revolution in Roman attitudes to Gaul. Transalpine Gaul came to be seen not only as a safe land route to Spain but also as an essential buffer zone against invasion from the north. When new developments in the middle of the first century BC threatened to destabilise the independent Gaulish tribes north of the Roman province, it was easy for Julius Caesar, newly appointed as governor of Gallia Transalpina, to persuade the Senate that military intervention was essential to protect Rome from attack. The threatened destabilisation of Gaul came from two sources. In 58 BC the Helvetii, a major Alpine tribe numbering over 300,000, decided to migrate across Gaul and resettle in Aquitania. The Helvetii had recently taken in many refugees from the Boii, who had suffered a catastrophic defeat at the hands of the Dacians a year or two earlier. Population pressure may therefore have played a part in the Helvetii's decision, but they must also have felt vulnerable where they were, squeezed between the Romans to their south and the increasingly powerful Germanic tribes to their north. At about the same time as the Helvetii were planning their migration, the Aedui appealed to Rome for support against their neighbours, the Arverni and the Sequani. The Sequani were allied with King Ariovistus of the Germanic Suebi, who crossed the Rhine in some force. The Suebi found they liked Gaul so much that they turned on the Sequani and began to occupy their land, raising the spectre of a replay of the invasions of the Cimbri and Teutones.

These disturbances gave Caesar all the excuse he needed to intervene in Gaul: not only did they threaten to spill over into Gallia Transalpina, they also threatened to disrupt Rome's lucrative trade with the Gauls. Caesar dealt with both the Helvetii and the Suebi quickly and with brutal effectiveness, dispatching both back to their original homelands after inflicting heavy casualties. But this was not enough for Caesar. Rome's rapid rise from city-state to empire had placed the republican form of government under increasing strain while the professionalisation of the army had transferred real power from the Senate to a handful of politically ambitious generals. No one understood the realities of Roman power politics better than Caesar. To achieve the political influence he craved, he needed not only to win a few battles but to make conquests. These would provide more than glory, useful though that was for impressing the Roman people: they would provide the opportunity to enrich himself with plunder, which he could use to buy the loyalty of his soldiers and to maintain a network of alliances within the Roman political class. Caesar's own brilliant, but hardly impartial, account of his campaigns in Gaul was part and parcel of his programme of political self-aggrandisement and was intended to be read aloud to gatherings of his supporters in Rome. The conquest of Gaul, the richest and most populous part of the Celtic world, would test even Caesar's considerable military abilities.

After repulsing the Helvetii and the Suebi and forcing the Sequani and Arverni to submit, Caesar wintered his army near Vesontio (Besançon), in the territory of the Sequani, well to the north of the Roman province (Caesar himself returned to Italy every winter during the war to take care of his political interests). Learning that the tough Belgic tribes were forming a coalition to oppose him, Caesar marched north with around 40,000 legionaries and 20,000, mostly Gallic, auxiliaries to the territory of the pro-Roman Remi, which he used as a base from which to launch an invasion of Belgica in April 57. Defeated in three hard-fought battles, the Belgae submitted in September. Recognising their inferiority on the battlefield, the Gauls subsequently tried to avoid open battle, preferring to use guerrilla tactics. The following year (56) Caesar campaigned against the Armorican tribes in the maritime north-west. In the first recorded naval battle in northern waters, a hastily built fleet of light Roman galleys defeated the larger sailing ships of the Veneti, probably in Quiberon Bay, by cutting their rigging with sickles fastened to the end of poles. Caesar may have had commercial, as well as military, aims in conquering the Armoricans. The Veneti and their northern neighbours the Coriosolites controlled the most important trade route between Gaul and Britain. A subsidiary force campaigned successfully in Aquitania, despite fierce opposition. In the last campaign of the year, Caesar returned to Belgica, and put down a rebellion of the Menapii and the Morini. They proved difficult to track down in the marshes and fens of their coastal homeland and the fighting dragged on through the winter.

The expeditions to Britain

Despite this, Caesar must have been confident that Gallic resistance had been broken because he began to prepare an invasion of Britain. Things did not go according to plan. First, Caesar was forced to delay the invasion because of another incursion by German tribes, who had crossed the Rhine and settled in the area of modern Maastricht. After butchering the unfortunate settlers, Caesar led a brief show of strength among the German tribes east of the Rhine to discourage further incursions. Finally, in August 55, Caesar crossed the Channel with two legions and landed, in the face of fierce resistance, near Dover. It was late in the campaigning season and he had underestimated the difficulties of sailing in the Channel and the likely strength of the British response: in short Caesar was lucky that his expedition did not turn into a disaster. After three weeks of hard fighting, Caesar withdrew, only to be attacked by the Morini on his return.

Caesar's troops spent the winter of 55–54 in intensive training for a follow-up expedition. This time Caesar embarked with five legions and 2,000 cavalry in 600 transports and 28 warships. The force was so imposing that the Britons did not dare contest Caesar's landing in Kent, waiting instead until he began to move inland. The Britons had elected Cassivellaunus, who may have been a king of the Catuvellauni, as their war leader. Under his leadership the Britons fought well, skilfully exploiting their knowledge of the ground and their greater mobility, but they still proved unable to defeat the Romans in open battle. After forcing a crossing of the Thames, Caesar entered Cassivellaunus' own territory and sacked his chief stronghold, which was probably at Verulamium (modern St Albans). Shortly before this, the Trinovantes of Essex met with Caesar and placed themselves under Roman protection. They had no love for Cassivellaunus, who had killed their king and driven Mandubracius, the heir to their throne, into exile with the Romans. These twin setbacks persuaded Cassivellaunus to treat for peace, much to Caesar's relief as it happened. It was getting late in the campaigning season and Caesar was now a long way from his ships. An attack on the fleet base by the Cantiaci had been defeated by its guards but the danger of being cut off was real enough. Caesar's terms were, therefore, not severe. Cassivellaunus was to provide hostages and pay tribute and had to allow Mandubracius to return from exile and assume the kingship of the Trinovantes. Archaeological evidence shows that the *oppidum* of the Trinovantes at Camulodunum (Colchester) subsequently became an important entrepôt for Roman goods, making it likely that they were rewarded with commercial advantages. Previously, most Roman goods had entered Britain at Hengistbury Head in Dorset, via Armorica.

What Caesar's real aims were and what he actually achieved in these campaigns have been much debated – Caesar knew as much about spin as any modern politician, and if he had intended to conquer Britain, as some believe, he was not going to advertise his failure – but they must have impressed his supporters back in Rome, where Britain was regarded as being beyond the bounds of the known world. In any case, Roman influence in

Plate 11 The Channel, coast of Britain

Source: John Haywood

southern Britain, through trade and diplomatic contacts, steadily increased after these expeditions, though perhaps it would have done so anyway once the conquest of Gaul was complete.

The Gauls fight back

If Caesar had left for Britain believing that Gaul was pacified, he was soon disabused of the notion on his return. Gaul had suffered a drought through the summer of 54 and the harvest had been so poor that Caesar had to disperse his legions across the breadth of northern Gaul for the winter to ease provisioning problems. Caesar ensured that the legions were no more than a hundred miles apart but the danger was obvious and he decided to delay his departure to Italy. One newly raised legion and an additional five cohorts from another legion (around 7,500 soldiers in all) were quartered on the Belgic Eburones. The Eburones were thought to be friendly – Caesar had, after all, stopped the neighbouring Atuatuci collecting tribute from them – but there was resentment at the prospect of feeding several thousand Roman soldiers through the winter. When the Eburones rebelled, this isolated and very surprised Roman army was wiped out almost to a man in a clever ambush planned by their leader Ambiorix. Many of the Roman dead would have been of Celtic stock as the destroyed legion had been raised in Cisalpine Gaul. Caesar's army also included thousands of Gauls – most of them cavalry – and, though some individuals spied on the Romans for their fellow Gauls, the vast majority proved loyal to their commander.

Ambiorix's victory showed that the Romans were not invincible, and the Atuatuci, Nervii, Menapii and Treveri (who were famed for their cavalry) quickly joined the rebellion. Fortunately for the Romans, other Belgic tribes, including the powerful Remi, remained loyal, and individual members of the rebel tribes, such as the Nervian noble Vertico, who arranged for messages to be passed through enemy lines, also actively supported them. Caesar cancelled his plans to return to Italy and took the field against the rebels even before the winter was over. There was little organised resistance as Caesar systematically devastated the Belgic countryside. The territory of the Eburones was singled out for especially rough treatment in the late summer of 53. Faced with overwhelming Roman force, Ambiorix ordered his followers to disperse and most, including he himself, evaded capture. Caesar felt confident that the fugitives would sooner or later die of starvation because he had destroyed the harvest, but Belgic resistance revived the next year and continued to the end of the war.

No sooner had Belgica been apparently pacified than a major rebellion broke out in central Gaul. This area, the most socially and economically advanced region in Gaul, had seen no fighting so far and was still filled with thousands of Roman merchants conducting business as usual. The outbreak started with the Carnutes, probably as a result of Druidical agitation. During the winter of 54–53, the Carnutes and the Senones had failed to attend a Gallic council meeting summoned by Caesar. Caesar, probably quite reasonably, believed that they had been plotting against him and by a timely show of force prevented the two tribes joining the rebellion. In the autumn of 53, after the end of campaigning against the Belgae, Caesar arrested and executed Acco, a chieftain of the Senones who was suspected to be the ringleader of the plot. The affair tidied up to his satisfaction, Caesar headed off to Italy for the winter.

Vercingetorix: architect of defeat

Caesar's action was badly misjudged. The execution of one of their own class shocked the Gallic nobility and made them fear for their own safety. Who might be next? The legions were dispersed in winter camps in the north and Caesar was tied down with political intrigue in Rome. A rising in central Gaul would cut the legions off from their commander and leave them paralysed. The Carnutes rose first, descending on Cenabum (Orleans) and massacring the Roman merchants there. An Arvernian noble called Vercingetorix quickly followed the lead given by the Carnutes. Vercingetorix took up the cry of Gallic freedom but he also had other motives. The

Plate 12 Coin bearing the effigy of Vercingetorix (72–46 BC) (metal); Gaulish (first century BC)

Source: Private collection/Giraudon/Bridgeman Art Library, www.bridgeman.co.uk

Arverni were ruled by elected magistrates and they had recently killed Vercingetorix's father Celtillus for trying to set himself up as king. Many of the tribal elite opposed rebellion – the Arverni had long been Roman allies – but Vercingetorix quickly raised a large armed following, seized the tribal *oppidum* of Gergovia (Gergovie, near Clermont-Ferrand) and was proclaimed king. Success in war would cement his hold on power.

One of the most charismatic leaders in Celtic history, Vercingetorix assembled the largest tribal coalition the Romans had yet faced. The Senones, Parisii, Turoni, Pictones, Lemovices, Cadurci, Aulerci, Andecavi and many other tribes of central Gaul joined in the rebellion; other tribes such as the Bituriges were coerced into reluctant participation. The Gauls were – almost – united against Rome, but it would all go horribly wrong. Vercingetorix ordered the Cadurci to invade Transalpine Gaul late in 53. He hoped this would tie Caesar down in the south and buy time for the destruction of the isolated legions in the north but he failed totally to anticipate the speed of Caesar's reaction. After driving the invaders out of the Roman province, Caesar did what the Gauls believed to be impossible and marched an army over the snow-covered Cévennes in January 52 directly into the heart of Arvernian territory. Now that he had tied Vercingetorix down in the south, Caesar left ravaging the territory of the Arverni to his future assassin, Brutus, and, with a small detachment of cavalry, made a dash to rejoin his legions in the north. Caesar had boldly turned the tables on his opponent.

The war now became a grim slogging match. Throughout the spring, Caesar tried to goad the Gauls into open battle by laying siege to their *oppida* and massacring or enslaving their inhabitants when they fell. The population of central Gaul was particularly vulnerable to this strategy because it was the most urbanised in the country. Vercingetorix resisted the provocation and responded with a desperate policy of scorched earth. This was intended to force the Romans to withdraw for lack of supplies but, by its very nature, it also inflicted great hardship on the Gallic peasantry. Caesar had still not drawn the Gauls into open battle when he laid siege to Vercingetorix's capital at Gergovia in late spring. At this point Caesar received news of a major setback: supporters of Vercingetorix had persuaded the Aedui to join the rebellion. His alliance with the Aedui gave Caesar secure communications back to Roman territory and, worse still, he had left his food reserves and hostages in their care. According to Caesar, a small clique among the Aedui's ruling elite was bribed into supporting the rebellion: they then won over their fellow tribesmen by spreading false stories about Caesar having executed two Aeduan nobles and ordered a massacre of Aeduan cavalry serving with the Roman army. Aeduan enthusiasm for the rebellion quickly cooled after a Gallic council meeting refused their claim to take command and instead confirmed Vercingetorix in his position, but they had robbed and killed or expelled the Roman citizens living among them, so there was no going back. The Bellovaci, a Belgic tribe that had a reputation for producing the best warriors in Gaul, now joined the rebellion and a great diplomatic effort was made to persuade the remaining neutral tribes to join in too. The defection of the strongest of his allies forced Caesar to attempt to take Gergovia quickly by storm, but his assault was beaten back with the loss of over 700 legionaries. Caesar's position was now untenable and he decided to withdraw all his forces from Gaul.

Scenting victory, Vercingetorix gathered together a huge force of 80,000 infantry and 15,000 cavalry. This comfortably outnumbered Caesar's army, which was only about 55,000 strong. Vercingetorix convinced his followers that they must not allow the Roman army to escape. If they did, he argued, the Romans would inevitably return with reinforcements and, for all their sacrifices, they would have won only a temporary respite. If their army could be trapped and destroyed, the Romans would never dare invade again and Gaul would be free forever. Vercingetorix may have been right – though other factors were at play, the great German victory at the Teutoburg Forest in AD 9, in which three legions were annihilated in a well-planned ambush, would effectively end Roman attempts to conquer Germany – but seeking open battle was a high-risk strategy and in the event it did not pay off.

Caesar was heading south through Burgundy towards the Rhône valley and safety in Transalpine Gaul. Vercingetorix stationed his army across Caesar's line of march, in hills above the little river Vingeanne (a tributary of the Saône), but his conduct of what could have been one of the decisive battles of European history was curiously half-hearted. Leaving his infantry holding the line of the river itself, Vercingetorix divided his cavalry into three squadrons and attacked the Roman column while it was still on the march. Despite being hard pressed, Caesar formed his infantry into an impregnable defensive square while his own cavalry, which had been heavily reinforced by German horsemen, eventually drove the Gallic cavalry from the field with heavy losses. The Gallic infantry never even joined the battle – they had been stationed too far away to support the cavalry attack and, when the cavalry fled, they fled too. Cavalry was the one arm in which the Gauls were generally superior to the Romans and this defeat was a crushing blow to their morale. Caesar, who had seemed so close to defeat that morning, once again held the initiative by nightfall.

Disaster at Alesia

Vercingetorix and some 80,000 warriors took refuge in the nearby *oppidum* of Alesia in the territory of the Mandubii. It was a disastrous tactical error. Caesar arrived the next day and immediately began to surround Alesia with two lines of ramparts, the inner one to prevent the inhabitants escaping, the outer to prevent any reinforcements or supplies getting in. Each rampart was about 14 miles (22 kilometres) in length and was protected with watchtowers, ditches, *chevaux de frises* and *lilia* (lilies), the Roman equivalent of a minefield – foot-deep pits containing a sharpened and fire-hardened wooden stake. Roman legionaries actually spent far more time digging than they ever did fighting. Vercingetorix had supplies for only one month and the Gauls made a desperate effort to break the siege. Though the Gallic council refused Vercingetorix's demand for a universal call-up of all warriors, forty-four different tribes from all parts of Gaul raised between them a relief army said to number nearly a quarter of a million men. It was a hugely impressive achievement, yet there were still a few tribes, the powerful Remi and the Lingones among them, who stood aloof, and it took weeks to gather such a large force.

By the time the relief army arrived at Alesia, the situation of the inhabitants was getting desperate. Vercingetorix tried to make his supplies last longer by sending out the women and children but Caesar refused to allow them through his lines. Three times the Gallic relief army tried to break through Caesar's defences and three times it was driven off after desperate fighting with heavy casualties on both sides. After its third assault, the relief army, its morale shattered, broke up and dispersed. Seeing that all hope was gone, Vercingetorix decided to surrender to spare his people further suffering. The Aeduans and Arverni among the captives were sent home – Caesar wanted to rebuild good relations with these powerful tribes as quickly as possible – but the rest were sent to the slave markets. Vercingetorix himself was imprisoned in Rome to be executed six years later when Caesar belatedly celebrated his triumph. It is hard not to feel sympathy for Vercingetorix: Gaul was thoroughly pacified by that time and his death served no purpose beyond providing a cruel entertainment for the Roman masses. Heroic figure though he was, it must be said that Vercingetorix's leadership was nothing short of a disaster for the Gauls. By concentrating so much of the armed strength of Gaul at Alesia, he simply gave Caesar a convenient opportunity to fight it on his own terms and destroy it. Had the Gallic council agreed to a universal call-up, the losses would only have been the heavier.

The fall of Alesia did not end the war, quite. Caesar's lenient treatment of the Arverni and Aedui worked: both tribes returned to their allegiance to Rome and their neighbours, the Bituriges, soon followed, but it took another year of campaigning before the last embers of Gallic resistance were extinguished. The Gauls decided to return to a strategy of opportunistic rebellions by individual tribes in order to keep Caesar hurrying from one end of Gaul to the other. But the casualties of the previous year and the enormous economic damage of Vercingetorix's scorched earth policy had sapped the will to resist. Caesar was occasionally brutal – when Uxellodunum (Puy d'Issou), the last major centre of Gallic resistance, fell, all those who had taken part in its defence had their hands cut off – but he was more often conciliatory, winning over the tribal elites with gifts and flattery and by not imposing new burdens on the exhausted Gauls. Caesar left Gaul pacified, so much so that when Rome collapsed into civil war in 49 BC there were no new uprisings. The price paid by Gaul for its resistance was high. Of its population of around seven million, perhaps a million had died and as many again were delivered to the slave markets.

Caesar's conquest of Gaul was probably not inevitable – it is clear that he greatly underestimated the fighting spirit of the Gauls, and after his failure at Gergovia he was staring defeat in the face – but from the beginning he held important advantages. No Gallic leader came close to matching Caesar's qualities as a general, particularly his ability to seize the initiative in the most unpromising circumstances. Though the Gauls usually had the advantage of numbers and certainly did not lack courage, unlike the Roman legionaries most fought without armour and lacked both training and discipline. Man for man the Roman legionaries consistently outfought the Gauls. The Gauls could win battles when they employed ambush and deception but in set-piece battles they were at a hopeless disadvantage. This Roman battlefield superiority need not have been the decisive factor it was, had the Gauls not given Caesar so many opportunities to exercise it. Even the huge armies Vercingetorix was able to raise were doomed. Raw courage and sheer weight of numbers have rarely been able to prevail on the battlefield in the face of technological or organisational superiority (and the Romans had both) unless the enemy commanders have been incompetent or foolhardy. The larger the army the Gauls brought to the battlefield, the harder it was to control once battle had been joined and the greater the casualties. Instead of following Vercingetorix, had the Gauls chosen to follow the example of Ambiorix, who dispersed his forces and survived, their resistance might easily have been prolonged beyond Caesar's term of office (which expired in 50). Many Romans viewed Caesar's rise with apprehension and would have been glad to see him defeated in Gaul, as others were to see his political ally Crassus defeated (and killed) in his vain attempt to conquer Parthia in 53. There is no evidence that the Romans had contemplated the conquest of Gaul before Caesar arrived on the scene, and whoever was chosen to succeed him might well have lacked the ability and determination to continue a war which had no end in sight, even if civil war had not broken out.

The last days of Celtic independence

With the conquest of Gaul complete, only two areas of continental Europe remained to the Celts, north-west Spain and the old Hallstatt heartland in central Europe. The civil wars (49–45, 44–30 BC) that heralded the collapse of the Roman Republic gave these remaining independent tribes a stay of execution. Octavian, the victor of the civil wars, did not try to resurrect the republic but ruled as emperor under the name Augustus. Augustus set about consolidating the frontiers of the Roman Empire along more defendable lines. This required an advance into central Europe north to the Danube, while the frontier in Spain was one that could be eliminated entirely. In 26 BC Augustus personally led a campaign against the Cantabri, Astures and Gallaeci. The mountainous terrain proved hard going for the Roman army, but within a year Augustus declared the war to be over. As so often for the Romans in Spain, he was premature in claiming victory. Revolts broke out in 24, 22 and 19. The last rebellion was rather brutally crushed by Augustus' son-in-law Agrippa, but only after he had restored morale and discipline to an army which had learned to fear the Cantabri. Even then there was another rebellion in 16 BC and it was only in 13 BC, after Augustus had personally reorganised its provincial government, that Spain was truly pacified. Spain subsequently became one of the most peaceful Roman provinces and only one legion was based there compared with three in Britain.

The Celts of central Europe had not only the Romans to contend with – they were also under pressure from the Germans and the Dacians. The Dacians probably first encroached on the Celts when they began to expand under King Rubobostes from their original homeland in Wallachia into Transylvania c. 170 BC. Dacia had become a major kingdom, occupying most of modern Romania, when its king Burebista began to expand aggressively westwards into the territory of the Boii, Taurisci and Scordisci in 60–59 BC. Burebista himself believed he was reconquering Dacian territory lost to the Celts during their migrations three centuries before. The Dacian attacks against the Boii were devastatingly successful, driving them out of what is now Slovenia and northern Hungary and probably Moravia as well, leaving only Bohemia itself. The Greek historian Strabo described this area as the 'desert of the Boii'. The survivors, who numbered over 30,000, fled across the Danube into the kingdom of Noricum, a coalition of Celtic tribes, which controlled most of the eastern Alps, and besieged the *oppidum* at Noreia (Neumarkt, Austria). Repulsed, they travelled through the Alps and found a welcome in the territory of the Helvetii. The Boii subsequently supported the Helvetii when they tried to migrate across Gaul in 58 BC, so unwittingly helping to give Caesar the pretext for his conquest of Gaul. Unlike the Helvetii, Caesar allowed the Boii to settle in Gaul. By this time they had had most of the fight knocked out of them and they played little part in the Gallic war, remaining loyal to Caesar until 52, when, probably as a result of coercion by their stronger neighbours, they sent a small contingent to join the Gallic relief army at the siege of Alesia.

Apart from Ariovistus' foray across the Rhine, the German expansion into Celtic territory is undocumented. The destruction and abandonment of the *oppidum* of Závist, near Prague, c. 25 BC probably marks the Germanic conquest of the remnants of the Boii. By around 16–8 BC all of the former Celtic territories north of the Danube were under the control of the Germans or the Dacians. By this time the Celts between the Alps, the Balkans and the south bank of the Danube had also succumbed to Roman rule. The Vindelici and Raeti of Bavaria were conquered in 15 BC, and the kingdom of Noricum was annexed peacefully very shortly afterwards. Noricum had been a Roman ally since 186 and the kingdom's elite had already adopted a highly Romanised lifestyle through the influence of a colony of Roman merchants at Virunum (Zollfeld), the royal capital. The Romans conquered the last independent Celtic tribes of continental Europe, in Pannonia and Illyricum (approximately western Hungary and Serbia), in three years, between 12 and 9 BC. There was little resistance: perhaps these Celts found the prospect of domination by the Romans, with whom they had much in common, less unwelcome than that of domination by the barbarian Germans.

6

THE LIMITS OF EMPIRE: THE ROMAN CONQUEST OF BRITAIN

Today our knowledge of Britain's boundaries rests not on hearsay and report, but on armed occupation: we have both discovered and subdued Britain.

Agricola, Roman general (AD 83/4)

Although Augustus famously advised his successors against any further conquests, the Roman Empire continued to grow for over a century after his death in AD 14. The most important of the new territories was Britain (or at least most of it, for the Roman conquest was never completed). The Roman conquest of Britain is usually seen in the context of the need of the new, and somewhat bookish, emperor Claudius (r. 41–54) for a military victory to secure his credibility with the army, but it is also clear that there were interests in Britain itself which favoured Roman intervention. After Caesar's invasion, the process of state formation in south-eastern Britain accelerated and tribal kingdoms began to emerge, the most powerful among them being those of the Trinovantes, Catuvellauni and the Atrebates. Semi-urban *oppida* began to replace hillforts as the main tribal centres. Increasing imports of wine, the adoption of a Roman-style coinage and the use of the Roman alphabet are evidence of the steady Romanisation of the British elite in the south-east. Some British kings, like Tincommius of the Atrebates and King Dumnovellaunos, who ruled lands in Essex and Kent, even visited Rome itself. The Roman historian Dio went so far as to describe Britain as being virtually Roman even before the conquest. By the early first century AD, therefore, south-eastern Britain was much like Gaul had been at the time of Caesar's conquest.

The hostility between the Trinovantes and the Catuvellauni, which Caesar had exploited, continued until the two peoples were united (*c.* AD 20) by Cunobelinus, who thereby became the dominant ruler of the south-east. Cunobelinus was of the Catuvellauni, but he made his capital at the prosperous *oppidum* of the Trinovantes at Camulodunum with its important commercial links with the Roman Empire. At around the same time the Atrebates came under the rule of Verica. Cunobelinus died *c.* AD 40 and his successors, his two sons Caratacus and Togodumnus, adopted a more aggressive and anti-Roman stance (a third son, Adminius, was exiled for his pro-Roman views). Possibly they were encouraged in this by Druids who were alarmed that the Romans had recently suppressed the Druids of Gaul. In 41 or 42, Caratacus and Togodumnus attacked the Atrebates and drove Verica into exile in the Roman Empire. The Romans had watched the rise of Caratacus and Togodumnus with concern, and Verica probably did not find it too hard to persuade Claudius to invade Britain to restore him to his throne. Besides, Claudius would have been well aware that the social and economic advancement of the south-east made it an ideal prospect for conquest and assimilation into the Roman Empire. What is not known is did Claudius intend only to conquer the south-east or were his sights set on the conquest of the whole of Britain? The rich mineral resources of Wales and south-west and northern England would certainly have made these areas worth controlling too, despite their relative backwardness, but north of the Tyne–Solway isthmus there was nothing much worth fighting over. The economy there was based on pastoralism and the local tribes were still highly decentralised societies whose elites were not at all Romanised. There was, therefore, little prospect of this area being easily or profitably assimilated into the empire, so it seems unlikely that its conquest was planned from the outset.

Claudius launched his invasion in early spring 43. Altogether four legions were embarked under the command of Aulus Plautius. Britain had not lost its air of mystery since Caesar's day and the legionaries almost mutinied on being told their destination. The main force landed in Kent, at Rutupiae (Richborough, then a fine natural harbour, now a few miles inland), where the Romans later erected an enormous commemorative arch, only the foundations of which now survive. Other forces landed on the south coast in the vicinity of Chichester Harbour. This was in the heart of Verica's territory and the Romans could expect a friendly welcome and a secure base there. There was probably also a third landing at an unidentified location. The Britons did not contest the Roman landings but waited until the Romans advanced inland. The Britons made a stand at a major river, usually identified as the Medway, but were defeated in a hard two-day battle and pursued by the Romans to the Thames. With a foothold secured, Claudius joined the army and led it on beyond the Thames to capture Camulodunum, which he entered triumphantly on the back of an elephant. Togodumnus died in the fighting and Caratacus fled. He would cause a lot of trouble for the Romans yet.

Claudius rewarded friendly British rulers with client kingdoms. Verica had probably died in the meantime, for there is no record of his returning to Britain, and his territories were given to Cogidubnos (probably a relative of Verica's?), who also received Roman citizenship. It is possible that the Roman palace at Fishbourne, near Chichester, was part of the reward

Plate 13 Maiden Castle
Source: English Heritage Photographic Library

for his cooperation. King Prasutagus of the Iceni of modern Norfolk and Queen Cartimandua of the Brigantes of northern England also became client rulers. Camulodunum became the first capital of Roman Britain. Claudius had the symbolic victory he needed and he left almost immediately, probably no later than the end of June 43. The real business of conquering Britain and organising it as a Roman province was left to Plautius.

Initially, the conquest proceeded smoothly enough. By the time Plautius' term of office expired in 47 all of Britain south-east of a line running roughly from Exeter to Lincoln was under Roman control. Only the Durotriges of modern Dorset had put up serious resistance and many of their numerous hillforts had to be taken by storm. One of these was Maiden Castle, where the remains of many of the British defenders have been discovered in a hastily dug war cemetery: one of them still had a Roman ballista bolt embedded in his spine. Plautius' achievement was impressive but the area he had conquered was precisely that which was most vulnerable to Roman intervention. The less centralised tribes in the country beyond were to prove much more difficult to subdue.

After putting down a minor rebellion by the Iceni and Trinovantes, Ostorius Scapula, Plautius' successor as governor of Britain, immediately resumed the advance west and north. The main resistance came from two tribes from modern Wales, the Silures and the Ordovices, who had adopted the fugitive Caratacus as their war leader. While the Britons stuck to guerrilla tactics, the Romans enjoyed little success. It was only when Caratacus unwisely made a stand against the Romans at a strongly fortified site in hills somewhere close to the river Severn (possibly the fort on Llanymynech Hill near Welshpool, which was destroyed around this time) that the struggle turned in their favour. The Britons proved no match for the Romans in open battle: as so often before when Celt fought Roman, it was a lack of armour that proved decisive. Caratacus' wife, daughter and brother were captured; he himself fled to the Brigantes, but Cartimandua promptly handed him over to the Romans. Caratacus was taken to Rome in 51, to be paraded in triumph before the people. His noble bearing and speech won Caratacus the sympathy of Claudius, who had a soft spot for Celts, and he fared better than Vercingetorix. Claudius pardoned him and allowed him to live out his days in some comfort in Rome.

Relieved of Caratacus' leadership, the Britons reverted to their effective guerrilla tactics, setting ambushes, harassing foraging parties and even defeating a legion. The Silures cunningly bound other tribes to the struggle by distributing booty and Roman captives among them. Resistance only stiffened when Ostorius, in exasperation, declared that the Silures must be completely annihilated or transported from their homeland. Ostorius was losing his grip on the situation, probably because of his poor health, when he died in 52. His successor immediately faced not only the intractable resistance of the Silures but also a crisis in the client kingdom of the Brigantes. Cartimandua's pro-Roman actions were resented by a strong faction led by her estranged husband Venutius (she was said to have ditched him for his dashing young armour bearer) and an attempt was made to overthrow her. She kept her throne only thanks to the intervention of a Roman legion. Venutius was an able commander – the Romans rated him second only to Caratacus among the Britons – and it took some years to put down his rebellion completely.

Gradually the Romans wore down the Silures and Ordovices. By 60 the last centre of serious resistance was the island of Anglesey. The Roman soldiers had to fight their way ashore, opposed not only by a host of British warriors but by Druids and wildly dishevelled priestesses waving torches and screaming curses and spells at them. The Roman soldiers, who were every bit as superstitious as the Celts, were momentarily paralysed with terror at the spectacle. But they were disciplined professionals and soon recovered their collective nerve. The Britons were put to flight and many of the Druids and priestesses were slaughtered. Some were burned with their own torches. Anglesey may have been an important centre for Druidism, as the Romans made a point of destroying all the sacred groves on the island.

Before the Romans could consolidate their victory in Wales, a serious revolt broke out among the Iceni. Prasutagus had recently died and willed his kingdom jointly to the emperor and his two daughters. However, the Romans had decided on the complete annexation of the kingdom and this provoked Prasutagus' widow Boudica into open revolt. It was said that the Romans had had Boudica flogged and had raped her daughters, which may or may not be true. What is certainly true is that the Roman procurator Catus Decianus treated the Iceni as if they were a conquered people. The rebellion spread quickly to the Trinovantes but, fortunately for the Romans, both Cogidubnus and Cartimandua remained loyal. The anger of the Britons focused on Camulodunum, which was seen as the symbol of their subjection. The temple of the Divine Claudius was especially resented because of the heavy costs of building and supporting it. The city was completely unfortified and had only a token garrison – most of the Roman forces were away in Wales with the governor Suetonius Paulinus – and its population of merchants and discharged veterans was almost defenceless. Despite forewarning of the British attack, nothing was done to evacuate the non-combatant population, while a 'fifth column' of Britons, who lived in the town but were sympathetic to the rebels, did their best to spread panic and confusion. The city fell easily to the rebels and was sacked. The garrison held out in the half-built temple for two days until it was stormed by the Britons. A legion that was marching to relieve the city was routed with heavy losses to its infantry. Contemporary reports did not exaggerate the fury of the Britons. Archaeological excavations have shown that the city was quite deliberately and methodically razed to the ground block by block in an attempt to remove all traces of Roman domination. Other towns that were sacked were Verulamium and Londinium (London). Paulinus, racing ahead of his legions, managed to reach Londinium, then an unofficial settlement of Roman merchants, before the rebels, but he judged it undefendable and abandoned the town to its fate. Most of the population fled, while those who remained were slaughtered on the spot or sacrificed to the war goddess Andrasta in gruesome rituals involving sexual mutilation. At Verulamium the victims were not Romans but Britons, the pro-Roman Catuvellauni. Archaeological excavations have shown that, like Camulodunum, both towns were burned to the ground. Altogether, the Romans and their loyal British allies were estimated to have suffered 70,000 casualties (quite possibly an exaggerated figure), but Decianus, the cause of all the trouble, was not among them: he had fled to Gaul.

The rebels do not appear to have had any clear strategic goals. As so often in Celtic warfare, their main interest was plunder. Crucially, this gave Paulinus time to gather a mixed force of about 10,000 legionaries and auxiliaries (regular soldiers who were not Roman citizens) before Boudica could rally her forces to drive the Romans out of Britain for good. It was a smaller force than Paulinus had hoped for as many isolated units could not, or dared not, move from their forts. The army Boudica raised to confront Paulinus was huge – the Roman historian Dio puts it at an improbably large 230,000 – and it was so confident of victory that the warriors even brought their wives and children along in wagons to watch the battle. Boudica raced around this vast disorderly throng in a chariot, encouraging her warriors with stirring speeches. The location of the battle is unknown. Paulinus' troops would probably have been marching south-east along Watling Street, the main Roman road between Londinium and the modern Welsh border, so somewhere close to this road in the east Midlands seems likely. The Britons' battle plan seems to have been simply to overwhelm the Romans by sheer weight of numbers, but Paulinus had taken up a good defensive position in a natural defile which could only be attacked easily from the front. Woods to the rear made it difficult for the Britons to use their superior numbers to outflank and envelop the Roman army. The Romans easily broke up the initial British attack with their javelins – few of the Britons had any body armour – and went over to the offensive. The Roman infantry adopted a wedge formation and, flanked by the cavalry, charged the Britons and drove them from the field. The wagons that the Britons had left in a semicircle to their rear as a kind of grandstand for the spectators now turned into a trap, obstructing their flight. The Romans broke ranks and fell upon the panic-stricken mass, indiscriminately massacring men, women, children and beasts of burden. The slaughter went on for hours. One report estimated that the Britons suffered 80,000 casualties, the Romans only 400.

The battle broke the back of the rebellion. Boudica, who escaped the battlefield, did not survive long, dying of illness according to one account, committing suicide according to another. The latter would have been quite appropriate behaviour for a defeated Celtic war leader. The Romans now disagreed among themselves about how to follow up their victory. Paulinus embarked on a campaign of scorched earth to punish the rebels, but the new procurator Julius Classicianus argued for a more conciliatory policy to encourage the native aristocracy to develop a positive loyalty to the empire. Julius was from an aristocratic Gallic family and so is likely to have had a better understanding of what was required than Paulinus. After an imperial inquiry, Julius won the argument and Paulinus was relieved of his post and replaced. Thereafter, Rome ruled the Britons with a lighter hand. Camulodunum was belatedly provided with a circuit of defensive walls, parts of which still stand, but it never recovered its original status. The Roman administration was moved to Londinium, which was more accessible from the sea than Camulodunum: Julius Classicianus died there. Remarkably his gravestone has survived and is now in the British Museum.

In June 68 the emperor Nero was driven from Rome and committed suicide. There was no obvious successor and a civil war broke out. Three emperors followed one another in quick succession until Vespasian, a veteran of the Claudian invasion of Britain, won a firm grip on power in the last weeks of 69 and established a new dynasty. Though there were no opportunist revolts in the area under direct Roman rule – the policy of conciliation had worked – there was serious trouble in the client kingdom of the Brigantes. Encouraged by the political chaos in the empire, Venutius had another go at ousting his hated ex-wife Cartimandua and this time he succeeded. The overthrow of Cartimandua was a serious setback for the Romans. The Brigantian kingdom covered all of Britain from the Mersey and the Humber north to the Tyne–Solway isthmus and probably even beyond to the foothills of the Southern Uplands in modern Scotland. Cartimandua's loyalty meant that, once they had conquered the Silures and Ordovices, the Romans would have had no hostile frontier to defend in Britain and there would have been a large buffer zone between the Romanised south and the unconquered tribes of the far north. Venutius' rebellion changed that permanently and forced the Romans, probably for the first time, to contemplate the conquest of the whole of Britain.

All the Romans could do at first was rescue Cartimandua and escort her to safety. Venutius was left in control of the Brigantes and free to make trouble with the other British tribes and stir them up against Rome. However, Rome recovered quickly from the civil war and by 71 it was able to concentrate on the task of bringing Venutius to heel. First, the Romans established control over the rich farmlands of the Vale of York by building a legionary fortress at Eburacum (York). Roads and forts were built along both sides of the Pennine Hills and across every major pass through them, until the Romans enjoyed complete freedom of movement and Venutius none. Venutius probably made his last stand at the *oppidum* of Stanwick in North Yorkshire, which was destroyed and abandoned around this time. Stanwick had been a modest 16.8-acre (6.8-hectare) hillfort at the time of the Claudian invasion. Large quantities of imported goods suggest that it may have been Cartimandua's capital. Around AD 50–70 new defensive ramparts were built at Stanwick, enclosing over 129 acres (52 hectares), and at the time of its destruction a new circuit of massive defensive ramparts enclosing nearly 743 acres (300 hectares) was under construction. By 73 at the latest, the power of the Brigantes was broken and the Romans controlled all of Britain south of the Tyne–Solway isthmus, the future line of Hadrian's Wall. What became of Venutius is unknown – he simply disappears from history. The victory over Venutius allowed the Romans to return to the unfinished business of pacifying the Silures and Ordovices. This task was completed in 78 by Agricola, who had just been appointed governor of Britain. Thanks to the biography written by his son-in-law Tacitus, we know more about Agricola than any other Roman governor of Britain. Tacitus portrays him as an ideal governor, a good soldier who fought to enlarge the empire but also a humane administrator who encouraged the advancement of the provincials. In fact, as recent archaeological discoveries have shown, Tacitus somewhat exaggerated his father-in-law's achievements for reasons of family prestige.

With the final suppression of the Silures and Ordovices, the main problem faced by the Romans in Britain was stabilising the northern frontier now that Cartimandua was no longer there to protect it. As Britain is an island, the logical solution was to conquer it all so that there would be no internal frontier to defend. Following Tacitus' biography, it had long been thought that the Roman advance north of the Tyne–Solway isthmus was begun by Agricola in the early 80s. However, recent excavations of a chain of Roman watchtowers on the Gask ridge south of Perth have proved that the Romans had in fact moved north and established a frontier deep inside Scotland immediately after the defeat of the Brigantes in 73. This frontier, which was marked by a road and a chain of forts and watchtowers, ran roughly south-west from the river Tay near Perth to Dunblane, near Stirling on the river Forth, and was probably intended to separate the Venicones of Fife (a rich agricultural area) from the Caledonians of the Highlands. The area between this frontier and the Tyne–Solway isthmus cannot have been thoroughly subdued because Agricola spent two or three years campaigning there before he was free to attempt the conquest of the Highlands. The east coast was already secure: the Votadini of Lothian had become Roman clients while the Venicones were prospering by supplying grain to the garrison on the Gask frontier. Agricola's operations were concentrated in the wild mountains of Galloway in the west. Pacification of this area would not only secure Roman communications to the north and eliminate potential allies for the Brigantes in any future rebellion: it was also an essential precursor to an invasion of Ireland. Though the Romans were quite well informed about Ireland, mainly from merchants' reports and occasional exiles – Agricola had an Irish chieftain in his retinue who he hoped might come in useful one day – they never attempted to conquer it. Agricola famously said that he believed Ireland could be conquered with one legion and a few auxiliaries, but he was certainly being ridiculously over-optimistic and his reputation would not stand so high today had he tried. The Irish would have proved to be just as hard to subdue as the Caledonians of the Scottish Highlands and for exactly the same reason: their lack of political centralisation.

An attack on an isolated garrison north of the Forth, possibly one of those on the Gask ridge, convinced Agricola that completing the conquest of northern Britain was a greater priority than invading Ireland. Agricola spent 82 campaigning in the region of the Gask frontier; the legionary fort at Carpow on the river Tay east of Perth may have been his base. The following year (83) he marched his army north up Scotland's east coast into territory which had never yet seen a Roman army. Over a dozen of Agricola's marching camps have been identified: the most northerly is at Cawdor and it is likely that he advanced as far as Inverness ten miles (16 kilometres) further west. Although no trace of a Roman camp has ever been found at Inverness (traces of temporary earthworks would have been obliterated long ago by later building), its strategic position at the entrance to the Great Glen that bisects northern Scotland would have made it an obvious objective and an ideal springboard for future campaigns in the northern Highlands. Throughout these campaigns Agricola used his fleet to launch raids ahead of his advance and some ships sailed as far north as the Shetland Islands.

Somewhere on his march north from the Tay, Agricola met and defeated a confederate army of the Highland Caledonian tribes at the battle of Mons Graupius (it is from this battle that the Grampian Mountains take their name, not vice versa). One plausible location for Mons Graupius is Bennachie in Aberdeenshire. Although not a high mountain, Bennachie has a prominent position on the edge of the Highlands and is easily recognisable in distant views because of its distinctive granite tors. A Roman marching camp, dating to Agricola's campaign, has been found at Durno, only a few miles north of the mountain. However, Tacitus' narrative is rather vague and it is quite possible that the battlefield is much further north. The Caledonians had united for a last-ditch effort to stop the Roman conquest of Britain, their leader, Calgacus, pointing out to them before the battle that, thanks to the Roman fleet, not even the sea offered them a way of retreat. At around 30,000 strong, the Caledonians' army was probably only slightly larger than the Roman army and the outcome of the battle was never in doubt. The Caledonians fought with real determination and, even after they had been driven from the battlefield, they constantly regrouped to try to ambush the pursuing Roman forces. Only the fall of night ended the fighting, by which time some 10,000 of the Caledonians had been killed. Roman losses were only 360. Once again, a large, united Celtic army had met the Romans in battle and been heavily defeated.

Tacitus presents Mons Graupius as a decisive battle: in reality it was anything but. Two-thirds of the Caledonian army had escaped and during the night it simply melted away into the landscape. The next day, Roman patrols found nobody. The Romans could not even burn the deserted farms because the Caledonians had done this themselves already. This was a far more effective strategy than trying to fight the well-oiled Roman war machine on its own terms: how could the Romans defeat an enemy they could not find? Agricola wintered in the Highlands, probably on Speyside, but the next year he was recalled to Rome by the emperor Domitian and he never returned to Britain. His successor, whose identity is not known for certain, withdrew from the most northerly conquests and established a frontier system along the 'Highland Line', which runs north-eastwards from the foot of Loch Lomond to Stonehaven, south of Aberdeen. Forts were built at the entrances to the main glens, so denying the Highland tribes freedom of movement. This system was certainly intended to be a springboard for the pacification of the Caledonians but this was never to happen. Faced with more serious problems elsewhere, the emperor Domitian began to withdraw troops from Britain and the aim of total conquest was quietly abandoned. Although this left Britain with an internal frontier to be defended, and there were fears that the remaining independent tribes might inspire the conquered Britons to rebellion, events would prove it to have been a wise decision. Even if the Highlands could have been conquered and pacified, which is far from certain, the costs would have greatly outweighed the potential rewards of adding this wild, remote and economically undeveloped region to the empire.

By 88 at the latest, the Romans had begun a gradual withdrawal from the Highland frontier. The withdrawal was a deliberate and planned process, not a panicky retreat, for the frontier forts were dismantled piece by piece and stripped of anything that might have proved useful to the natives. It is

Plate 14 Hadrian's Wall from Housesteads fort
Source: John Haywood

likely that the failure to pacify the tribes immediately behind the frontier was as important a factor in this decision as pressure from the Caledonians beyond it. By 105 the Romans had pulled back to the Tyne–Solway isthmus. At first the frontier was marked by a chain of forts strung out along a military road known as the Stanegate, then in 119 the emperor Hadrian ordered the construction of his famous 70-mile (112-kilometre) long wall from coast to coast 'to separate the Romans from the barbarians'. The wall was built a mile or two north of the Stanegate to take advantage of a steep escarpment of hard volcanic rocks which gave extensive views to the north. Hadrian's Wall is still impressive even today, when it nowhere stands to more than half its original 20-foot (6-metre) height (and much less in most places) – the impression it created on the Britons can only be guessed at. Quite probably they were overawed by this demonstration of Roman organisation and building skills. The building of Hadrian's Wall did not immediately stabilise the frontier – it was temporarily pushed north again to the Forth–Clyde isthmus between around 142 and 163, and the emperor Severus campaigned deep into the Highlands at the beginning of the third century – but it was a powerful, if unintended, symbol of the Roman failure to complete the conquest of Britain.

7

THE CELTS IN THE ROMAN WORLD

[Claudius] made up his mind, you know, to see the whole world in
the toga, Greeks, Gauls, Spaniards, Britons, and all.
Seneca, Apocolocyntosis (c. AD 54)

The Romans were highly successful at assimilating conquered peoples and
turning them into loyal provincials and, eventually, Roman citizens, whose
manpower contributed to yet further conquests. Thus the descendants of
conquered Cisalpine Gauls helped Rome conquer Gaul, while Gauls later
took part in the Roman conquest of Britain. Assimilation was not pursued
by deliberately attacking local cultures, languages and identities: the Roman
Empire was actually one of the most successful multi-cultural societies ever
created. This success was based on religious tolerance, which removed the
most serious potential obstacles to assimilation. True, all citizens were
expected at times to make token sacrifices to the official state gods, but this
was a political act, a declaration of loyalty to the empire. The Romans did
not care at all if those making the sacrifices actually believed in the existence
of Jupiter, Mars and the rest. The Romans tried to stop human sacrifice,
and they had difficulty taking some of the Egyptians' animal gods seriously, but the only religions that ever faced persecution were monotheistic
Judaism and Christianity. The insistence of Christians and Jews that they
alone had a monopoly of religious truth, and their refusal to sacrifice to the
state gods, fully justified their persecution as this intolerance threatened the
cohesion of the empire. Not surprisingly, the empire became a much more
totalitarian state after the triumph of Christianity in the fourth century.
Religion, perhaps even more than language, played such an important part
in cultural identity in the ancient world that the empire's tolerance allowed
the local identities of its subjects to continue to flourish, be they Gauls,
Britons, Greeks, Egyptians and so on. This continued to be the case even
after the emperor Caracalla extended Roman citizenship to all free inhabitants of the empire in 212.

For the bulk of the empire's subjects, the peasants, Roman rule changed little: they continued to speak their native languages and worship their traditional gods; they continued to till the land in the same way that they always had, live in the same kind of houses they always lived in, and were exploited by the rich in the same old way too. Where the empire did begin to undermine local identities was at the top. For all their tolerance, the Romans had unshakable confidence that their way of life was the best and they encouraged their subjects to emulate it, but with mixed success. In the Hellenised east, the Romans had conquered a civilisation that was older and more sophisticated than theirs. The Romans could teach the Greeks little and were open-minded enough to realise they had much to learn from them. Rome was not a model of sophistication for the Greeks, and attempts to popularise entertainments such as gladiatorial combats were not very successful. It was very different in the Celtic west, where the social elite had, to varying degrees, already adopted elements of a Romanised lifestyle before they were actually conquered. Converted into a provincial aristocracy, the old Celtic ruling class gradually adopted a Romanised material culture, while their role in local government encouraged them to learn Latin and worship the state gods. This last was made easier by the Roman custom of twinning their gods with local gods, for example, in the Celtic world, the thunder god Taranis with Jupiter and the warlike god Teutates with Mars. This process of conflation was what Tacitus called the *interpretatio Romana*. Another Romanising influence was the army. Service in the legions was open only to Roman citizens but provincials could join the auxiliaries. Though the pay was inferior and the period of service longer, the award on discharge of Roman citizenship made service attractive. This was especially so in the Celtic west where military service was an honourable substitute for the old warrior tradition. The military life was thoroughly Roman. The language of the army was Latin. Every fort had its bathhouse and shrine to the state cults. After 25 years' service recruits were very Romanised, but the flow was not entirely one way as the cult of the Celtic goddess Epona was spread widely through the empire by cavalrymen attracted by her role as protectress of horses.

That it was the Celts themselves who largely controlled the pace of their Romanisation is confirmed by burial practices. Four burials at Goeblingen-Nospelt in Luxembourg, dating from 50 to 15 BC, show both continuity with La Tène traditions and gradual change. The earliest two graves (50–30 BC) were typical La Tène elite cremation burials with horse gear and weapons and only one Roman object between them, an amphora. A third, slightly later grave (30–20 BC) contained similar war and horse gear but also imported Italian pottery and a wine-serving set, together with locally made pottery incorporating native and Roman decorative motifs. The most recent grave (25–15 BC) contained a long Celtic slashing sword and horse gear, showing that the deceased had still identified with native aristocratic warrior tradition, but in all other respects the material culture represented by the grave goods was almost completely Romanised. A Roman wine-serving

Plate 15 Relief of Epona, Gaulish goddess, protector of horses, riders and travellers, from Gannat, Allier, *c.* 50 BC–400 AD (clay); Gallo-Roman

Source: Musée des Antiquités Nationales, St-Germain-en-Laye, France/Lauros/Giraudon/Bridgeman Art Library, www.bridgeman.co.uk

set and dinner service show that more than Roman material culture had been adopted – Roman table manners had too. The graves of three aristo-cratic Celtic women from Heimstetten, near Munich, dated to AD 30–60, show a similar picture of acceptance of the new and retention of traditional cultural identities. In some areas of eastern Gaul it remained common to place weapons in male graves until the third century; in other areas almost completely Romanised burial practices, in which there are few distinctions between male and female burials, had been adopted well before the end of the first century AD. Clearly different communities took Romanisation at their own pace.

Cisalpine Gaul and Spain

The first Celtic area to be completely assimilated into the Roman system was also the first to have been conquered, Cisalpine Gaul. The situation here was untypical of the Roman Empire as a whole because of the removal of much of the Celtic population to make way for Roman and Latin settlers in the decades after the war with Hannibal. Elsewhere in the Roman Empire there was no great exodus of Roman settlers from Italy to the conquered provinces. Even the discharged veteran soldiers who settled in the colonies that were founded specially for them in the provinces (for example, Colonia Agrippina, modern Cologne) were mostly neither Roman nor even Italian but recruits from other provinces. However extensive the land confiscations may have been, the Romans did not succeed in removing all the Gaulish population. Celtic cults, like that of the Matronae (triple mother goddesses), continued into imperial times, as did Celtic personal names such as Boduac. The Celtic language continued to be spoken into the first century AD and even in the second century some northern Italians still spoke with a 'Gallic' accent. By this time though what remained of the Cisalpine Gauls had clearly long accepted Roman rule, as all of the region's free population had been granted citizenship as early as 49 BC. Northern Italy developed a strong literary and poetic tradition in early imperial times and some of the greatest Latin poets, including Horace and Catullus, may have been of Celtic descent.

The coastal areas of Spain, which had long been influenced by the Greeks, Phoenicians and Carthaginians, were very quickly and completely Romanised. Though it was politically loyal to the empire, the Celtic interior was only superficially Romanised while the tribes of the mountainous north-west, the Gallaeci, Cantabri and Astures, remained largely uninfluenced by Roman civilisation. Romanisation was most obvious in religion. As throughout the empire, there was a rapid conflation of native and Roman cults. The nameless chief god of the Celtiberi was identified with Jupiter, for example, the underworld goddess Ataecina with Proserpina, and the native war god Tarbucelis with Mars. Religious images became Romanised, but they are often only thinly disguised native deities. Images of Venus and Diana are probably native mother goddesses. Worship of various nature spirits, such as the female xanas of Asturias, which were usually portrayed in Romanised fashion as nymphs and fauns, continued for centuries and they survive in local folklore to this day. All temples and shrines, whether of native or Roman deities, were built in Classical styles. Religious beliefs were least Romanised in Galicia. In most of imperial Spain, Roman deities eventually came to outnumber native ones. In the north-west, however, the numbers were about equal. The eastern mystery cults of Isis, Cybele and Mithras spread to Spain, and in the third century Christianity became important. The Celtic cults declined as Christianity took over in the fourth century, and the latest known inscription mentioning a Celtic god is to the otherwise unknown Erudinus, which was made at Santander in 399.

The old Celtic tribal identities still survived in north-west Spain even in the fifth century, where the Vaccaei, Gallaeci, Astures and Cantabri all resisted the invading Visigoths and Suevi, while there was no resistance in the more Romanised areas. Kin-based clans (called *gentes* by the Romans) also persisted throughout the period of Roman rule. In the north-west, the pre-Roman settlement pattern continued unchanged. The Romans saw cities as being synonymous with civilisation, but in north-west Spain their attempts at urbanisation failed and Celtic *castros* (hillforts) remained occupied until the end of the Roman period and beyond. One, Castro de Mohias near Oviedo, was occupied continuously from the Iron Age until the sixth or possibly even the ninth century. No Roman-style public buildings, such as theatres, are known from the area. Round stone huts continued to be built even in what passed for towns. Celtic symbols such as sun discs were used on funerary stelae (upright stone slabs with carvings or inscriptions) and pre-Roman decorative styles re-emerged in late Roman times, showing a conscious revival of identification with the Celtic past. Torcs were still made well into the imperial period, and Celtiberian type javelins continued to be used even in the thirteenth century. The majority of personal names in the north-west continued to be Celtic throughout Roman rule. How long Celtic languages survived after the Roman conquest is unclear. Certainly Hispano-Celtic was still in ordinary use in the first century AD and, as modern Portuguese and Galician contain many words of Celtic formation, it must have survived until late Roman times when Latin began to break up into the precursors of the modern Romance languages. It is clear that it was not Roman conquest that killed Celtic Spain but Christianity and the subsequent Germanic and Moorish invasions.

Gaul

Gaul became the most Romanised of the empire's Celtic provinces and the Gauls themselves have a fair claim to being regarded as the truest heirs of Roman culture in the west. The Gauls never lost their distinct identity, but by the end of Roman rule they had ceased to be Celtic in any meaningful sense. The most Romanised part of Gaul was the southern province of Gallia Transalpina, which was renamed Narbonensis after Caesar conquered the rest of Gaul. Because of their long contacts with the Greeks of Massalia and their already Mediterraneanised economy, the Gauls of this region became de-tribalised and almost entirely Romanised in culture and language. The thoroughgoing nature of Romanisation here gave Provence a distinctive cultural and linguistic identity that endured right through the Middle Ages and made its absorption into the kingdom of France a sometimes bloody affair. If Narbonensis was civilised Gaul, northern Gaul was long regarded as a barbaric region, sometimes nicknamed Gallia Comata, 'Long-Haired Gaul'.

The assimilation of Gallia Comata into the Roman system began in 27 BC when it was divided into three provinces, Gallia Belgica, Gallia Lugdunensis and Gallia Aquitania, known collectively as Tres Gallia, the Three Gauls. The Gauls had little fight left in them after Caesar had finished with them, but a number of small rebellions in the first century AD fed the Roman's anxieties and prejudices about them, so creating a barrier to their complete assimilation. The most serious of these rebellions was led by the Batavian chief Julius Civilis in AD 69 in an attempt to create an independent

'Empire of the Gauls'. Civilis was actually a Romanised German and most of his supporters were Germans from both sides of the Roman frontier: he got very little support from the Gauls themselves. The Gallic provinces were divided up into administrative districts called *civitates* and elective magistracies and other Roman institutions of civil government were introduced. The native aristocracy was encouraged to seek public office by the offer of Roman citizenship, which brought many legal privileges, as a reward. Roman Gaul was governed by Gauls. The *civitates* were based on the Iron Age tribal territories and their capitals were usually the old tribal *oppida*. If the site of the *oppidum* was unsuitable, because it was on a confined hilltop for example, then the Romans founded a new town nearby. The *civitas* capitals survive today as modern towns, and it is a sign of the durability of tribal identities under Roman rule that their modern names are derived from the tribal names rather than the names that the Romans gave to them. Hence Paris (Roman Lutetia) was the capital of the *civitas* of the Parisii, while Reims (Roman Durocortorum) was the capital of the Remi. To encourage the adoption of a Romanised lifestyle, the *civitas* capitals were given all the usual amenities of Roman civilisation, such as baths, aqueducts, metalled roads, theatres, amphitheatres and Classical-style temples.

A symbolic landmark in the Romanisation of Gaul was the decision of the emperor Claudius (r. 41–54) to allow members of the Gallic aristocracy to become senators, making it possible for them to identify themselves with the empire's ruling class. The privilege was first extended to Rome's long-time allies, the Aedui. In practice few Gauls were actually appointed to the Senate as the old Roman families guarded their status jealously. The aristocracy first became bilingual in Gaulish and Latin, but Latin eventually took over completely. Late Roman Gaul produced many important literary figures, including the poets Sidonius Apollinaris, Ausonius and (St) Paulinus of Nola, all of whom wrote in Latin. Even among the lower classes, Gaulish was beginning to give way to Latin in Narbonensis as early as the first century AD. Gaulish disappeared from public inscriptions in the rest of Gaul around the same time (implying widespread literacy in Latin); it continued to be the first language of the majority into the fourth century, however. By the middle of the fifth century a Latin vernacular, the forerunner of French, was beginning to take over, but in Auvergne and Armorica (Brittany), and perhaps a few other areas, the common folk still spoke *Celtice* or *Gallice*. The Roman state cults, often assimilated with local deities, spread across Gaul but traditional Celtic cults continued to flourish. Iron Age sanctuaries, such as those at Ribemont-sur-Ancre and Gournay, continued to be used, and elaborated, through the Roman period, and there is some evidence that human sacrifice and the head cult survived despite official prohibitions. Traditional Celtic temples and sanctuaries continued to be built, though now using stone, brick and concrete in the Roman manner. Most were simple buildings consisting of a central shrine surrounded by an ambulatory, but they occasionally reached massive proportions, as with the so-called Temple of Janus at Autun.

Plate 16 Roman walls at Carcassonne (late third century AD)
Source: John Haywood

Gaul suffered terrible devastation during Caesar's conquest, but the stabilisation of the Roman frontier on the Rhine at the beginning of the first century AD became the key to recovery. The permanent presence of seven legions and dozens of regiments of auxiliaries on the frontier was a great stimulus to agriculture and industry in Gaul. Intensive grain production transformed the landscape of northern Gaul and Gallic landowners built comfortable villas on the proceeds. The demand for grain even led to an early venture in mechanised agriculture, the invention of an effective reaping machine. By the second century Gaul had probably even overtaken Italy in wealth. Gaul's prosperity was shaken in the third century. East of the Rhine, the first signs of political centralisation can be seen among the Germanic tribes by the late second century. Smaller tribes were forming confederations and adopting new identities. The name of one of these, the Alemanni, means simply 'all men'. Another important confederation was the Franks. Like the Iron Age Celtic tribes, the Germanic confederations were dominated by warlike chiefs and warrior elites who found the wealth of the Roman Empire an irresistible temptation. The frontiers held, despite continuous Germanic pressure, but the economic cost was so great that in the third century the empire collapsed into political anarchy. Of the 26 emperors who ruled between 235 and 284 all but one died by violence (the one who died in bed was not so lucky either – he caught the plague). As rivals for the throne fought one another, the border defences were neglected, allowing the German tribes to break through repeatedly and raid deep into Gaul and, sometimes, even Spain and Italy.

The Gauls responded to the collapse of central authority by setting up their own independent 'Gallic Empire' under the general Postumus in 260. Postumus won popularity by concentrating on restoring the Rhine frontier rather than by trying to win power in Rome, and his authority was also accepted in Spain, Britain and Raetia (now southern Germany and Switzerland). For the first and only time, almost the entire Celtic world was independent and united under a single ruler. Although this was not a 'nationalist' revolt so much as demand for better imperial government, it contributed to a marked increase in Gallic self-confidence. When Postumus was assassinated in 268, Spain returned its allegiance to Rome. Postumus' successor Victorinus lost Raetia and most of Narbonensis to Claudius II around 269 and the rest of the Gallic Empire was recaptured by Rome after the defeat of its last emperor Tetricus in 274. Gaul's importance was at its greatest in the fourth century, when Trier became one of the capitals of the empire. The demands of defending the Rhine frontier meant that many emperors spent far more of their time in Gaul than in Italy. Rome itself rarely saw an emperor. Aristocratic Gauls were proud of their contribution to the empire and proud also of the way they had made Classical culture their own. But they were still proud to be Gauls, no more so than when a Gaul, Avitus, became Roman emperor in 455. This enthusiasm for the empire was not shared by the Gaulish peasantry, as it was on them that the high cost of defending the empire mainly fell. High taxes progressively impoverished the peasantry and many ran away from the land to join bands of peasant brigands called *bagaudae*.

In the course of the fifth century the Romans gradually lost control of Gaul to the Germanic Visigoths, Burgundians and Franks. The Franks proved the strongest of these, and they had won control of all of Gaul by 534. There was very little popular resistance: high taxation had undermined the loyalty of the empire's subjects. The transition from Roman to Frankish rule was certainly not entirely peaceful – the Franks had Roman, Visigothic and Burgundian armies to fight – but Gaul was not left in smoking ruins or overrun by Germanic settlers. Only the Rhineland and what is now Belgium and north-east France saw much Germanic peasant settlement. Everywhere else the Franks formed a political and military elite but were a small minority living among the native Gaulish population. Even the Gallo-Roman aristocracy survived. Yes, they grumbled about the barbaric habits of their new rulers, like using rancid butter as hair oil, but they came to terms with the new order and got to keep most of their estates and retained political influence by supplying the Frankish kingdom with most of its literate administrators and bishops. The Frankish homeland was on the lower Rhine, and long contact with the empire had given them a healthy respect for Roman civilisation. Although they were still pagan when they invaded Gaul, the Franks soon converted to Christianity, so removing the main obstacle to their assimilating with the Gauls. The Franks came to identify with the superior Christian-Roman civilisation of their subjects, eventually adopting their language too. The Gauls for their part came to identify politically with their conquerors and adopted their Frankish identity. From this fruitful fusion of Roman, Celt and German, the modern French identity gradually began to develop. Even though they do not consider themselves to be Celts, the French have always considered the Gaulish past to be an important part of their identity and celebrate it today not only in scholarship but in popular culture too, as exemplified in the cartoon character Asterix.

Britain

Britain remained the least Romanised of the empire's Celtic provinces, though any fears the Romans initially held that Ireland and the unconquered north would prove to be unsettling examples of freedom proved groundless. The Britons came to regard the Caledonians and Irish as barbarians and enemies. Not that there is any reason to suppose that they had ever regarded them as friends anyway. The part of Britain under Roman control became the province of Britannia, ruled by a governor based in London. By *c.* 100 most of the province had been subdivided into *civitates* based on the Iron Age tribal territories, much as had been the case with Gaul. Roman rule increased the pace of urbanisation. Colonies (*coloniae*) of Roman citizens, mainly discharged veteran soldiers, were founded at Chelmsford (Caesaromagus), St Albans (Verulamium), Gloucester (Glevum), Lincoln

(Lindum) and York (Eburacum) to act as agents of Romanisation. Some of the late Iron Age tribal *oppida*, such as Silchester (Calleva), were adopted as *civitas* capitals. In other cases new towns were founded to replace old hillforts. In this way Dorchester (Durnovaria), the *civitas* capital of the Durotriges, replaced the nearby hillfort of Maiden Castle. In the economically advanced lowland zone the native aristocracy was readily accommodated within the administrative hierarchy of province and *civitas* and they took up the burdens of building temples and other public buildings. Their lifestyles, appearance and dress, even their names, became Romanised. Tacitus wrote, somewhat sneeringly, of the Britons being enslaved by baths and banquets and proudly describing this aping of Roman manners as *humanitas* ('civilisation'). Not all Romans were so superior. As far as the Roman poet Martial was concerned, his British lady friend Claudia Rufina positively exemplified *humanitas* – flattery indeed. Classical sculpture, wall painting and mosaics were introduced, though they were often adapted to local taste. A spectacular example of this is the very unclassical Medusa's head carving from the temple of Sulis-Minerva at Bath. Despite this, the insular La Tène style remained popular for personal jewellery, especially in the north. As in Gaul, the Romans tried to win over the locals by introducing them to the amenities of urban life, such as hot baths and amphitheatres. In the south-east, the aristocracy reorganised their lands into large-scale farming estates and built villas for themselves, but in the west and north farming and building techniques remained unchanged by the Roman conquest. Even in the south-east, small farmers still remained outside the imperial cash economy in the third century. Much of Wales and northern England was economically too under-developed to be incorporated into the normal pattern of civil administration. These mineral-rich and strategically important areas remained under direct military government throughout the Roman occupation. Tribal identities remained strong in these regions throughout the period of Roman rule, but they seem to have declined in importance in the south-east.

Though the imperial cults were introduced into Britain, Celtic paganism remained strong. Often, as was common throughout the Roman empire, native cults were assimilated with Roman cults, as happened in the temple of Sulis-Minerva at Bath, where the Celtic goddess Sulis was equated with the Roman goddess of wisdom Minerva. Celtic paganism was still going strong in the late fourth century, when a temple to the local agricultural god Nodens was built at Lydney in Gloucestershire. Despite official prohibitions, human sacrifice and the head cult continued to be practised publicly almost to the end of Roman rule. One example, dating to *c.* 200, is the skull of a teenage boy, which had been de-fleshed and displayed on a post in a temple at St Albans before being buried in a ritual pit. The boy had been battered to death. Impressive Christian mosaics at the fourth-century villa at Hinton St Mary show that Christianity had begun to win converts in the upper classes by the early fourth century, but its progress was slow before the emperor Theodosius officially banned all pagan cults in 391. The conversion of the Britons to Christianity thereafter must have taken place

Plate 17 Head of Medusa from the temple of Sulis-Minerva, Bath
Source: Roman Baths Museum, Bath, Avon, UK/Bridgeman Art Library, www.bridgeman.co.uk

over a very short period of time. Certainly the writings of St Patrick and Constantius of Lyon, who wrote an account of the visit of St Germanus, bishop of Auxerre, to Britain in 429, betray no evidence at all of surviving paganism. Nor are anything other than Christian symbols ever found on fifth-century memorial inscriptions.

Britain produced no great literary figure to compare with Sidonius or Ausonius, though St Patrick was a Romano-Briton. So was the theologian Pelagius (d. *c.* 418), who rejected the orthodox Christian teaching that humankind's salvation depended on divine grace, preaching instead that man had free will to choose between good and evil and so was responsible for his own salvation. He was declared a heretic in 417. There were British poets who could write elegant verse in Latin but only a few couplets have survived on tombstones and mosaics. The only one known by name lived towards the end of the fourth century – Silvius Bonus, who was mocked by the Gallic poet Ausonius, who said he could not be a good poet because no Briton could be a good poet ('French' contempt for 'British' culture started early). Scenes from the *Aeneid* and images of Roman gods and Greek myths on mosaics and tableware show that the British elite were familiar with Classical authors, including Homer, Virgil and Ovid, and wanted to display the fact to visitors. A red jasper intaglio bearing a portrait of Socrates, found in Gloucestershire, indicates that some educated Britons had an interest in Classical philosophy. The elite quickly learned to speak and write Latin, but they were always bilingual. The majority remained Celtic-speaking. Even the rich, such as Quintus Natalius Natalinus, the owner of a villa at Thruxton in Hampshire, still had Celtic names in the fourth century. Latin was purely a language of culture and administration and no British vernacular version of the language developed as it did in Gaul and Spain. The Brithonic language borrowed around 800 words from Latin but it remained Brithonic.

Britain survived the empire's crisis years in the third century relatively unscathed either by barbarian invasion or civil war, though it was independent from central Roman authority as part of the Gallic empire and again under the usurpers Carausius and Allectus, who ruled a short-lived 'British Empire' between 286 and 296. The fourth century has, with good reason, been described as the 'Golden Age' of Roman Britain. The sea did not perfectly insulate Britain from the troubles suffered by Gaul – raids by Saxon, Pictish and Irish pirates required a considerable and continuing attention to coastal defences – but the province was relatively secure in comparison. The insecurity on the continent even benefited the British economy. The Rhine frontier was under constant pressure from the Germanic tribes and the provisioning needs of the Roman army stimulated agriculture in Britain. Luxurious villas sprang up across important grain-growing areas like the Cotswolds. Britain's relative immunity to invasion ended with the 'barbarian conspiracy' of 367. The Roman province was assailed by a formidable alliance of Scotti (from Ireland), Attacotti (origin unknown) and Picts (from northern Britain), who attacked from the north and west, and Franks and Saxons, who attacked the Channel coast. The garrison got no warning of the attack because the agents placed to supervise the northern tribes had been bribed. Britain's cities, by now mostly walled, seem to have held out, but plundering bands overran the countryside and the commander of the coast defences was killed. The invaders were driven out in 368 after reinforcements arrived from Gaul, but a pervasive sense of insecurity remained and the fabric of Roman Britain began to unravel. Barbarian raids, or even just the fear of them, hit the countryside the hardest. Some villas and farms can be shown to have met violent ends but most were simply abandoned or allowed to fall into disrepair: very few survived into the fifth century. Towns had never flourished in Britain in the same way they had in Gaul, and they too went into decline as they lost their administrative functions due to political instability.

Though fourth-century Britain was politically loyal to the empire, the province won a reputation as a breeding ground for usurpers, most of them ambitious generals. The trend was set by Constantine the Great, who was proclaimed emperor at York in 306 (of course Constantine won and so is not usually considered a usurper – that status is reserved for losers). Later usurpers, such as Magnus Maximus (the Maxen Wledig of Welsh legend) who rebelled in 383, withdrew troops to fight in civil wars on the continent, so weakening the garrison and leaving the province exposed to barbarian raids. The last British mint had closed by 388 and, as money supplies from the continent were intermittent, coins gradually went out of circulation. In 407 another usurper, Constantine III, led another army out of Britain to Gaul in pursuit of his political ambitions. By this time it seems that the Britons had had enough; the empire was no longer working for them, and in 410 they expelled Constantine's administration and organised their own defences against the barbarians. Britain thus became the only province ever to leave the empire of its own volition. Pelagius had many followers in Britain, and his doctrine of spiritual self-help may well have influenced the Britons in their momentous decision to break with Rome.

8

THE MAKING OF WALES

On the departure of the Romans, the Picts and Scots . . . occupied all the northern and most distant parts of Britain up to the wall. Here a dispirited British garrison stationed on the fortifications pined in absolute terror night and day, while from beyond the wall, the enemy constantly attacked them with hooked weapons, dragging the cowardly defenders down from the wall and dashing them on the ground.

Bede, *Ecclesiastical History*, I.12 (731)

The collapse of the Roman province of Britannia left the Britons poorly prepared for independence and ill equipped to defend themselves against the depredations of their wild Celtic neighbours, the Picts of northern Britain and the Scots of Ireland. The demoralised and terrified Britons invited the Saxons, pagan pirates from the North Sea coast of Germany, to come and defend them in return for land to settle on. The Saxons soon defeated the Picts and Scots but, seeing what a feeble and cowardly bunch the Britons were, they sent back to Germany for reinforcements and began to take over the country for themselves. The Angles and Jutes from Denmark joined the Saxons to grab a piece of the action and, if they were not slain, the hapless Britons either fled abroad or were driven to seek a comfortless refuge in the mountainous west as the victors set about laying the foundations of England. Such is still the popular image of the fate of the Britons after the end of Roman rule. It provides a heroic foundation myth for the English and legitimises the lovingly nurtured victim culture of modern Celtic nationalism. In fact, this picture of moral collapse was created by later ecclesiastical writers to serve their own didactic purposes. The decision of the Britons to break with Rome – they were the only provincials to leave the empire by choice – does not suggest that they lacked confidence in themselves. The Britons were, in reality, the most successful of all the inhabitants of the former Roman Empire in resisting the Germanic barbarian invasions.

The responsibility for creating the myth of the helpless Britons lies firmly with Gildas, a British monk, who lived around the middle of the sixth century. Gildas was the author of one of the very few literary works to have survived from the period, *De excidio Britanniae* ('On the Ruin of Britain'), a gloomily doom-laden jeremiad about the state of Britain and the Britons. *De excidio* is essentially an extended sermon in which Gildas argues that the various troubles experienced by the Britons since the end of Roman rule had been inflicted on them by a just God because of their wicked behaviour. Gildas had received a good Classical education, and knew his Bible and the works of early Christian theologians, such as Jerome and Salvian, who had interpreted the decline of the Roman Empire in a very similar light. Indeed, this remained a standard Christian approach to history throughout the Middle Ages. God allowed bad things to happen to his people because they were sinful. The depredations of the Huns, Goths and Vandals, as well as those of the Angles, Saxons, Picts and Scots, not to mention plagues and famines, were all amenable to explanation in these terms. The only certain way to stop such awful things happening was the path of moral reform. Because of the moralistic nature of his work, Gildas had an interest in painting as grim a picture as possible of the state of immediate post-Roman Britain. It is hardly surprising that English historians from the Venerable Bede (d. 735) onwards accepted Gildas's testimony uncritically (not that they had anyone else's to compare it with). As a monk, Bede shared Gildas's gloomy worldview. As an Angle, Bede was not inclined to be sympathetic towards the Britons, who were in any case members of the schismatic Celtic church and so quite obviously less righteous than the Angles and Saxons, who by this time had converted to orthodox Catholicism and accepted the authority of the pope.

The independent Britons

Following the end of Roman rule, power devolved on the local Romano-British elites who were responsible for local government under Roman rule. Many aristocratic Britons initially retained the titles of their Roman magistracies – St Patrick's father was a decurion (a town councillor) and in 429 Verulamium (St Albans) was ruled by a man claiming the power of a tribune – and it is likely that they tried to preserve a Roman-style adminis-tration. After all, this was the only example of government they would have known. In the longer term, political and economic dislocation made this both unsustainable and unnecessary and local aristocrats set themselves up as kings and *tyranni* ('tyrants'). In some cases these kingdoms were based on a Roman city: Gloucester, Cirencester and Bath all had their own kings in the sixth century. In the less Romanised west and north, it was the old Iron Age tribal identities that formed the basis of emerging kingdoms. The Cumbrian kingdom of Rheged was formed by the Novantae or Carvetii, the north Welsh kingdom of Gwynedd by the Ordovices, and in Devon and Cornwall the kingdom of Dumnonia by the Dumnonii. It might be expected that efforts to maintain a Romanised administration would have been strongest in the wealthy south-east, but this was the first area to be overrun by the Anglo-Saxons, so little is known about political structures there. It is not clear either what efforts were made to preserve a degree of unity in the face of the external threats faced by the Britons, but there were some rulers such as the 'great tyrant' Vortigern ('overlord') and Ambrosius Aurelianus whose leadership was widely recognised by the Britons. It was, in fact, the clergy, rather than secular rulers, who preserved the most important aspects of Roman influence on the Britons – the Latin language and the Christian religion – ensuring that no matter how politically frag-mented it became, Britain remained culturally a part of the late Roman world after 410. The so-called Celtic church developed only in the later fifth century, after the pagan Anglo-Saxons overran south-eastern Britain. Communication between the British church and Rome became more difficult, allowing doctrinal differences, notably in calculating the date of Easter, to develop.

The most objective picture of what was actually happening in Britain in the century following the end of Roman rule comes from archaeology. Pervasive insecurity and economic dislocation had already led to a decline in urban life and the abandonment of most country villas by the end of the fifth century. Nevertheless, for a time at least, the Britons attempted to maintain the infrastructure of a Romanised lifestyle. For example, the bath complex at Bath was maintained until as late as *c*. 470. At Verulamium the forum remained in use, and water mains and new mosaic floors were being laid in high-status houses until as late as *c*. 475. Wroxeter in Shropshire bucked the trend completely and saw a major redevelopment in the middle of the fifth century, when new shops and a large timber mansion – pos-sibly the residence of a local king – were built. Carlisle also saw new build-ings in the early fifth century, including a large timber hall, which may have been an assembly place for the local kingdom of Rheged. There may be other such halls awaiting discovery in other Roman cities, which retained a symbolic importance as centres of power long after they had ceased to function as true urban centres. The headquarters building of the legionary fortress at York was maintained for centuries, probably as the headquarters of the British, and later Anglian, kings of Deira. A few Roman forts, such as Birdoswald on Hadrian's Wall, developed into villages, occupied no doubt by descendants of their original garrisons, but, perhaps surprisingly in view of their well-built stone walls, they were not attractive places for the Britons to settle.

Though urban life of some sort seems to have continued into the early sixth century at Carlisle and Wroxeter, by this time many of the towns of Roman Britain had been abandoned, supplanted by hillforts. Some of these, such as South Cadbury in Somerset, were reoccupied Iron Age hill-forts but most were new foundations. These post-Roman hillforts were much smaller than their Iron Age antecedents and were clearly intended only to accommodate a local chieftain or king and his elite warriors and servants, rather than an entire tribal population. Their builders exhibited a marked preference for natural strongholds – small, steep rocky hills – such as Dinas Emrys in the heart of Snowdonia and the limestone crag of Dinas Powys near Cardiff. In this way the former Roman province came to resemble the un-Romanised area north of the wall, or even Ireland.

These power centres may have been cramped and exposed but they were certainly not isolated. Fortified power centres from Castle Dore in Cornwall to Dunadd in Argyll, well north of the Romanised area, have produced evidence of trade contacts reaching as far afield as the eastern Mediterranean in the shape of wine amphorae and other goods. The spread of Christianity made obtaining wine important for religious as well as social reasons because of its use in celebrating the Eucharist (or 'Mass'). Early monastic sites, such as that at Tintagel in Cornwall, shared the same wide-ranging trade connections as the elite power centres. Now that the old Roman port towns had been abandoned, goods were landed at informal beach sites on sheltered estuaries like a recently excavated site among sand dunes at Bantham in south Devon that produced huge amounts of pottery from the Aegean, Anatolia, Syria and North Africa. Negotiations held here between the merchants and the local elite were treated as major social events, accompanied by feasting on cattle, sheep, pigs, deer and other mammals and wildfowl, which were roasted over huge outdoor hearths.

It is clear that the newly independent Britons believed the greatest threat to their way of life came from their un-Romanised and still pagan fellow Celts, the Picts and the Scots/Irish, rather than the Saxons. The Picts were fierce raiders but the Scots were the more dangerous because they came as conquerors and settlers too. Historical traditions and memorial stones inscribed with the Irish ogham alphabet provide evidence of Irish settlements in Devon and Cornwall, south-west Wales, north Wales, the Isle of Man and Argyll. In the long term, the settlement in Argyll was to be the most significant, but that was mainly a problem for the Picts. The tyrant Vortigern is said to have reacted to the threat of the Picts and Scots by ordering Cunedda, a prince of the Gododdin (i.e. the Votadini), to North Wales to drive out the Irish invaders, which he duly did. Cunedda succeeded in establishing himself as ruler of the Ordovices and it was from him that the kings of Gwynedd claimed descent. Later historical traditions of Gwynedd claimed that Cunedda also drove out the Irish from south-west Wales, but this was a fiction intended to bolster the dynasty's claims to overlordship of all Wales. Medieval Welsh genealogies include Irish names among the early kings of Dyfed (in south-west Wales), showing that the Irish here established a successful dynasty. However, these Irish settlers were soon assimilated with the native Britons, as ogham and Old Irish was soon superseded on memorial stones by the Roman alphabet and the Latin language. The Irish settlers in Cornwall and Devon were also assimilated with the natives, but the Isle of Man became completely Gaelicised. At least in part, the Britons' success against the Picts and Scots may have been due to the support of Saxon mercenaries who were invited to settle in Britain in return for military service. The Saxons proved to be dangerous allies.

The coming of the Saxons

In the fourth century, Saxon pirate raids on the east coast of Britain were so common that it became known as the 'Saxon Shore'. The coast was heavily fortified, but the frequent withdrawal of troops to fight in civil wars on the continent gave the Saxons plenty of opportunities to slip through the defences. Perhaps the Angles and Jutes joined in these raids too, but we do not know. The Britons never tried to distinguish between the different Germanic tribes that raided and settled in Britain – they just called the lot Saxons (Welsh *Saesneg*, Gaelic *Sassenach*): the convenient custom of calling these Germanic invaders 'Anglo-Saxons' was actually begun by the Franks across the Channel in Gaul. For their part, the Anglo-Saxons simply described the Britons as *waelisc*, that is 'foreigners', whence 'Welsh' and 'Wales'.

Neither the exact date nor the circumstances of the first Anglo-Saxon settlements are known for certain. The traditional version of events, derived from Gildas and Bede, is that Vortigern invited the Saxons to settle in Kent in 449, three years after the Britons had appealed unsuccessfully to Rome for help against the Picts and Scots. The story of the subsequent rebellion of the Saxon leaders Hengest and Horsa, their calling in of reinforcements from across the North Sea and their treacherous slaying of the British leaders at a peace conference is a rattling good yarn but it is, alas, unlikely to be true. Archaeological evidence, most of it from pagan cemeteries containing warrior burials with Germanic weapons and metalwork, proves that Anglo-Saxon settlement actually began within a decade of the time that Britain became independent. By around the 450s Anglo-Saxons were settled in some numbers in Kent, the Thames valley, East Anglia, Lincolnshire and around the Humber estuary and York. If Vortigern did settle Angles or Saxons in Britain, they certainly were not the first. Possibly the Anglo-Saxons were unwelcome immigrants from the start, but it is not unlikely that British rulers invited the first settlers in. With the benefit of hindsight, this would seem not just unwise but positively reckless – Gildas said that it was like letting wolves into a sheepfold – yet settling Germanic tribes as 'federates' (allies) in return for military service was a long-established Roman practice and it would not be surprising if Romanised British rulers chose to emulate it. Nor would it be surprising if, once established, the Angles and Saxons took advantage of periods of British weakness or internecine strife to enlarge their territories, just as the Franks, Visigoths and other federates were doing at the same time in the Roman Empire.

By the end of the fifth century the Anglo-Saxons had seized control of most of south-east Britain. This was a considerable achievement for a group of tribal peoples with no common leadership and whose social and economic organisation was a lot less sophisticated than that which the Britons had inherited from the Romans or, for that matter, than the Britons had had even before the Roman conquest. Because it had the best farmlands, the south-east was the wealthiest region of Britain and supported the densest population. It was also the most Romanised part of the country, but this was not the advantage for the Britons it might seem. The traditional bonds of Celtic society were at their weakest here and it was also here that the Roman administration, with its tax collectors, had been at its most efficient. By the fourth century, the cost of defending the Roman Empire against German pressure was enormous. The rich, of course, used their influence to avoid paying taxes, so the burden fell heavily on the peasants, undermining their loyalty to the empire.

When the Roman frontiers finally collapsed in the fifth century, the invading Germanic tribes faced little popular resistance anywhere, not even in Italy. Conditions probably even got better for the peasantry under their new Germanic rulers, whose lack of administrative expertise made them inefficient tax collectors. The British elite of the south-east was proud of its Romanised lifestyle, but their enthusiasm is unlikely to have been shared by the peasants whose labour paid for it all. Lacking also the bonds of tribal solidarity, British resistance to the Anglo-Saxons probably collapsed quickly in the south-east. Once again, centralisation had failed the Celts and made them more vulnerable to conquest. It was a different matter in the less Romanised west and north, where the Iron Age tribal identities survived to provide a focus for loyalty and state formation: British resistance to the Anglo-Saxons continued here for centuries.

The battle of Mount Badon

The rapid advance of the Anglo-Saxons faltered soon after 500. A Romanised British warlord called Ambrosius Aurelianus united a large part of the Britons under his leadership and their combined forces inflicted a crushing defeat on the Anglo-Saxons at Mount Badon. The site of this famous battle has never been found, but Badbury or Baydon, both in Wiltshire, are possibilities as this area was at the western edge of the area controlled by the Anglo-Saxons. Bath is another possibility. The victory at Mount Badon was later credited to King Arthur, but there is actually no contemporary historical evidence whatsoever for this, or even that Arthur really existed at all. Gildas, who was writing within a generation of the battle, is quite clear that the British leader at Mount Badon was Ambrosius and he makes no mention of Arthur anywhere in his works. Arthur may simply be a folkloric figure who was historicised when real events became associated with his name. If Arthur did exist, then the most likely possibility is that he and Ambrosius are actually one and the same person: Arthur, which means 'bearman', being perhaps originally a nickname given to the tough warrior by his men. Badon probably gave the Britons their best chance to expel the Anglo-Saxons – and there is actually evidence that some Anglo-Saxons did return to Germany after the battle – but the unity of purpose achieved by Ambrosius was short-lived. Once the Anglo-Saxon advance had been halted, the feeling that they were a common threat to all Britons evaporated and the victory was not followed up. The Britons of the south-western kingdom of Dumnonia diverted their energy into over-seas colonisation, in Brittany (see p. 146) and Galicia, where the little-known colony of Britonia flourished briefly in the sixth century.

Badon was clearly a serious reverse for the Anglo-Saxons, but their control over the south-east gave them great powers of recovery and they were able to resume their advance by *c.* 550, though more slowly than before. After their victory over the Britons at Dyrham in the Cotswolds in 577, the West Saxons captured Gloucester, Cirencester and Bath. This left the British kingdom of Dumnonia cut off and isolated in the south-west. In the north, King Urien of Rheged tried to destroy the Angles who had seized control of the British kingdom of Bernicia, but he was killed while besieging their stronghold at Bamburgh *c.* 590. Soon after this the Bernicians took over the neighbouring Anglian kingdom of Deira, based on York, to form the powerful kingdom of Northumbria. An attempt by the Gododdin of Lothian to destroy Northumbria was crushed at the battle of Catraeth (Catterick) in Yorkshire, probably in 600. One of the survivors of the battle is thought to have been the poet Neirin (or Aneirin), who composed the epic poem *Y Gododdin* ('The Gododdin') in honour of the British dead. The Britons suffered a further blow when the Northumbrians captured Chester in 616. This drove a wedge between the Britons in Wales and those in Cumbria and Strathclyde in southern Scotland. The isolated British enclaves created by the Anglo-Saxon advance developed their own versions of the Brithonic language: Cumbric in the north, Welsh in the centre and Cornish in Dumnonia. The future for the north Britons looked bleak when the Northumbrians conquered the Gododdin *c.* 638 and Rheged a few years later, but their days of expansion at the expense of the Celts were ended by a defeat by the Picts in 685. The West Saxons kept Dumnonia under constant pressure and had overrun most of Devon by 700, but Cornwall (from *Cornwalas*, 'the peninsular Welsh'), or West Wales as it was often called by the Anglo-Saxons, was not so easily subdued. It was only after 838, when the West Saxons defeated an allied Cornish–Viking force at the battle of Hingston Down, just west of the river Tamar, that Cornwall finally lost its independence. Even then Cornwall still kept its own vassal kings until at least 900 and the Cornish were not completely subdued until the reign of King Athelstan (924/5–39). The Midland Anglo-Saxon kingdom of Mercia had expanded to the foothills of the Cambrian mountains some time before 700, but it made little progress after that: this is still more or less where the modern English–Welsh border runs.

The origins of Wales

So far in this book, the term 'Wales' has been used only as a convenient geographical term. It was in the course of the seventh century that Wales, in the modern sense as the country of the Welsh, came into existence. By this time the Britons had begun calling themselves *Cymry*, the people of *Cymru*, the British word for the country that then included not only modern

Wales but also the surviving British kingdoms Rheged and Strathclyde in what are now north-west England and south-west Scotland. After Rheged and Strathclyde fell to the Anglo-Saxons and Scots, *Cymru* and *Cymry* came to be applied only to modern Wales and its people, but traces of the original wider identity survive in the names of Cumbria (the Lake District) and the Clyde's Cumbrae islands. Wales was divided into several kingdoms, which, though small, were far from impotent. The powerful kingdom of Mercia, which successfully bullied its Anglo-Saxon neighbours into submission in the eighth century, went to enormous trouble to fortify its Welsh border with a series of defensive earth ramparts. The most impressive and best preserved of these is Offa's Dyke, named for King Offa (r. 757–96) who ordered its construction, which was an 18-foot (5.5-metre) high rampart running 64 miles (102 kilometres) from Llanfynydd near Wrexham to Kington in Herefordshire. The Dyke is often thought of as merely an impressive attempt by the Mercians to define the frontier, but there are no gates in it as might be expected if people were still going to be crossing it on normal business. The Mercians clearly feared the Welsh. The building of the Dyke is best understood in the context of the Pillar of Eliseg, near Llangollen, a weathered stone monument with an inscription commemorating the success of Eliseg, king of Powys in the mid eighth century, in winning back Welsh territory from the English by nine years of warfare. The Welsh later won back more territory from Mercia as the course of the Dyke now lies mostly in Wales. Small successes like this kept Welsh hopes alive. When he toured Wales in the late twelfth century recruiting for the Third Crusade, the churchman Gerald of Wales noted that the Welsh 'boast and confidently predict that they will soon reoccupy the whole island of Britain'. However, by this time Norman lords had seized control of much of the south and the boast was sounding rather hollow. Gerald described it as an 'illusion'.

Genocide or peaceful co-existence?

The Anglo-Saxon invasion of Britain and the settlement of what came to be called England was not a peaceful affair. The *Anglo-Saxon Chronicle* records many violent incidents, such as the storming of an old Roman fort at Pevensey in Sussex in 491, when the victorious Saxons massacred all the local Britons who had taken refuge there. Genocide, however, there certainly was not. The genetic characteristics of the population of eastern Britain (there is no Anglo-Scottish genetic border) are similar to those of the population of the North Sea coast of continental Europe, proving that there was a considerable influx of Anglo-Saxon settlers to Britain (later reinforced by Danish Viking settlers). But this Germanic imprint diminishes towards the west, where the genetic characteristics of the modern population show greater continuity with the prehistoric population. Therefore, if there was any genocide or large-scale ethnic cleansing of the native Britons, it could have taken place only during the earliest stages of the

Anglo-Saxon settlements: most modern English people must, it seems, have ancient Britons among their ancestors. This genetic pattern is mirrored in place names. Apart from the names of major rivers, few Celtic place names survive in the east, but they increase in numbers towards the west. What the place name and genetic evidence indicates is that though the initial Anglo-Saxon invasion was a folk movement, which overwhelmed the natives in parts of eastern Britain, the later stages were more in the nature of a political conquest of a settled British population, which then became assimilated to Anglo-Saxon ways. This is borne out by the early Anglo-Saxon kingdom of Bernicia (between the Tees and the Forth), which has a Celtic name and only limited evidence for pagan Anglo-Saxon settlement, most of which is concentrated around the royal centre at Yeavering. What probably happened is that relatively small numbers of Anglo-Saxons succeeded in displacing a native ruling dynasty and taking over its kingdom intact. The Britons transferred their loyalties to the new ruling elite and adopted its language, culture and identity. Elsewhere, British aristocrats may have successfully integrated with the Anglo-Saxon aristocracy. The evidence for this is especially good in Wessex, the kingdom that would eventually unify England. The early laws of Wessex prove that it had a mixed Anglo-Saxon and 'Welsh' population and its founder Cerdic (Caradoc) had a Celtic name. This integration may not have been as difficult as it seems. By the time Cerdic lived in the early sixth century, warrior aristocracies with very similar values ruled both the Britons and the Anglo-Saxons: there was only the language barrier to overcome. Anglo-Saxon warriors would certainly have understood the heroic sentiments expressed by Neirin in *Y Gododdin*, while British warriors would have appreciated *Beowulf*. However, the low status that most Britons must have had under Anglo-Saxon rule is starkly reflected in the English language. The victorious Anglo-Saxons adopted barely half-a-dozen British words into Old English.

Even in the south-east, where the Anglo-Saxons settled most thickly, there is considerable evidence for the survival of the native population. Fifth-century 'Romano-Saxon' pottery has Anglo-Saxon decorative motifs but it was made using Romano-British techniques, that is, British potters were working for Anglo-Saxon customers, adapting their craft to suit the tastes of the newcomers. British metalworkers did the same. At Dorchester-on-Thames a cemetery remained in use for Christian burials through the fifth and sixth centuries and, after he converted to Christianity in the seventh century, the Saxon king Cynegils allowed the Italian missionary St Birinus to found a monastery there. The likelihood is, therefore, that it had been occupied by a British Christian community throughout the period of Anglo-Saxon paganism, coexisting peacefully alongside the incoming pagan Anglo-Saxons. British communities survived for centuries even in areas which were conquered by the Anglo-Saxons in the fifth century. When the Anglo-Saxon St Guthlac travelled through the East Anglian Fenlands *c.* 700 he found them still populated by Celtic speakers. The survival into the twentieth century of traditional shepherds' counting systems based on Welsh across western England from Wiltshire to the Lake District shows that Anglicisation was not necessarily a rapid process. But Anglicisation was thorough. Cornwall alone has never been completely Anglicised and remains the only county of England where the inhabitants will not automatically identify themselves as English.

Despite the contribution of the Britons to the modern population of England, the English, unlike the French, have never really found a place for the Celts in their national mythology. Centuries of warfare have conditioned the English to see the Celts as historical enemies and as having nothing very much to do with them. The Anglo-Saxon homelands were distant from the Roman Empire, and they knew less about Roman civilisation than the Franks and respected it less. The Britons also were less Romanised than the Gauls had been, so the Anglo-Saxons may have seen less to admire in their culture. The fifth-century Britons were not really that different from the invaders, so it was they who were assimilated by the Anglo-Saxons. The one aspect of the Celtic heritage that the English did take to was the legend of King Arthur. As the supposed ruler of all of Britain and conqueror of Gaul, the legendary Arthur was a suitable role model for England's expansionist post-Conquest Norman and Plantagenet kings. A greater understanding of the origins of the legends enabled the British Celts to reclaim Arthur in the twentieth century (though the Welsh, Cornish and Scots cannot agree on which of them he belongs to).

Wales and England

After Offa built his dyke in the eighth century, the border between the Anglo-Saxons and the Welsh remained fairly stable. There were wars – the Welsh gained a little ground in the north, the English a little in the south – but there was also cooperation against the Vikings. In the tenth century, the sons and grandsons of Alfred the Great of Wessex unified the Anglo-Saxons and the kingdom of England was born. England was self-evidently the strongest kingdom in Britain and its kings came to exercise a real but undefined hegemony over its Celtic neighbours. The *Armes Prydein* ('The Prophecy of Britain'), a Welsh poem composed *c.* 930, called on the Celts of Britain, Brittany and Ireland to unite with the Vikings of Dublin and drive the English out of Britain. In 937 the Scots, the Britons of Strathclyde and the Dublin Vikings did unite against the English, but their crushing defeat at the battle of Brunanburh (location unknown) was a convincing demonstration of English power. The English hegemony was played out symbolically in 973 when King Edgar was rowed along the river Dee at Chester by eight kings from Wales, Strathclyde, Scotland and the Isle of Man while he steered the boat.

The mountainous terrain of Wales did not encourage national unity. The areas of fertile land were widely scattered and each naturally tended to become the focus of an independent dynasty. The Severn valley was the heartland of Powys; Gwynedd's was Anglesey and so on. Nevertheless, the number of Welsh kingdoms tended to decline as the stronger ones took over the weaker. From nine in 900, there were only three major Welsh kingdoms left by 1000: Gwynedd in the north, Powys in mid-Wales and Deheubarth in the south-west, plus three minor kingdoms in the south-east that were more often than not dependencies of the larger kingdoms. Individual Welsh kings, like Hywel Dda (r. *c.* 900–50) of Deheubarth and Gruffydd ap Llywelyn (r. 1039–63) of Gwynedd, achieved positions of overlordship over most, or, in Gruffydd's case, even all, of Wales but, like the high kings of Ireland, they never exercised direct rule throughout their dominions, ruling indirectly through their vassal kings. These overlordships never lasted more than a generation. Partly this was because of the Welsh practice of partible inheritance, partly because succession disputes were common as nephews and cousins as well as sons were eligible to succeed to kingship, and partly because of English intervention. The English did their best to keep the Welsh disunited but they appear to have had no territorial ambitions in Wales. For instance, when Gruffydd ap Llywelyn's ambitions became too big for Wales alone, Harold Godwinson (the future King Harold) invaded and restored the independence of his subject kingdoms. Gruffydd himself was hunted down and killed but no territory was taken.

The Norman invasion

The conquest of England by duke William of Normandy in 1066 changed things, not just for the English but also for their Celtic neighbours. England in 1066 was probably the most centralised kingdom in Europe, with power and landownership concentrated in very few hands. The three great battles of that year thinned the ranks of the English royal family and nobility, making the subsequent task of the Normans of consolidating their conquest much easier. There were fierce peasant rebellions but they were uncoordinated and lacked credible leadership. By 1070 it was all over and England's new French-speaking ruling class was secure in its possession of the country. The Normans practised strict primogeniture. Younger sons of the nobility would be given a good training in war and then left to shift for themselves. This surplus of landless warriors made the Normans natural colonists, in Italy and the Holy Land, as well as Britain. William the Conqueror was always more interested in Normandy than Wales, but he was happy enough to allow Hugh the Fat, Roger of Montgomery and William Fitzosbern, of the marcher earldoms of Chester, Shrewsbury and Hereford, to enlarge their lordships at the expense of the Welsh.

At first the Normans made rapid progress into Wales. The small kingdoms of Brycheiniog (Brecon), Gwent and Morgannwg (Glamorgan) had all been conquered by 1093, and by 1114, when Henry I launched a massive three-pronged invasion of Wales, the Normans had overrun most of Deheubarth, penetrated Powys along the valleys of the Dee and Severn and occupied the coastal areas of Gwynedd from the mouth of the Dee as far as Anglesey. Something like 500 earth and timber motte and bailey castles were built to consolidate these conquests, and more than a dozen new marcher lordships were created ('march' is cognate with German 'mark' and means 'border'). A complete Norman conquest seemed only a few years away, yet their reach had far exceeded their grasp. Civil war in England during the reign of King Stephen (1135–54) deprived the marcher lords of royal support and the Welsh recovered around half the territory they had lost. The areas where the marcher lords held on most securely – the fertile farmlands of Gwent, the Vale of Glamorgan, the Gower and south Pembrokeshire – were those which had been suitable for the transplantation of the English manorial system and were attractive to English, and also Flemish, peasant colonists.

Stephen's successor Henry II (r. 1154–89), one of medieval England's most able rulers, launched several campaigns to try to restore the English position in Wales. They all failed. Henry's sons, Richard and John, and his grandson Henry III would all fare no better in their campaigns against the Welsh. The churchman Gerald of Wales (1146–1223), a prolific writer on Wales and Ireland, accurately identified the reasons for the failure of English campaigns. One of the reasons, he thought, was a moral one. 'The English are striving for power, the Welsh for freedom; the English are fighting for material gain, the Welsh to avoid a disaster; the English soldiers are hired mercenaries, the Welsh are defending their homeland.' Because the Welsh were more lightly armed and armoured than the English, they could not fight them on equal terms. Therefore, the Welsh avoided open battle and employed harassing tactics, making the best use of rugged terrain, where the less mobile English were at a disadvantage. It was impossible, Gerald thought, 'to conquer in one battle a people which will never draw up its forces to engage an enemy army in the field, and will never allow itself to be besieged inside fortified strong points'. Gerald, too, was keenly aware of the financial costs. Campaigns in Wales were expensive and little in the way of plunder could be expected to defray the costs. Henry II's campaign of 1165, for example, cost £7,500 at a time when his income from the crown lands was less than £10,000 a year. This was an enormous amount of money down the drain with nothing at all to show for it. There was also the problem that the post-Conquest kings of England were frequently distracted by the need to defend their French lands from the king of France. If only the Welsh would unite under one leader, mused Gerald, the English would never conquer them.

The dominating figure of later twelfth-century Wales was Rhys ap Gruffydd (r. 1155–97), king of Deheubarth, also known as the Lord Rhys, who conquered several of the marcher lordships in mid and south Wales. A 'moderniser' who built stone castles and championed church and monastic reform, Rhys was also a notable patron of Welsh culture and held the first recorded eisteddfod in 1176. Succession disputes broke up Deheubarth after Rhys's death but it was Gwynedd, not England, that was the main beneficiary of this. England was paralysed by a civil war that broke out at the end of John's reign (1199–1216), and the king of Gwynedd, Llywelyn ab Iorwerth (r. 1195–1240) was able to conquer the other Welsh kingdoms without English interference. For this feat he earned the title Llywelyn the Great. Llywelyn tried to ensure that his kingdom remained intact after his death by breaking with custom and appointing his son Dafydd (d. 1246) as his sole heir. Unfortunately, Dafydd proved to be an inept ruler and his kingdom collapsed as a result of rebellions and English intervention. Welsh unity was restored by Dafydd's nephew Llywelyn ap Gruffydd (r. 1246–82), who adopted the title 'Prince of Wales' in 1258.

Devastating attacks on the marcher lordships forced Henry III of England to recognise Llywelyn's title and his overlordship of Wales by the Treaty of Montgomery in 1267. This was a step on the way towards the creation of a national kingship that a stronger English king would surely have refused, but at least Henry forced Llywelyn to acknowledge that he held his title as a vassal of the English crown.

Hammer of the Welsh

When King Henry III of England died in 1272, Llywelyn ap Gruffydd, Prince of Wales, felt secure in his domains. Llywelyn had always got the better of Henry and he expected that things would be the same with his son and successor Edward. Success had made Llywelyn overconfident and he began to ignore his obligations as a vassal of the English crown. The signs that Edward would be a different sort of king from his father were already there for all to see. A lover of tournaments in his youth, he had fought with distinction during the barons' revolt and was crusading in the Holy Land when his father died. Edward had a taste and an aptitude for war that his father conspicuously lacked. Summoned, as custom demanded, to attend Edward's coronation in London in 1274, Llywelyn failed to turn up. Llywelyn subsequently refused to perform homage to Edward, in effect denying his subordinate status. By these needlessly provocative actions, Llywelyn would lose his lands and his life and the Welsh their independence.

In 1277 Edward led an army of 800 knights and 15,000 foot into Gwynedd. Smaller English armies invaded Powys and Deheubarth while the English fleet landed troops on Anglesey, Gwynedd's breadbasket, to seize the all-important grain harvest. The mountains of Snowdonia might have been a natural stronghold but their defenders could be starved into submission once they had been cut off from Anglesey. Llywelyn found he could not rely on the loyalty of the Welsh rulers he had conquered during his rise to power, and even his own brother Dafydd defected. The war was over in months. By the Treaty of Aberconwy, Llywelyn's principality was broken up, native rulers were restored to Deheubarth and Powys, and Dafydd was given his own principality of the Four Cantrefs in north-east Wales (a cantref was a territorial unit comprising one hundred hamlets). Edward had balked at the cost of conquering Wales outright. Had Llywelyn kept his head down, the Welsh might have long retained a considerable measure of self-government, and who knows what opportunities might have come his way when the Scottish wars of independence began in 1296.

Plate 18 Harlech Castle, built by Edward I, 1285–90, for £8,000
Source: John Haywood

But Llywelyn became a victim of circumstances. Dafydd was unhappy with the pay-off for his treachery and he rebelled against Edward in March 1282 and attacked Hawarden castle near Chester. After weeks of dithering, the widespread popular support for the rebellion persuaded Llywelyn to back his untrustworthy brother. Not to have taken part would have undermined his claim to leadership of the Welsh, especially if the rebellion was successful, but to join in was to invite massive English retaliation. No wonder he hesitated.

At first the war went well for the Welsh and they inflicted defeats on the English in the south and on the Menai Straits in the north. Many castles were taken too. Edward I is often portrayed as a scheming mastermind of English imperial expansion, but it was only at this point that in frustration he decided on the outright conquest of Wales. He did so with his eyes open, justifying the enormous cost to his subjects on the grounds that it would save money in the long run if the Welsh problem was solved once and for all. Then in December, Edward had a lucky break: Llywelyn was killed in battle at Irfon Bridge near Builth in mid-Wales. It was the kind of battlefield coup that Gerald of Wales had thought to be impossible. Leadership of the Welsh passed to Dafydd, but his treacherous career had made him many enemies and he lacked Llywelyn's authority. Without credible leadership, resistance began to collapse. The last stronghold in Welsh hands, Castell-y-Bere near Machynlleth, surrendered in March 1283 and Dafydd was betrayed to the English in June of that year. The last native Prince of Wales, Dafydd was executed at Shrewsbury in October. To consolidate his victory Edward immediately began the most ambitious programme of castle building ever seen in the British Isles. Including money spent on castles, the cost of Edward I's campaign of 1282–3 was close on £150,000, over ten times his annual income from the crown lands. The difference had to be made up by borrowings and a tax on the moveable goods of Edward's English subjects. The contribution to costs made by revenue from Wales and from the sale of treasure captured during the campaign came to less than £400.

By the Statute of Rhuddlan in 1284, Edward established direct crown control over the Principality of Wales and introduced English criminal law. English colonisation of North Wales was encouraged but it was mainly confined to walled towns close to the protection of Edward's new castles at Caernarfon, Conwy, Rhuddlan and elsewhere. There were Welsh rebellions in 1287 and 1294–5, when Madog ap Llywelyn tried to revive the title 'Prince of Wales', but these were defeated after hard fighting. When Edward I proclaimed his eldest son Edward Prince of Wales in 1301, it was not an act of conciliation but a reminder to the Welsh that the days of independence were over. However, the perpetuation of the title also helped to ensure that Wales retained a distinct identity within the kingdom of England. Although many Welshmen entered the royal administration and tens of thousands served in English armies in the Scottish wars and the Hundred Years War in France, the Welsh remained unreconciled to English rule. Minor rebellions were common in the fourteenth century, until in

Plate 19 Llywelyn, Prince of Wales, kneels to be beheaded watched by Edward I at the window (English with Flemish illuminations); Ms 6 f.167v. St Alban's Chronicle (late fifteenth century)

Source: Lambeth Palace Library, London, UK/Bridgeman Art Library, www.bridgeman.co.uk

1400 a century of simmering discontent boiled over into a nationwide rebellion, which saw the English hold on Wales reduced to a few castles and walled towns.

Glyndwr's revolt

The leader of the rebellion was Owain Glyndwr (b. 1359), lord of Glyndyfrdwy near Llangollen in north-east Wales. Though he was descended from a royal house, there is nothing in Glyndwr's early career to suggest that he was a potential Welsh 'Braveheart' figure. He studied law at the Inns of Court, became a squire to the earl of Arundel and fought loyally in Richard II's army in Scotland. Richard's deposition by Henry IV in 1399 may have strained Glyndwr's loyalty, but it was a property dispute with his neighbour Lord Grey, the English lord of Ruthin, that tipped him over into open revolt. Angry that Grey had seized land he thought his own, Glyndwr burned Ruthin in September 1400. After Glyndwr's supporters proclaimed him Prince of Wales the revolt spread with electrifying speed. Welsh students even ran away from Oxford to join in. The English reacted quickly but to little effect. Glyndwr rarely sought open battle, preferring the irregular tactics that had served the Welsh so well in the past. By the end of 1403 the English hold on Wales appeared to have been broken: even parts of the English border shires came under Welsh control. Just a few dozen isolated English garrisons hung on grimly in their besieged castles. Henry IV's usurpation had made him enemies of the powerful Percy and Mortimer families, who allied with Glyndwr. If they succeeded in over-throwing Henry, they agreed that Glyndwr would be granted a principality that included all of Wales, plus the English shires of Cheshire, Shropshire, Herefordshire and part of Gloucestershire. Glyndwr laid ambitious plans for an independent Principality of Wales, with its own parliament, civil service, universities and independent church with an archbishopric at St David's in Pembrokeshire. The defeat of his English allies at the battle of Shrewsbury in 1403 probably doomed Glyndwr's rebellion to ultimate failure – to be secure in the long term he needed the recognition only a sympathetic English government would willingly provide – but this was not immediately apparent because he soon found new allies in the French, who sent an expeditionary force to Wales in 1405. The French proved to be faint-hearted allies. They invaded England, took Worcester but retreated at the first sign of opposition and went home in 1406, having achieved nothing.

The withdrawal of the French was the turning point of the rebellion. With no possibility now of outside support or recognition, Glyndwr's supporters began to waver, Henry IV had by now got over the political

Plate 20 Seal of Owain Glyndŵr
Source: Patricia Aithie/Ffotograff

troubles of his early years and was able to concentrate on reconquering Wales. By 1408, resistance was confined to the mountains of the north, where it continued for another four years or so. Glyndwr went into hiding after 1410 and was never apprehended by the English. It is thought likely that he died and was buried secretly at his daughter's home at Monnington Court in Herefordshire sometime after Henry V offered him a pardon, which he refused, in 1415, but there remains considerable uncertainty about his last years. Even in the sixteenth century, the belief persisted that he was still holding out in the hills, biding his time. The immediate legacy of Glyndwr's revolt was a devastated countryside and a raft of repressive anti-Welsh legislation that remained in force until Henry VII, of the Welsh Tudor family, came to the throne in 1485. The failure of the revolt effectively killed off Welsh aspirations for independence, and in future Welsh political ambitions were focused on achieving equal status with the English. In cultural terms, this was not achieved until the twentieth century, but in legal terms it came with the Act of Union in 1536 which abolished the marcher lordships and all legal distinctions between the English and Welsh, saw the country divided into shires and gave it the right to parliamentary representation. Wales thereby lost its legal identity, but the Act did ensure that, at a local level at least, the Welsh would be governed by 'magistrates of their own nation'. This guaranteed that Wales would not come to be thought of as simply part of England. The Act of Union made English the language of law and administration and this posed an obvious threat to the Welsh language. That the Welsh language was able to hold its own was largely an unintended consequence of the Reformation, which was of course taking place at the same time as the Act of Union. While the Reformation failed to win popular acceptance in England's other Celtic dependency of Ireland, Protestantism (and later Nonconformity) put down deep roots in Wales. This was because, in contrast to Ireland, religious texts were quickly made available in the native language. Welsh translations of the Lord's Prayer, the Creed and the Ten Commandments were published as early as 1547. Translations of the Prayer Book and the Scriptures followed. The Roman Catholic church had forbidden the translation of the Scriptures into vernacular languages but now any literate lay person could get a religious education. The opportunity was seized upon eagerly, and as a result Welsh found a new role as the language of religion, so ensuring both its survival and its continuing central role in the identity of the Welsh people.

9

ALBA

*When the Romans returned home, then eagerly there emerged . . .
the foul hordes of Scots and Picts, like dark throngs of worms that
wriggle out of fissures in the rock when the sun is high and the
weather grows warm. They were somewhat different in their customs
but they were in perfect agreement in their greed for bloodshed: and
they were readier to cover their villainous faces with hair than their
private parts with clothes.*

Gildas, On the Ruin of Britain (*c.* 540)

Unconquered though it was, northern Britain was not immune to the influence of the Roman Empire. The abandonment of the Antonine Wall in 163 marked the end of Roman attempts to control the British tribes between Hadrian's Wall and the Forth–Clyde isthmus by imposing direct rule. Henceforward, these tribes were supervised by Roman agents and kept sweet with gifts of treasure. A particularly favoured tribe was the Votadini, whose stronghold at Traprain Law in Lothian has yielded a large hoard of both complete and hacked-up Roman silver vessels. The Celtic warrior elite needed to acquire prestige display objects to maintain its status. Such gifts by the Romans took away much of the incentive to raid. Traprain Law was originally an Iron Age hillfort, but in the Roman period it grew into a small town. Large quantities of Roman artefacts, from coins, glass and pottery, to weapons, jewellery and manicure sets, show that its leading inhabitants led a superficially Romanised lifestyle. This informal empire survived until 367 when the Britons bribed the Roman agents to look the other way while they joined the Saxons in plundering the British province.

The Painted People

Direct Roman contacts with the Caledonian tribes living to the north of the Forth–Clyde isthmus were limited to occasional military expeditions, such as Septimius Severus' genocidal campaign in 209–11. The Caledonian tribes responded to the Roman threat by forming tribal coalitions. By the third century, the dozen or so tribes encountered by Agricola had been replaced by just two, the Verturiones or Maeatae, centred on Fife and Strathmore, and the Caledones in the Highlands proper. A century later, these two were reduced to one, the Picts. The abandonment of most brochs and duns in these centuries was probably a result of this process of political centralisation. The name, which means 'painted people', is thought to have originated as a nickname among Roman frontier garrisons, perhaps because the Picts decorated their bodies with tattoos. The Picts seem quickly to have adopted the name for themselves. Though they had a common identity, the Picts were divided into a number of regional kingdoms, ruled from small forts on craggy hilltops or coastal headlands. The names of some of these kingdoms have survived in modern place names: Fortriu (Forteviot), Fib (Fife), Athfolta (Atholl) and Cait (Caithness). The earliest historical Pictish king was Bridei mac Maelcon (r. c. 550–84), who ruled his kingdom of Fidach from the stronghold of Craig Phadrig near Inverness. Bridei exercised a form of high kingship over all of Pictland and other rulers sent hostages to his court. After Bridei's death in battle, power, and the high kingship with it, shifted to the southern Pictish kingdom of Fortriu, which was based on the territory of the Verturiones in fertile Strathmore. In the mid seventh century the Northumbrians began to expand into Pictish territory, conquering Fife and exacting tribute from the Picts. A Pictish rebellion around 670 was crushed, but in 685 King Bride mac Bile of Fortriu overthrew the Northumbrian dominion at the battle of Nechtansmere, near Forfar. A beautifully carved stone cross at nearby Aberlemno showing a battle between Pictish and Anglo-Saxon warriors is thought to commemorate this battle, which established the Picts as the main power in northern Britain.

Little is known about the Pictish language: the few surviving records are limited to personal and place names and a handful of inscriptions in the Roman and the Irish ogham alphabets, which have so far defied translation. Some linguists believe that a few Pictish words are derived from a lost pre-Celtic non-Indo-European language, but most are clearly related to the Brithonic form of Celtic spoken by the Britons. Certainly, the Romans considered the Picts to be close kin of the Britons, but more barbaric because they were not Romanised. The most easily recognised Pictish place-name element is the prefix *pit-* (as in Pitlochry and Pittenweem), which derived from *pett* meaning a parcel of land. The distribution of these place names suggests that the main area of Pictish settlement was in Fife, Perthshire, Angus, Aberdeenshire and around the Moray Firth, but it is likely that it was actually much more widespread. Because of the later settlement of Gaelic speakers in the Highlands and of Norse speakers in Caithness and the western and northern isles, and the effects of rural depopulation in the nineteenth century, it is likely that many hundreds of 'pit' place names have been lost. When the Picts first appeared they were a pagan people. Nothing is known of their gods, but like other Celtic peoples they practised human sacrifice and venerated springs, wells and caves. The Briton St Ninian began the conversion of the southern Picts to Christianity in the fifth century,

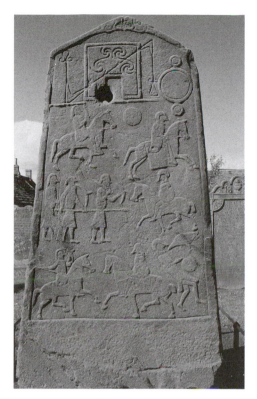

Plate 21 Battle of Nechtansmere, Aberlemno
Source: © Crown Copyright reproduced courtesy of Historic Scotland

while the Irish St Columba began the conversion of the northern Picts in 565. During his mission, Columba had the earliest recorded encounter with the Loch Ness monster, which tried to eat one of his monks. Columba's intervention saved the day, of course, and, as far as is known, the monster has not tried to eat anyone since.

The Picts are best known for their enigmatic carved symbol stones. About 40 to 50 different symbols are known; the most common are the 'Pictish beast' (a strange mythological creature likened to a swimming elephant), the mirror and a variety of geometrical figures based on crescents and circles. The meanings of the symbols are unknown, and will probably remain so, but they probably did not have religious significance as they continued to be used after the conversion to Christianity. The earliest known symbols appear on metalwork in the fourth century and their use on stones dates only to the fifth or sixth century. Pictish symbols are usually used in combinations of two to four, with the particular combination of symbols perhaps identifying an individual, family or tribe. The purpose of the symbol stones is as uncertain as their meaning, but several have been discovered in association with burials. It would seem, therefore, that at least some were tombstones, a practice that must surely have been adopted as a result of contacts with early British Christians.

Dál Riata

As well as the pushy Northumbrians, the Picts also had to cope with the territorial ambitions of the Scots. Confusingly, the Scots came from Ireland. The name was first used by Irish pirates and meant simply 'raiders' (rather as Scandinavian pirates would later describe themselves as Vikings), but the word came to be applied to all the Irish, whether or not they were pirates. The decline of Roman power gave the Scots great opportunities for raiding and settlement along the west coast of Britain. The Britons had little difficulty in assimilating these Irish immigrants but for the Picts it was another story. Pictland became Scotland. Traditionally, King Fergus MacErc (d. 501) of the northern Irish Dál Riata dynasty was regarded as the leader of the first Scottish settlement in Pictland. Some time in the late fifth century, Fergus was said to have conquered the Kintyre peninsula, while his brothers Loarn and Oengus conquered Lorn and Islay. The story is likely to have been invented to explain the traditional division of Scottish Dál Riata (modern Argyll) into the three tribes of Cenel Loairn, Cenel nOengusa and Cenel nGabrain (named for Fergus's grandson Gabran). Fergus and his successors ruled both Irish Dál Riata and Argyll as a single kingdom until 637 when the two parts of the kingdom became independent of one another. Some modern historians have questioned this traditional account of Scottish settlement, doubting that Argyll really was Pictish territory when Fergus won control over it. They point out that, at its nearest point, Argyll is only about 12 miles (19 kilometres) from northern Ireland, a very short sail in favourable conditions. While Argyll was linked to Ireland by the sea, it was separated from the rest of Pictland by the Highlands, which would have been a real barrier to communications in ancient times. It is therefore possible that Argyll had been essentially Irish in culture and language – that is, Gaelic speaking – for a long time before Fergus took over. The hypothesis is attractive but probably beyond proof.

The Scots chose as the site of their capital the hill of Dunadd, which rises abruptly and craggily from the flat mossland at the mouth of Argyll's Kilmartin valley. The site had many advantages: it was a natural stronghold that could be easily fortified and it was on a narrow isthmus at the neck of the Kintyre peninsula with easy communications to the Atlantic to the west and the Firth of Clyde to the east. However, what may have made Dunadd even more attractive to the Scots was its position in the heart of one of the most remarkable prehistoric landscapes in Britain. An amazing concentration of standing stones, stone circles, henges, carved stones, burial cairns and barrows, spanning a period of 3,000 years, marked the Kilmartin valley out as a site of extraordinary significance, a place of power that, as newcomers, the Dál Riata dynasty will have wanted to associate themselves

Plate 22 Royal inauguration site, Dunadd
Source: John Haywood

with as a means of establishing their legitimacy. Dunadd was not a spacious site but, as well as the royal household, it housed a colony of skilled metalworkers that made brooches and other jewellery. Large amounts of imported pottery and glass discovered in excavations show that Dunadd had regular trade contacts with Gaul. On rocks on the summit of the hill are carvings, ogham inscriptions and a foot-shaped depression, which was used in rituals for the inauguration of kings.

For a long time, the Scots were confined to Argyll, but their cultural influence was spread into Pictland by the Irish missionary church on the Hebridean island of Iona, founded by St Columba in 563. This eventually came to be seen as a threat, and King Nechton (r. 706–24) mended fences with the old enemy Northumbria and brought the Pictish church into line with practices of the Roman church. One result of this shift was a fusion of Pictish, Irish and Northumbrian decorative styles that produced some of the most distinctive Christian sculpture known in early medieval Britain. The Picts reached the peak of their power under Oengus mac Fergus (r. 729–61). Oengus captured Dunadd in 736 and conquered the Scots before turning his attentions to the Britons of Strathclyde in 750. In alliance with the Northumbrians, Oengus besieged the British capital at Dumbarton in 756 and was disastrously defeated. Pictish power began to wane, and some time before 768 the Scots under Aed Find not only regained their independence but also began to attack Pictland. In the decades that followed, southern Pictland came more and more under Scottish control. Several kings of Fortriu had Gaelic names and were probably of Dál Riatan origin. The final straw for the Picts appears to have been the Vikings, who began raiding the British Isles at the end of the eighth century. The Vikings conquered and settled the Pictish territories of Shetland, Orkney, Caithness and the Outer Hebrides. The Picts here – those that survived at least: genetic studies suggest that 40–60 per cent of the population of Orkney and Shetland are of Scandinavian origin – were completely assimilated by the newcomers. A few symbol stones are the only reminders of the Picts there; not even place names survive.

Union or conquest?

The Scots also suffered at the hands of the Vikings, who seized Kintyre and the Inner Hebrides, but, somehow, they were able to take advantage of the Picts' misfortunes. After a devastating Viking raid on Fortriu in 839 left two Pictish kings dead, the Scottish king Kenneth mac Alpin (Cinaed mac Alpin) conquered all of Pictland. The traditional date for this is 842/3, but the conquest was probably only completed in 848 when Kenneth transferred relics of St Columba from Iona to the chief centre of the Pictish church at Dunkeld. It was a gesture of thanks by the king to the saint for the support of his church. Kenneth, or one of his immediate successors, commemorated his conquest by commissioning a Pictish sculptor to carve the 23-foot (7-metre) high monolith, known as Sueno's Stone, which stands on the outskirts of Forres in Moray. One face of the stone is covered from top to bottom with scenes of battle and mass executions of Pictish kings and nobles. The message it conveyed to the conquered Picts was a bleak one indeed. It would seem that by conquering Fortriu the Scots took control of the Pictish high kingship and then secured their conquest by defeating the Pictish sub-kings. Many a Pictish high king had had to do this too, but Kenneth went a step further, and by killing the defeated sub-kings and their aristocracy deprived any attempted Pictish rebellion of leadership. Sueno's Stone was one of the last Pictish works of art. Pictish symbols fell out of use, as did the Pictish language, which was replaced by Gaelic. The last contemporary reference to the Picts dates to 904. Thus the Picts became the only one of the Celtic peoples known to have inhabited Britain in historical times to have become completely extinct. The Scots had no great interest in preserving the memory of the Picts, and in later medieval writings they had become folkloric figures, a race of pygmies who lived underground. This odd belief may be derived from the many souterrains that the ancestors of the Picts built as cool underground storerooms for perishable foodstuffs.

The Scots adopted many of the trappings of Pictish kingship, along with its places of power, such as Scone, near Perth. Their old royal centre at Dunadd was abandoned: it was too vulnerable to the Vikings and the Pictish lands were far richer than Argyll. Kenneth and his immediate successors used the title 'king of the Picts', but this was abandoned by Donald II (r. 889–900), who adopted the title 'king of Alba'. Though Alba is the Gaelic word for Scotland, 'Scotland' in 900 did not mean what it does now but referred only to the area between the Forth and the Spey. In the course of the tenth century, however, Scotland began a period of steady territorial expansion, which continued for over 200 years. Weakened by a devastating Viking attack on its capital at Dumbarton in 870, the British kingdom of Strathclyde became a satellite kingdom of Scotland before it was finally annexed around 1018. The English king Edgar ceded English-speaking Lothian to Kenneth II around 973 in return for his submission and Malcolm II's victory over the English at Carham in 1018 established the Tweed as Scotland's southern border. The eleventh century was marked by a struggle with a rival Scots dynasty that had established itself in Moray. Macbeth, Moray's most famous ruler, became king of Scotland in 1040 but was driven out after his defeat by Malcolm III Canmore ('big head') at Dunsinnan in 1054. After Macbeth was defeated and killed by Malcolm at Lumphanan three years later, Moray declined and was completely incorporated into Scotland by 1130. The Norse colonies in Caithness and Sutherland followed soon after. When Norway ceded the Hebrides to Scotland in 1266, the country had reached almost its modern borders: Scotland's last territorial acquisitions were Orkney and Shetland, ceded by Denmark in 1468–9 in lieu of a princess's dowry, which the bankrupt country could not afford to pay. The islanders still have a strong sense of their Scandinavian heritage and in recent years there have been somewhat tongue-in-cheek calls for the restoration of Danish sovereignty.

A kingdom without a nation

By the beginning of the twelfth century Scotland was well established as the second most powerful kingdom in the British Isles, but it was still a multi-ethnic state – there was no Scottish nation. The English of Lothian still thought of themselves as being English, the Britons of Strathclyde still thought of themselves as being Britons. As for the Scots, they still considered themselves to be Irish. The forging of a common identity probably began during the reign of David I (1124–53). David spent his formative years in England and he achieved high office in the government of Henry I before inheriting the Scottish throne in 1124. David had been impressed by the power of the English monarchy and he began to introduce Anglo-Norman practices into Scotland, beginning the dilution of the Celtic character of his kingdom. David's Anglo-Norman friends, members of the Bruce family among them, were granted feudalised lordships, many of them in areas where royal authority was still weak, such as Galloway and the Highlands. English and Flemish burgesses were also invited to settle in Scotland to promote trade and urbanisation. Under David, Scotland got its first native coinage. This settlement greatly raised the status of English, which became the language of the court and began to replace Cumbric in Strathclyde and Gaelic in Fife and Angus. As a result of these changes, Scots began to reject their Irish origins as they became increasingly aware of themselves as a distinct people in their own right. The Irish too noticed the change and began to see the Scots as foreigners. In modern times, this rejection of Irish origins has led to a rehabilitation of the Picts as the authentic ancestors of today's Scots, while their takeover by the MacAlpin dynasty is presented (for nationalistic reasons) as a cosy consensual union, rather than the bloody conquest it clearly was.

There remained a deep, and often troublesome, division in Scotland between the Gaelic-speaking Highlands and the feudalised English-speaking Lowlands, but a sense of common nationhood was confirmed by the experience of the wars of independence from England (1296–1328). In the twelfth century Anglo-Scottish wars were usually caused by the Scots trying to push their borders south into northern England, but in the thirteenth century peace generally prevailed and relations between the two kingdoms became friendly and cooperative. This ended abruptly when Edward I's high-handed mediation in a succession dispute alienated the Scots and permanently embittered Anglo-Scottish relations. Although neither of the two main leaders of Scottish independence, William Wallace and Robert Bruce, were Celts, the Highlands proved crucial to Scotland's survival as an independent kingdom. The English could and did achieve military dominance of the Lowlands but they lacked the resources to dominate the Highlands, which were home to nearly half the population of medieval Scotland. With this secure reservoir of manpower behind it, Scotland was effectively unconquerable. After his victory at Bannockburn in 1314 united the Scots behind Robert Bruce, it was only a matter of time before the unsupportable financial and political burden forced the English to recognise Scotland's independence.

If the Highlands were a great asset to the kings of Scotland in times of war with the English, they could also be a considerable problem at other times. The same geographical and economic factors that made it difficult for the English (and before them the Romans) to campaign in the Highlands also made it difficult for the king of Scots to impose his authority effectively on the independent-minded Gaelic chiefs of the region. The relative poverty of the Highland economy was an almost insuperable obstacle, as there was no chance that the subjugation of the region would pay for itself by increasing the slender resources of the Scottish state. Even the fertile island of Islay, which the crown acquired in the 1490s, proved economically almost worthless. The cost of moving the island's considerable food rents (cattle and grain) to the Lowlands was so ruinous that the crown simply sold them straight back to its tenants. Islay was soon granted to a clan chief. Perverse though it might seem, Celtic Scotland survived in large part because it was poor.

Highlander and Lowlander

The foundation of Anglo-Norman lordships in the Highlands in the twelfth century had not achieved what was hoped for of them because the new lords had soon gone native and adopted the Gaelic clan system. Because they were the best ways for chiefs and warriors to win prestige, private warfare and cattle raiding were endemic in the Highlands and often spilled over into the Lowlands. Mutual suspicion and loathing characterised relations between Highlanders and Lowlanders. The attitudes of Lowlanders towards the Gaels were remarkably similar to those of the Greeks and Romans towards the Gauls. If we believe the fourteenth-century Scots chronicler John of Fordun, the Lowlanders were civilised and possessed almost every virtue imaginable while the Highlanders were 'fierce and untameable, uncouth and unpleasant, much given to theft, fond of doing nothing, but their minds are quick to learn, and cunning. They are strikingly handsome in appearance, but their clothing is unsightly. They are always hostile and savage, not only towards the people and language of England, but also towards their fellow Scots because of the language difference.' In his poem *The Dance of the Sevin Deidly Synnes* the poet William Dunbar infests the lowest circles of Hell with Highlanders, where they drive the Devil mad with the unintelligible racket of their 'Irish' (i.e. Gaelic) speech. From the Lowlander's point of view, the Highlanders were bar-bar barbarians. Medieval Scotland was a half-Celtic hybrid, and by the end of the Middle Ages the Celtic half was steadily declining in cultural prestige, which makes today's idealisation of the Highlander all the more remarkable.

The Lordship of the Isles

The most powerful of the semi-independent Gaelic lordships of the Highlands was the MacDonald Lordship of the Isles. The Lordship of the Isles was in a sense the successor to the Norse Kingdom of the Isles, which had been ruled from the Isle of Man in the eleventh century. The downfall of the kingdom was begun by Somerled, a chieftain of Argyll who was of mixed Gaelic and Norse descent. In a naval battle fought by moonlight on a winter's night in 1156, Somerled defeated King Godred II of Man and won control of most of the Hebrides. Preferring a far-distant lord to a near one, Somerled acknowledged the ultimate sovereignty of the king of Norway over his island possessions, but this brought him into conflict with the Scots king Malcolm IV, who had been greedily eyeing the Hebrides himself. Somerled was killed while raiding in Scotland, in battle near Renfrew in 1164, but the Hebrides remained in the possession of his descendants. Long since converted to Christianity, the Norse settlers in the Hebrides soon became assimilated to Gaelic ways. When Norway finally ceded the Hebrides to Scotland in 1266, these semi-independent Gaelic lords simply transferred their allegiance to the king of Scots and carried on as before.

The Lordship of the Isles was founded by Angus Og MacDonald, a grandson of Somerled's grandson Donald. Angus backed Robert Bruce in his struggle for the Scottish throne with the rival Comyn family and was rewarded by being made Lord of Islay in 1307. After he led the men of the Isles into battle at Bannockburn, Angus was further rewarded with the mainland districts of Morvern, Ardnamurchan and Lochaber. Through advantageous marriages, Angus's son and successor John of Islay added the rest of the Hebridean islands to his inheritance, as well as the mainland districts of Kintyre, Knapdale and Garmoran. In 1353 John formally adopted the title *Dominus Insularum*, 'Lord of the Isles': significantly, in Gaelic he used the title *rí*, 'king'. Sea power and some 30 stone castles held this vast lordship together. The castles of the lordship were almost all sited on the coast where they could control the sea-lanes by sending out fleets of galleys to intercept shipping. These Highland galleys, or 'birlinns', were swift and seaworthy descendants of the longships that had dominated the northern seas in Viking times. They remained popular with Scottish and Irish pirates well into the seventeenth century. The only important castle of the lordship to be sited inland was on an island in a loch at Finlaggan on Islay, and so confident were the lords in their control of the Hebridean seas that its fortifications were more symbolic than functional. Finlaggan was the official capital of the Lordship, where, on a second island linked to the castle by a causeway, the Council of the Isles met. The scant ruins that survive today give little impression of the former importance of the place. The lordship was a self-consciously Irish-orientated polity in a way the kingdom of Scotland had long ceased to be. The inauguration ceremony of the lords was reminiscent – deliberately so – of that of the ancient Scottish kings of Dál Riata as it involved the use of a square stone on which was carved the shape of a man's footprint. The new lord was expected to place

Plate 23 Effigies of galloglasses on fifteenth-century gravestones from Kilmory
Source: © Crown Copyright reproduced courtesy of Historic Scotland

his foot in the print as a sign that he would walk in the footsteps and uprightness of his predecessors. Gaelic was the language of administration and high culture and, like Irish kings, the lords were surrounded by hereditary functionaries, such as the *seanchaidhean* or clan historians. Literary and artistic links with Gaelic Ireland were actively cultivated. So too were political links: the marriage of John Mor, a younger son of John I, to Margery Bisset, the heiress of Antrim, extended the influence of the MacDonalds to northern Ireland in the 1390s. Thousands of Irish galloglasses crossed the North Channel to serve in the armies of the lordship.

Royal authority had never been strong in the Highlands, but the Lords of the Isles were powerful enough to pursue an independent foreign policy, which often conflicted with the interests of the Scottish kingdom as a whole. The dangers of this became glaringly apparent to the Scottish crown when John I allied with Edward III of England in 1335 to place the compliant puppet Edward Balliol on the Scottish throne. King David II sentenced John to forfeiture of his lands for his treachery. Being justifiably confident that David could not enforce the sentence, John simply ignored it. Donald, the second lord, also allied with English kings, reaching defensive agreements with both Richard II and Henry IV. Donald also tried to take advantage of the minority of James I to win control of the Earldom of Ross, to which he had a claim through his wife. Donald was defeated in 1411 by a royal army under the earl of Mar at Harlaw, about 20 miles (32 kilometres) from Aberdeen, but his son Alexander, the third lord, finally acquired the disputed inheritance in 1424. The acquisition of Ross brought the lordship to its greatest territorial extent and made Alexander the greatest magnate in the Highlands. James I tried to cut Alexander down to size, capturing him by an act of bad faith and imprisoning him in Tantallon castle. James sent his army to invade the lordship but it was defeated at Inverlochy in 1431 by Alexander's cousin Donald Balloch, who went on to ravage the lands of the Mackintoshes and Camerons who had allied with the crown. Outraged, James demanded Donald's head as the price of peace. A severed head was duly delivered and Alexander was released, but the king had been duped: Donald was alive and safe in Ireland. The unfortunate former owner of the head is unknown.

The fortunes of all medieval principalities and kingdoms rested heavily on the abilities of their rulers. An internationally recognised kingdom could survive a weak or incompetent ruler but this could easily prove fatal to even the grandest and most independent lordships because they were essentially just collections of estates and rights, not sovereign entities. The run of able Lords of the Isles came to an end with the accession of John II in 1449. It was no help to him that he was still a boy, but even as an adult he lacked the forceful character necessary for successful rulership. A contemporary described John as a meek and scholarly man, better suited to be a churchman than a chieftain. John's weakness allowed the martial figure of Donald Balloch to secure a controlling influence over the lordship's foreign policy. Today, Donald would be described as a hawk and he pushed for an aggressive policy towards the crown. In 1451 John seized royal castles at Inverness and Urquhart; the following year Donald led the Lordship's fleet of galleys into the Clyde to ravage James II's crown lands.

Under Donald's influence, John negotiated the Treaty of Ardtornish with Edward IV of England in 1462. In return for their support, Edward promised to share all of Scotland north of the Forth between John and Donald if he conquered the country. Such an ambitious alliance threatened not only the crown but all the Highland magnates too. After Edward reached a peace agreement in 1474, James III was free to deal with the Lordship of the Isles. In 1475 James declared Ross, Kintyre and Knapdale forfeit for treason, and a willing alliance of Highland magnates led by the earls of Huntly and Atholl invaded the Lordship and forced John to submit in 1476. John's authority was badly damaged, and the different branches of Clan Donald and other leading clans, the MacNeills, MacLeods and MacLeans, began to struggle with one another for 'headship of the Gael' in what was left of the Lordship. John seems to have concluded that the best chance to preserve the Lordship was to keep a low profile, but he was frustrated by his warlike son Angus, who set out to recover the lost lands by force. Angus seemed to be on the brink of success when, at the instigation of the Mackenzies of Kintail, an Irish harpist cut his throat while he slept one night in 1488/9. John's nephew Alexander of Lochalsh continued the fight, but his defeat by the Mackenzies near Strathpeffer in 1491 proved he was not a warrior of Angus's stature. Meanwhile the Lordship descended into chaos as John ceased to take any active part in its government. James IV saw his opportunity and formally abolished the Lordship in 1493 and divided it among the local clan chiefs. John was grateful to retire to the royal court on a generous pension: he died in 1503. No clan would be allowed to build up such a powerful lordship again but, though the threat to the crown was ended, the abolition of the Lordship did little to increase the effectiveness of royal government in the Highlands. There were many rebellions aimed at restoring the Lordship of the Isles, the last in 1545, and clan rivalries, which had been suppressed by a common loyalty to the lords, re-emerged with a vengeance. The 'danting of the isles' – the sub-jugation of the Highlands – would be a major concern for Scottish govern-ments for the next 200 years and the task would not be completed until after the Act of Union.

10

IRELAND AND ITS INVADERS

> *Ireland is one of the worst countries in the world to campaign in or subdue, for it is a strange, wild place consisting of impenetrable forests, great lakes, bogs and uninhabited regions. It is hard to find a way of making war on the Irish effectively for, unless they choose, there is no one there to fight and there are no towns to be found.*
>
> Jean Froissart, *Chroniques* (*c.* 1410)

The discovery of large quantities of Roman artefacts on a fortified headland near Drumanagh in County Dublin in the early 1990s briefly threatened a revolution in thinking about late prehistoric Ireland. Had the pristine Celtic world of Ireland been violated by a Roman invasion after all? As it turned out, no it had not. Drumanagh was a native stronghold with trading links to the Roman world. Other sites have provided evidence for trade with the Roman Empire and even for the presence of resident Romano-British merchants in the shape of British-type burials with British and Roman grave goods. Merchants from the Roman world must have been frequent visitors because the Romans had a good knowledge of the Irish coast and even of major ceremonial centres inland, such as Emain Macha (Navan), which they called Isamnion. Despite these contacts, surprisingly few Roman artefacts have been found in Ireland. It seems that the Irish elite felt no urge to adopt the trappings of a Romanised lifestyle as the continental and British Celtic elites had done and that Roman coins and metalwork were simply melted down and recycled into La Tène artefacts more in keeping with native tastes. Contacts with the Roman world do not seem to have had any impact on social developments either, as there was no acceleration in state formation, urbanisation or settled agriculture. Ireland remained a world of tribes and chiefdoms and of cattle rearing and cattle raiding as portrayed in the epic *Táin Bó Cúailgne* ('The Cattle Raid of Cooley'), which is believed to be set in the fourth century. One of the few overt signs of Roman influence was the development of the ogham alphabet in the third or fourth century. Ogham was designed to be simple to carve and was used for memorial inscriptions, which are the earliest records of the Irish language. Another Roman influence was the introduction of Christianity, a development that effectively brought an end to Irish prehistory.

Early Christian Ireland

The first Christians to live in Ireland were probably British slaves, rather than missionaries. The decline of Roman power in the fourth century gave the signal to the Irish to begin pirate raids on the British coasts. A Roman poet wrote that 'the sea foamed with the beat of hostile oars'. One Irish king, Niall of the Nine Hostages, was credited with leading seven expeditions to Britain, and his mother, Cairenn, was said to have been a freed British slave. Another British slave was St Patrick, who was captured as a teenager in the last days of Roman Britain and carried off to Ireland, where he tended sheep for six years before he escaped, only to return *c.* 435 as a missionary bishop. Patrick later wrote that thousands of Britons had been slaughtered in these Irish raids. Although Patrick is popularly regarded as the apostle of Ireland, he was far from the first missionary to preach the gospel there. The first missions were sent by the church in Gaul in the late fourth or early fifth century, and by 431 there were sufficient converts to justify Pope Celestine appointing Palladius of Auxerre as bishop of the Irish. Other continental missionaries who were active around this time included St Auxilius, St Iserninus and St Secundinus. The continental mission was concentrated on Leinster; Patrick's mission was to the still completely pagan northern half of the country. A rough guide to the area evangelised by Patrick comes from the distribution of early churches with the name *Domnach Pátraic* ('church building of Patrick'), only one of which is found south of a line drawn between Dublin and Galway. After St Patrick's arrival, British missionaries gradually took over the work of conversion from the Gauls. This had an important influence on the development of early Irish Christianity, as it drifted out of the control of the Roman church. The British method of calculating the date of Easter was used along with other 'Celtic' practices, such as an informal diocesan structure and a more eremitical tradition of monasticism than that practised in areas controlled by the hierarchical and authoritarian Roman Catholic church. The conversion of Ireland was largely complete by the sixth century: it had been a peaceful process and, according to Irish tradition, no martyrs were made. The transition was probably eased by the policy of locating Christian centres close to ancient pagan ritual centres. St Patrick's church at Armagh, for instance, was close to the seat of the kings of Ulster at Emain Macha, while St Secundinus' church at Dunshauglin was close to Tara, which retained its symbolic association with kingship despite having been abandoned centuries before. The introduction of Christianity must have led to the destruction of much of the culture of pagan Ireland, yet it remained acceptable even for monks to enjoy the mythological tales of the ancient Irish heroes and their magical gods, and to pass them on and eventually write them down for posterity. In medieval Europe, only the Icelanders had a comparable respect for their pagan past.

Early Christian Ireland was a complex mosaic of hundreds of local kingdoms and dozens of over-kingdoms. An ordinary king (*rí tuathe*) was the ruler of a *tuath*, which was defined as a 'people' or 'community', rather than as a territorial unit. The territory of a *tuath* could be very small, often less than 100 square miles (160 square kilometres). Each *tuath* would have its capital, usually a small ringfort or a crannog; a church or monastery; and an inauguration site, usually a prominent prehistoric barrow that was believed to be the grave of an illustrious royal ancestor. The people of a *tuath* were, in theory at least, an extended kinship group and the king was the head of the senior lineage. The king was responsible to his people for the fertility of their land and cattle, hence their prosperity: this was no doubt a legacy of pagan times. Kings also had duties of lawmaking, judgement and leadership in war. In return all the free families of the *tuath* owed the king tribute (paid in kind – coins were not used in Ireland before the Viking Age) and military service. Clerics and learned poets performed what little administration these simple kingdoms required. Ordinary kings might themselves owe tribute (usually cattle), hospitality and military service to an overking (*ruiri*), who in turn might owe it to a king of overkings (*rí ruirech*). Overkings, therefore, did not exercise direct rule outside their own *tuath* – their power rested upon their ability to call on the resources and services of their client kings. Sometimes, an exceptionally powerful king might be described as king of Ireland (*rí Érenn*) but the high kingship did not develop as a formal institution until the late tenth century. The relationships between kingdoms were not fixed. An ordinary king with military ability and ambition could build a strong war band and use it to make himself an overking. Nevertheless, even by the seventh century some stable dynasties of overkings had emerged, the most powerful of which were the Northern and Southern Uí Néill dynasties of north-east Ulster and Meath respectively. To an outsider, early Christian Ireland would have appeared to be a deeply divided country and, indeed, small-scale warfare was endemic. Yet this highly decentralised political structure was to prove remarkably resilient, well able to absorb the shock of invasion and constantly renew resistance.

The early Irish church was a mirror image of the country's decentralised political structures. The rigid hierarchy of the Roman Catholic church, with its dioceses and provinces, was modelled on the administrative structure of the late Roman Empire. In Ireland bishops were respected but the church was dominated by the abbots of monasteries, which played the leading role in pastoral care for the laity. Monasticism was introduced to Ireland from Britain during the period of the conversion. British monks, such as St Finnian of Clonard (*fl. c.* 500), founded the first monasteries and trained Irishmen like Columba (Colum Cille) who themselves went on to become prolific founders of monasteries and churches. Monasticism was open to women as well as men, but there was a reluctance to donate land for nunneries, so they were fewer, smaller and less influential than male houses. Monasteries that were believed to share a common founder were grouped in *paruchiae* (parishes) but, unlike dioceses, these were not territorial units: the monasteries of a *paruchia* could be widely scattered.

The Golden Age

The church introduced literacy in Latin. Irish monks enthusiastically took up the study of patristic and Classical literature and were themselves soon producing a wide range of literature in both Latin and Gaelic, including biblical commentaries and hagiography, law, grammar, computation, annals and poetry. Irish monasteries soon had well-stocked libraries. The standard of Irish monastic scholarship was the equal of any to be found in the early medieval West, but what particularly impressed foreigners was the high average standard of education of the monks: possibly because they were importing an alien culture, Irish scholars paid great attention to providing good teaching materials for novices. Monasteries also became important

Plate 24 Book of Durrow (*c.* 650–700); carpet page with trumpet and spiral decoration and six-ribbon interlacing, Irish, from Durrow, County Offaly (vellum); Ms 57 fol. 3v

Source: The Board of Trinity College, Dublin, Ireland/Bridgeman Art Library, www.bridgeman.co.uk

Plate 25 Monasterboice High Cross, eighth century
Source: John Haywood

centres for craftsmanship and the visual arts. Monasteries were great land-owners, and many became wealthy on the rents of their tenants and the offerings of the pilgrims who visited in search of forgiveness for sins or cures for illnesses and injuries. Kings needed divine favour if they were to fulfil their responsibilities to their subjects and they became frequent visitors to monasteries along with their retinues. The belief that the saints protected them led many kings to entrust monasteries with their treasur-ies. Because they were wealthy centres of consumption, merchants and craftsmen were attracted to the monasteries to cater for the needs of the monks and their visitors, and they settled in villages close by. By the end of the ninth century some of the more important monasteries had developed into small towns. These included Armagh, thanks to its association with St Patrick the main centre of Christianity in Ireland, and Clonmacnoise, which was situated at a strategic crossing of land and river routes in the centre of the country. Under the patronage of the monasteries, Irish crafts-men produced superb works of art in stone and metal, such as the sculp-tured high crosses, many of which still stand, and the silver chalices of Ardagh and Derrynaflan. The finest Irish artistic achievements of the period are, unquestionably, the intricately illuminated gospel books, such as the Book of Durrow and the Book of Kells (actually made on Iona). Though in later ages the credit was given to angels, these were made by the monks themselves as acts of devotion. The art of what has come to be called the 'Golden Age' was a harmonious fusion of late Insular La Tène geometrical patterns and interlaced animal ornaments borrowed from the Anglo-Saxons, which art historians know as the Hiberno-Saxon style. Irish metalworkers also adopted from the Anglo-Saxons the technique of making decorative patterns using filigree (fine twisted wires of gold or silver) and soon ex-ceeded them in skill.

Despite the close involvement of the leading monasteries with the secular world, Irish monasticism also had a strong tradition of asceticism, inherited from the desert fathers. Monks following this tradition sought complete solitude for contemplation and built their monasteries on the windswept islands off Ireland's west coast, the most spectacular of which clings almost impossibly to the cliffs of the precipitous islet of Skellig Michael. Another expression of this ascetic tradition was the Culdee reform movement (from *Céile Dé*, 'Client of God') that flourished from the eighth through to the twelfth centuries. Though life in places like Skellig Michael must have been cold and hungry, it was not tough enough for some monks. Placing their fates in the hands of God, small parties of monks set sail in flimsy hide boats in search of ultimate solitude in uninhabited lands. Many must have finished up at the bottom of the sea, but others found safe harbours and later made it back home to tell of their adventures. The most fantastic of the tales of these seafaring monks is the *Voyage of St Brendan*, which some believe is a description of a voyage to North America. The tale mixes plaus-ible information, such as a description of a fiery mountain in the sea, which could well be a volcanic island, with pure fantasy, making it a difficult work to interpret. A modern replica of a hide *currach* has successfully crossed the

Atlantic, but that was with the benefits of modern weatherproof clothing and navigational equipment and the reassuring presence of a rescue boat. However, Irish monks certainly reached the Faroe islands and Iceland long before the Vikings got there.

The Irish called their practice of religious travelling *peregrinatio* ('travelling for God'), while foreigners called it 'the Irish fashion of going away', so distinctive was it to them. Not all *peregrini* had their minds fixed only on solitude, however, and the present-day isolation of many Irish monasteries is deceptive. Columba's monastery on the delectable Hebridean island of Iona offered plenty of solitude but it was not really remote in an age when travel by sea was always faster than on land. Iona was in fact an excellent base from which Columba could lead the conversion of the northern Picts, as well as maintain his influence in Ireland, which was only a day's sail away. Another Irish monk from Iona, St Aidan (d. 651), played the leading role in the conversion of Northumbria. Other Irish missionaries, such as Columbanus (d. 615) and Fursa (d. 650), took themselves to the powerful Frankish kingdom and Italy to spread the ascetic brand of Irish monasticism. The Irish did much to raise the rather relaxed standards of continental monasteries, but their refusal to accept diocesan authority, and their adherence to other Celtic practices, brought them into conflict with local bishops. Columbanus had a particularly stormy career and at one point was escorted from the Frankish kingdom under armed guard, though he was soon back. Because of their high reputation, many Irish monks found a welcome at the court of the Frankish emperor Charlemagne (r. 768–814) who fostered a revival of learning known as the Carolingian Renaissance. Outstanding Irish scholars who contributed to the renaissance included the geographer Dicuil, the poet Sedulius Scottus, and John Eriugena ('Irish born'), whose treatise *Of the Division of Nature*, a discussion of the evolution of the universe, was one of the few truly original philosophical works of the early Middle Ages. The practice of *peregrinatio* gradually declined in the ninth century as a result of the rising influence of Benedictine monasticism, with its emphasis on stability, which forbade monks to wander from their monasteries. However, Irish monasteries, known as *Schottenklöster*, remained influential in southern Germany and Austria until the Reformation.

How important was the civilisation of Ireland's 'Golden Age' in a global context? Did the Irish, as has been claimed, save civilisation? Though it was never the only light in the so-called Dark Ages – sophisticated cultural life never died out in Italy and Gaul, and Anglo-Saxon England had its own (though partly Irish-influenced) great cultural achievements – by the standards of contemporary western Europe, Irish civilisation was undeniably outstanding. Significant though the Irish achievement was in western European terms, when viewed in a global context it serves only to emphasise the early medieval West's cultural backwardness. No cultural centre of seventh- to eighth-century western Europe could compare with those of the Byzantine Empire, China, India or even the central-American Maya civilisation, which was then at its height. The greatest cultural centre of all was Baghdad, the capital of the Islamic Arab Caliphate, where the study of Classical science and philosophy flourished. Arab scholars played a more important role in preserving and disseminating the wisdom of Graeco-Roman antiquity than even the Byzantine Greeks, who showed surprisingly little interest in the achievements of their pagan forebears. When medieval Europeans eventually rediscovered the works of Aristotle and other ancient philosophers it was from Arabic translations of the Greek originals. In today's atmosphere of popular Islamophobia, it is sobering to reflect that, if anybody saved *Western* civilisation, it was the Arabs.

Longships and *longphorts*

The Vikings brought Ireland's Golden Age to an end. The earliest known Viking raids were on England: Portland in Dorset was sacked *c*. 789 and the Northumbrian monastery of Lindisfarne got the same treatment in 793. Two years later a Viking fleet sailed south through the Hebrides, sacking Iona before descending on the Irish coast, where several other monasteries were sacked. Wealthy and unprotected, monasteries became a favourite target for the Vikings, who took full advantage of their swift ships to launch hit-and-run raids, plundering, kidnapping and withdrawing before the locals could organise a defence. As the Vikings became bolder they sailed up Ireland's many navigable rivers right into the heart of the country: the Shannon became a Viking highway and longships anchored on Lough Neagh and Lough Erne. Ireland's fragmented political structure meant that there was no coordinated response to the raids and at times it seemed as if the Vikings could go anywhere and do anything they wanted. The saints seemed impotent to defend their monasteries – Armagh was sacked three times in one month alone in 840. Much of the damage done by the Vikings was short term. The loss of crops and livestock would cause hunger but they could be replaced in a season or two. Most Irish houses, even those of kings, were built of wicker and thatch and what burned easily was also easily rebuilt. The losses of manpower (and womanpower) to Viking slave raids must have been a more serious long-term blow to farming communities but the better off, at least, stood a chance of being ransomed. The cultural damage caused by the attacks on the monasteries was, however, immense and long lasting. Books were destroyed for the sake of their decorated covers and reliquaries and vessels made of gold or silver were hacked up to make it easier for the raiders to share out the loot among themselves. Worst of all, the communities of learned monks were dispersed; many of them were killed or sold as slaves.

In the 840s the Vikings began to build fortified camps called *longphorts* around the coast, to use as bases from which to raid all year round. By the tenth century, some of these – Dublin, Wexford, Waterford, Cork and Limerick – had developed into Ireland's first port towns. In contrast to England, where the Vikings conquered and settled large areas of countryside, in Ireland they were never able to win permanent control over any land outside the immediate vicinity of their coastal bases. On the face of it,

Plate 26 Devenish monastic round tower; belfry, treasury and refuge from Viking raiders

Source: John Haywood

it would have seemed that Ireland's disunity should have made it more vulnerable to conquest by the Vikings than England, which was divided into only four powerful centralised kingdoms. In fact the opposite was true. In early medieval Europe it was always the centralised kingdoms that got conquered most easily. After the 'Great Army' of Danish Vikings invaded England in 865, the kingdoms of Northumbria and East Anglia both collapsed as soon as their kings had been killed in battle. Mercia too collapsed when its king decided he would prefer not to get killed and fled the country. Only Wessex survived to prevent England becoming Daneland. The centralised nature of the Anglo-Saxon kingdoms meant that it was relatively easy for the Vikings to destroy the small ruling class and take over; just one battle might do the trick. Little trouble would then be expected from the leaderless peasantry. Ireland, however, had hundreds of kings and even more lineages from which new kings could be chosen. Many Irish kings did die in battle against the Vikings. Six were killed in one battle alone at Islandbridge near Dublin in 919. But with such decentralised leadership no victory could ever have the decisive knockout effect it could in England. Nor was there much chance of a lasting peace agreement with so many kings to negotiate with. Once they were settled in their towns, the Vikings lost their main military advantage over the Irish, that is their mobility, and they became more vulnerable to counterattack. By 1000 all the Viking towns had been forced to acknowledge Irish kings as their overlords and had become integrated into Irish political life, tolerated for the trade they brought and their fleets of warships, which made them useful allies in the wars of the Irish kings. Converted to Christianity, and in many cases Gaelic speaking, the Irish Vikings had, by this time, become known as Ostmen, to distinguish them from real Scandinavians.

Brian Boru and the high kingship

Traditionally, Ireland's Viking Age is held to have ended with Brian Boru's victory at the battle of Clontarf in 1014. Brian was already 50 years old when he became king of Dál Cais in Munster after his brother was murdered in 976. As a younger son Brian had not expected ever to rule, let alone become Ireland's most famous high king, but he soon showed that he had a real talent for war when he defeated the Limerick Vikings in 977. The following year Brian defeated and killed his brother's murderer, Maél Muad, the overking of Munster. In 984 Brian began to extend his power outside Munster by imposing tributary status on the kingdom of Osraige in Leinster. He campaigned almost annually until in 997 he forced the Southern Uí Néill high king Maél Sechnaill to recognise him as overlord of all of the southern half of Ireland. There was the briefest of peaces before Brian, his sights now set on the high kingship itself, went back onto the offensive against Maél Sechnaill. Finally defeated in 1002, Maél Sechnaill resigned his title in favour of Brian and accepted him as overlord: it was the first time anyone other than an Uí Néill had been high king. Two more years of campaigning and every kingdom in Ireland had become tributary to Brian, hence his nickname *bóraime*, 'of the tributes'.

Brian's achievement was a considerable one but he did not in any meaningful sense unite Ireland: outside his own kingdom of Dál Cais, he exercised authority indirectly, through his tributary kings, and he created no national institutions of government. The obedience of Brian's tributaries was not assured and he faced, and put down, several rebellions. The most serious of these began in 1013 when Leinster allied with the Dublin Vikings against Brian and called in an army of Vikings from Orkney and the Isle of Man. It was this alliance that Brian's army met and defeated at Clontarf, now a suburb of Dublin. The octogenarian king was too frail to take any part in the fighting, but a Viking who had fought his way through the lines killed him at the moment of victory. Lacking any institutional foundations, Brian's hard-won hegemony immediately collapsed. Maél Sechnaill recovered the high kingship but the Uí Néill stranglehold on the title had been broken. Competition for the high kingship became intense, spurring developments in government as rival overkings sought to exercise direct rule throughout their dominions. The big losers were the ordinary kings who lost their royal status. The title *rí tuathe* went out of use and was replaced by *taoiseach*, meaning chief. Kings also adopted the theocratic principle of divine ordination common to other European monarchies, so that it was no longer necessary for the king to be, or pretend to be, of the same kin as his subjects. A conquered king could now be deposed and his lands annexed by the victor. In the process kingship became more territorial in nature, but before a national kingship could develop Ireland was invaded by the Anglo-Normans.

In 1155, at the instigation of the archbishop of Canterbury, Pope Adrian IV (the only English pope) issued the bull *Laudabiliter*, authorising England's new king Henry II to conquer Ireland in the interests of reforming the church there and granting him the title Lord of Ireland. The Irish church had been slow to recover from the ravages of the Vikings: the priesthood had become hereditary, many bishops and abbots were laymen and monks lived openly with their concubines. Native kings such as Muirchertach Ua Briain of Munster had already taken up the task of bringing the Irish church into line with Roman Catholic practices, but their progress had been limited. One of the successes of the reformers was the setting up of a regular diocesan structure for the country. In the process, the archbishop of Armagh was given primacy over the Irish church (in 1152), so ending the archbishopric of Canterbury's long-standing rights to appoint bishops to the Ostman towns. Thus *Laudabiliter* was part of Canterbury's campaign to recover its lost influence. In today's terms, the papal commission was the equivalent of a United Nations resolution authorising the use of force, but Henry was not interested; he already ruled lands stretching from the Scottish border to the Pyrenees and there was nothing in Ireland worth fighting over. The bull lay forgotten about until one of Henry's own vassals, Richard FitzGilbert, popularly known as Strongbow, won control of Leinster in 1171. This created a potential threat that Henry understood only too well. Henry held his French lands as a vassal of the king of France, but with the resources of the kingdom of England at his command he could defy his theoretical overlord whenever it suited him.

The coming of the Anglo-Normans

Strongbow inherited his claim to Leinster from his wife Aífe, the daughter of King Diarmait MacMurchada. After he tried unsuccessfully to win the high kingship in 1166, Diarmait had been expelled from his kingdom and sent into exile in England. While in England, he was given permission by King Henry to recruit Norman, Flemish and English mercenaries from the marcher lordships in South Wales to help him recover his kingdom. Strongbow, who was out of favour with Henry and had little to lose, was Diarmait's most important recruit. In 1167, Diarmait went home with a small force of Anglo-Norman knights and archers and quickly recovered his kingdom. A larger force arrived in 1169 and helped Diarmait capture the Ostman town of Wexford. Then in August 1170 came the event that the *Annals of Ulster* retrospectively described as 'the beginning of the woes of Ireland'. Strongbow himself landed near Waterford with 200 knights and a thousand archers. Within days he captured Waterford for Diarmait: his reward was Aífe's hand in marriage. A few weeks later he captured Dublin and invaded the kingdoms of Meath and Bréifne. When Diarmait died in May 1171, without any direct male heirs, Strongbow assumed the kingship. This was against Irish custom – kings were elected and had to have royal blood – and he was opposed by Diarmait's nephew Muirchertach. The high king Rory O'Connor (Ruaidrí Ua Conchobhair) rallied the forces of Connacht, Ulster, Meath, Airgialla and Bréifne to support Muirchertach, but Strongbow easily defeated this vast army (it was perhaps 30,000 strong) outside Dublin. Almost as alarmed by these developments as the Irish, Henry dusted off *Laudabiliter* and set off to invade Ireland himself, bringing with him an army of some 500 knights, 3,000 archers and a siege train. Henry landed near Waterford in October 1171 and marched through Munster before heading for Dublin. Henry's was by far the most powerful army Ireland had ever seen and no one was inclined to resist it. Strongbow submitted and agreed to hold Leinster as Henry's vassal. Most of the Irish kings also submitted to Henry, as did the Irish church.

Henry spent Christmas at Dublin, feasting and flattering the Irish kings, but when he left Ireland in the spring of 1172 he had established effective English rule in Leinster, Meath, Dublin, Waterford, Wexford and no more. It was left to Strongbow and other opportunistic Anglo-Norman barons like Hugh de Lacy to complete the conquest of Ireland. At first they seemed invincible and in 1183 Rory O'Connor abdicated from the high kingship, his authority shattered by his failure to stem the English advance. The Anglo-Norman combination of armoured knights and archers proved absolutely devastating to Irish armies whose soldiers fought with spears and shields and with so little armour that the English often described them as fighting 'naked'. At Dundonnel (near Waterford) in 1170 an Irish army

Plate 27 Carrickfergus Castle, the oldest stone castle in Ireland (1180s)
Source: John Haywood

of 3,000 was routed by just ten Anglo-Norman knights and 70 archers. This marked battlefield superiority remained an important factor throughout the history of Anglo-Irish warfare. English armies were usually better equipped and better trained than the Irish, and when they met the Irish in open battle they won more often than not. The English consolidated their conquests with fortifications and settlements, much as they had done in Wales. Motte and bailey castles were built in their hundreds, to be replaced gradually by a smaller number of strong stone castles, from which the Anglo-Norman barons and their knightly vassals could dominate the surrounding countryside. Where the Anglo-Normans conquered, the ancient Irish landscape of dispersed settlements and pasture was transformed by the imposition of the English manorial system, with its nucleated villages and ploughlands. These villages were populated by English and Irish peasants attracted by favourable terms. Walled towns, like Galway and Athenry, were founded and populated by English burgesses to act as agents of Anglicisation. Yet despite this methodical approach, the pace of conquest slackened after 1200 and by the end of the thirteenth century it had become depressingly clear to the English that they were not going to be able to dislodge all the native Irish dynasties.

After Rory O'Connor's abdication there were no more claimants for the high kingship, but Irish resistance continued under the leadership of local kings and chiefs, who were determined to maintain their independence. While it may have been Ireland's disunity that had let the invaders in, it now became an asset in just the same way as it had in the Viking Age. Had Ireland in 1170 been as centralised a kingdom as England was in 1066, it would have been conquered just as easily. But no such battlefield coup as happened at Hastings was possible in twelfth-century Ireland, so the Irish had time to adapt. The odds on the battlefield were evened to some extent in the thirteenth century when Irish kings began to recruit galloglasses (heavily armoured infantry) from western Scotland, but usually the Irish, like the Welsh, preferred to avoid open battle. The lightly armed Irish were more mobile than the English. While the English chased around vainly trying to bring the Irish to battle, the weather, disease, exhaustion and supply shortages steadily thinned their numbers. English foraging parties were ambushed and stragglers picked off. Plashing woods (building brushwood fences between the trees) made them impenetrable obstacles for the English cavalry, preventing pursuit. The persistence of Irish resistance discouraged English settlement and there was also a geographical obstacle to the policy of Anglicisation. Outside the fertile south-east, most of Ireland was not well suited to the imposition of the manorial system and, just as was the case in Wales, the English could not easily, or profitably, dominate areas that did not have a settled peasantry. English armies conquered huge areas of western Ireland in the early thirteenth century but, as they could not be colonised, they were left under the rule of Irish kings who simply waited for a suitable opportunity to rebel. Rivalries between the leading settler families, such as the FitzGilberts and the de Burghs (Burkes), also meant that at times the English were almost as disunited as the Irish.

The English were not helped either by their preoccupation with other theatres, especially France. War in France was popular, the weather was good and there were excellent prospects for plunder and ransoms. Their heavy armour meant that, for knights at least, there was not even so serious a chance of death in battle, and the code of chivalry ensured that, if captured, they would be well treated while their relatives at home raised the cash for their ransom. Ireland was wet and poor and prisoners were usually killed, as was normal in Celtic warfare. This last practice convinced the English that the rules of 'civilised' warfare need not be applied in Ireland. The English preoccupation with France is not hard to understand, but it condemned them to a stalemate in Ireland. A complete English conquest of the island became a remote prospect.

After the successful rebellion of the Leinster Irish in the last years of the thirteenth century, the English position in Ireland began gradually to deteriorate. The Scottish Wars of Independence briefly seemed to offer the prospect of expelling the English altogether. Robert Bruce made an appeal to the Irish to support the Scots on the grounds that both peoples had a common origin and sent his brother Edward to invade Ireland in 1315, hoping to divert English forces away from Scotland. Ulster rallied to his cause, but this was the area of Ireland that had always had the closest links to Scotland. Elsewhere in the country, the Scots seemed to be just as foreign as the English and the Irish stood aside to let the two fight it out between themselves. Edward Bruce was a good soldier but the lack of local support eventually proved fatal and he was defeated and killed by local English forces at the battle of Faughart, near Dundalk, in 1318. Even though they had seen the Scots off, the English had suffered much economic damage and they lost control of most of Connacht and Ulster to the Irish in the 1330s.

The decline of the English colony

The arrival of the Black Death in Ireland in 1348–50 swung the balance further in favour of the Irish. The disease spread along the main trade routes and positively flourished in the unhygienic and crowded medieval towns. The highly urbanised English were therefore hit hard, and around 40 per cent of them died, while the more numerous rural Irish were largely spared. These losses could not be made up by immigration. Thanks to the Black Death, England had a labour shortage and wages were rising fast. Faced with physical insecurity in Ireland and new economic opportunities in England, many English colonists voted with their feet and left. Military pressure and depopulation were not the only problems faced by the settlers: there was also the more insidious threat of assimilation with the Irish. The colonists clung tenaciously to their English identity (they would never have described themselves, as they usually are today, as 'Anglo-Irish'), but intermarriage with Irish families and the multitude of everyday contacts with the Irish meant that they were gradually becoming Gaelicised. In 1366 the English government in Dublin introduced the Statutes of Kilkenny in a desperate attempt to keep the English in Ireland distinct from the Irish. The most important measure was the requirement for all those living in the English colony to use only the English language, English personal names and English law. Even horses had to be ridden in the English way (the Irish did not use stirrups). Intermarriage was outlawed, as was keeping an Irish concubine. Irish priests could not serve in the colony, nor could Irish monks enter monasteries there. Playing Irish sports and keeping Irish minstrels and kerns (Irish mercenaries) were banned, so too was selling arms and horses to the Irish. Taken together, these measures vividly illustrate the extent of Irish influence on the colonists and, in fact, colonists who visited England were, much to their annoyance, often taken for Irishmen. Other measures in the statutes provided for maintaining a permanent stance of military readiness and for avoiding unnecessary wars. The English clearly felt themselves to be under siege.

By the end of the fifteenth century the area obedient to the English crown had shrunk back to the Pale, the thoroughly Anglicised area that approximated roughly to the counties of Dublin, Meath and Louth. Even the Pale was not secure, however, as it was regularly raided for 'black rent' by the MacMurroughs of Leinster. Outside the Pale, the great Anglo-Irish magnate families of the Butlers of Ormond and the Fitzgeralds of Kildare and Desmond ruled most of the south in semi-independence at 'the king's command'. Some Anglo-Irish baronial families, like the Berminghams and the MacWilliam Burkes, had been completely assimilated to Gaelic culture, while even the nominally loyal Butlers and Fitzgeralds had adopted a highly Gaelicised lifestyle and were bilingual. It was beginning to look as if the English colony might go the same way as the Ostman towns.

The decline of the English colony was matched by increasing Irish self-confidence. This found expression in a vigorous resurgence of Gaelic culture, led by a number of learned families, each with its own hereditary specialism in poetry, medicine, law, history or music. Traditional inauguration rites, abandoned after the Anglo-Norman invasion, were revived and carried out at ancient centres like the Navan that had been associated with kingship since prehistoric times. Traditional provincial overlordships were also rebuilt, for example by the MacMurroughs in Leinster and the O'Neills in Ulster. However, if Irish kingship had survived the Anglo-Norman invasion, its institutional and ideological foundations had withered. Although poets might still address them by the traditional royal title of rí, Gaelic rulers of late medieval Ireland no longer saw themselves as kings but as lords much like the great Anglo-Irish magnate families: their kingdoms had become landed estates and their subjects had become tenants who paid rent which the lords used to hire professional armies of kerns and galloglasses to make war on their enemies, Irish as well as English. In truth, Irish kings had become little more than warlords. This essentially limited concept of their sovereignty was a weakness that a stronger English government could exploit. Whatever the reality on the ground, the king of England was still internationally recognised as the legal overlord of Ireland.

11

THE LAND FACING
THE SEA

Maximus crossed the Channel and went first to the kingdom of the Armoricans, which is now called Brittany. . . . He summoned Conan to him, out of hearing of his troops, and said to him with a smile: 'We have captured one of the fairest kingdoms of Gaul. . . . I will raise you to the kingship of this realm. This will be a second Britain, and once we have killed off the natives we will people it with our own race.'

Geoffrey of Monmouth, *History of the Kings of Britain*
(*c.* 1136)

The only remaining Celtic-speaking region on the European continent today is Brittany in north-west France. Brittany today preserves its Celtic identity not only in its language – Breton – but also in its folk culture and popular festivals. The survival of Celtic language and identity in Brittany is truly remarkable. While in the British Isles Celtic speakers remained the majority of the population well into the Middle Ages, the Bretons were from the outset greatly outnumbered by their Romance-speaking neighbours. For much of its history, Brittany has had more in common with south-west England and south-west Wales than it has had with France. All are peninsulas of ancient rocks pushing out into the Atlantic Ocean. All, too, display a rampart of cliffs to the sea, are hilly inland and have temperate, if sometimes stormy, climates, dominated by the proximity of the surrounding Atlantic. Even the place names are similar. To the modern mind, used to fast transport by land, the sea separates the three peninsulas, but, until comparatively recent times, it was a high road between them – travelled in turn by megalith builders, merchants, settlers, saints and pilgrims. These maritime links to Britain have been central to the survival of a Celtic Brittany.

The Gauls knew Brittany's wild coastline as *Armor*, 'the land facing the sea', from which the whole region was known in ancient times as Armorica. Iron Age Armorica prospered by its strategic position on the main trade route between the Mediterranean and Britain. Few Mediterranean merchants were prepared to risk the wild Atlantic and sail direct to Britain, so Armorican tribes, such as the Veneti, became middlemen, selling British tin to the Romans and Roman wine to the Britons. Trade helped push the Armoricans towards statehood. Around 100 BC the first *oppida* were built and native rulers began to mint spectacular gold coins, which were used for official payments to retainers and warriors. Armorica's Atlantic orientation was abruptly ended by the Roman conquest in 57–56 BC. The Romans deliberately broke Armorica's links with Britain by shifting trade away from the Atlantic towards the Rhône–Rhine corridor. At the same time the Romans' roads linked Armorica more closely with the rest of Gaul than it had ever been before. The local tribal territories were organised into *civitates* and planned towns replaced the old tribal centres. Villas and other Romanised buildings sprang up in the countryside and fish salting centres developed along the coast to supply the Romans' craving for piquant fish sauces. But, although Armorica became administratively and economically integrated with the empire, its cultural integration was much more superficial. The vast majority of personal names known from dedications and graffiti are Celtic, and outside the towns knowledge of Latin spread slowly. Even in the fifth century, when in the rest of Gaul local dialects of Latin had developed and were beginning their long evolution into the modern French language, Armorica remained mainly Celtic speaking. Yet this was a moribund Celtic society. Such elements of Celtic culture as survived did so solely by virtue of the region's isolation and the innate conservatism of farming peoples. In time Armorica would have become as Romanised as the rest of Gaul: what prevented this from happening was the collapse of Roman power in the fifth century and an influx of confident, expansionist, Celtic-speaking Britons which followed hard on its heels. It was these newcomers who transformed Armorica into *Britannia Minor* – 'Little Britain' – from which the modern name Brittany (Breton *Breizh*, French *Bretagne*) is derived.

Armorica into Brittany

British emigration to Armorica seems to have begun in a small way soon after 300. During the crisis that shook the Roman empire in the mid third century, Frankish and Saxon pirate raids hit Armorica hard. Pollen samples from peat bogs in Finistère point to a decline of agriculture and a corresponding advance of woodland. Many coastal villas and other settlements were abandoned; others survived in much reduced circumstances. The fish salting industry collapsed. Coin hoarding, a classic sign of insecurity, increased and the impoverished peasantry turned to brigandage. When stability finally began to return *c.* 300 there was a modest economic recovery. Some of the sites abandoned during the crisis were reoccupied by people who used pottery from southern Britain, while a mid-fourth-century cemetery at St Urnel (Finistère) contained skeletal types more closely resembling those of south-west England and south-west Wales than the native Armoricans. Armorica had become depopulated during the third century, so this limited British settlement may have been encouraged by landlords desperate to attract new tenants. No contemporary writer noticed the arrival of these newcomers, but in his famous *History of the Kings of Britain*, the twelfth-century author Geoffrey of Monmouth records the legend of Conan Meriadec. Conan was a British noble who went to the continent with the Roman emperor Magnus Maximus in 383 and was granted Armorica as a reward for his loyalty. The Britons slaughtered the locals and repopulated the province with 100,000 settlers and 30,000 soldiers who were brought over from Britain, turning Armorica into 'a second Britain'. There is no independent evidence that Conan was a real historical person – and the massacre of native Armoricans certainly never happened – but many Britons did serve in the Roman army on the continent in the fourth century so there may be some kind of factual basis to the story. Armorica's recovery began to run out of steam *c*. 350, economic decline set in again, and by the end of the century most, if not all, villas had been abandoned, this time for good. Then, soon after 410, the Armoricans, 'emulating the example of the Britons' across the Channel who had just expelled the Roman administration, rebelled against Roman rule and set up their own government. It did not last long. The Roman general Exuperantius recovered control in 417 but, while Rome retained nominal control until the 460s, Armorica collapsed into ungovernable anarchy in the 420s as a result of repeated peasant rebellions.

The hundred years or so between the mid fifth century and mid sixth century are critical, for they saw the main wave of British immigration, which transformed Armorica into Brittany. Yet our sources of information are so meagre that we do not even know for certain if the British settlement was a mainly violent or peaceful process. There seem to have been two waves of migration. The first had taken place by the 460s under the leadership of a king called Riothamus. This may have taken place with the agreement of the Romans, as Riothamus was an ally of the emperor Anthemius against the Visigoths. A second and more sustained migration took place in the first half of the sixth century. Later traditions recorded in the *vitae* (religious biographies) of early Breton saints suggest that this migration was organised by aristocrats with close links to the royal family of Dumnonia, a British kingdom roughly comprising modern Devon and Cornwall. By the later sixth century three main regional powers had emerged: Cornouaille (Cornovia) in the west; Broërech, named after its founder Waroc, in the south-east; and in the north Domnonée (Dumnonia), which long preserved its political and social ties with its namesake across the sea. The migration was accompanied by a major movement of British clergy – most of them from South Wales – who introduced the practices of the Celtic church. The *vitae* tell of priests and monks, such as St Paul Aurelian, founding churches and monasteries on the sites of abandoned villas and deserted Roman towns inhabited only by wild animals. Others, following the tradition of the *peregrini*, sought out wild and remote islands for their settlements.

The Britons had a similar material culture and way of life to the Armoricans so it has proved difficult for archaeologists to identify any of their settlements. The most important evidence of the British settlement comes, therefore, from place names. The similarities between Breton and Cornish and Welsh place names are immediately obvious, even to a non-linguist. Common Breton place-name elements of British origin include Plou (Welsh *plwyf*, 'people'), Lan (Welsh *llan*, 'church'), tré (Welsh *tref*, a subdivision of a parish), ker (Welsh *caer*, 'hamlet'), coët (Welsh *coed*, wood) and lis or lez (Welsh *llys*, a hall, i.e. the residence of a notable person). These British-influenced place-name elements are concentrated in northern and western Brittany and probably give a good idea of where British settlement was concentrated. In the south-east place names derived from Gaulish are common, suggesting that there was little British settlement there. The British settlement is evidenced not only in place names, of course, but also in the Breton language itself, which is closely related to Welsh and Cornish.

Refugees or colonialists?

According to the monk Gildas, writing in Britain *c.* 540, the Britons who migrated to Armorica were refugees from the Anglo-Saxon invasions of Britain. Though this explanation meshes well with the hoary tradition of presenting the British Celts as the persecuted victims of the English, it does not really hold water. As we have seen, Gildas's purpose in writing was not to record history but to excoriate the Britons for their sinfulness. If we believe Gildas, the Britons were too feeble to defend themselves against the Anglo-Saxons, yet they managed to win control of a large part of Gaul (which was itself subject to invasion by other Germanic peoples), and then maintain their independence against powerful neighbours for nearly a thousand years. This does not sound like the achievement of a beaten people. And these Britons had not been beaten; they came from areas that had driven off the Anglo-Saxon invaders. In reality, Geoffrey of Monmouth's fanciful tales are probably truer to the spirit of the British settlers than Gildas's gloomy jeremiad. The British settlement of Armorica was a self-confident expansionist movement, intended to take advantage of the yawning power vacuum left by the collapse of Roman power to seize land in a sparsely populated region. We should not underestimate the ambitions of the Britons – after all, King Arthur himself was said to have conquered Gaul.

Not long after the first Britons began to settle unnoticed in Armorica, the Franks, a Germanic people, began to infiltrate across the Roman empire's Rhine frontier and settle in what is now Belgium. The Romans had more pressing problems elsewhere on their long frontiers and they agreed to recognise the Franks' settlements in return for their providing recruits for the army. The Romans probably saw this as a temporary expedient, but there was always some new problem facing the declining empire and as, by and large, the Franks kept their side of the bargain, they stayed. Only after

Roman power entered its terminal decline in the 470s did the Franks begin the aggressive territorial expansion that had made them masters of most of Gaul by the early sixth century. There is no evidence for Frankish settlement in Armorica, but they apparently laid claim to it from the time of King Clovis (r. 481–511), who defeated an army of Britons on the Loire around 490. The Britons may have established a garrison as far east as Orléans in 530, but by the end of the century the Franks had pushed them back roughly to the line of the river Vilaine. This remained the Frankish–Breton frontier for the next 200 years.

Although Domnonée was briefly forced to accept vassal status in 635, the Franks generally left the Bretons, as we can now call them, in peace until the reign of Pippin III (r. 751–68), the first of the Carolingian kings. The Bretons seem to have tested the strength of the new dynasty by raiding Frankish territory and Pippin retaliated by occupying Vannes. To contain the Bretons, the Franks created a military frontier, the Breton March, based on the counties of Vannes, Nantes and Rennes: its earliest known count was the French hero Roland who was killed when the Basques attacked the rearguard of Charlemagne's army at Roncesvalles as it crossed the Pyrenees in 778. The emperor Charlemagne (r. 768–814) and his son Louis the Pious (r. 814–40) between them launched six campaigns to conquer Brittany but the result was always the same. In the face of overwhelming Frankish force, the Bretons submitted, bided their time and at the first opportunity rebelled and won back their independence. The Franks found the Bretons' light cavalry and guerrilla tactics hard to deal with, but the main reason for their failure lay, paradoxically, in the Bretons' lack of unity. As the Breton leaders, usually described by the Franks as counts (*comes*), were independent of one another, there was no central authority to negotiate with or enforce a peace agreement.

The kingdom of Brittany

In the 820s Louis began to turn away from this fruitless confrontational policy and instead encouraged Breton nobles to enter imperial service voluntarily. He believed this would open their eyes to the potential rewards of cooperation with the wealthy Frankish empire, and he was right. One Breton who joined the Franks and rose to a position of honour and trust at the imperial court was Nomenoë. In 831 Louis appointed Nomenoë as *missus imperatoris* (imperial representative) for Brittany. Nomenoë was required to become an imperial vassal but he received the county of Vannes and virtually regal powers over all of Brittany as his reward. The arrangement was mutually advantageous. Nomenoë gained a clear superiority of status over the Breton counts and could rely on the support of Europe's most powerful ruler in any disputes. For his part, Louis gained a clear title to lands that he did not actually control and was also able to start bringing the Breton church into line with Roman practices. Brittany as a united political entity was born.

Louis's policy might well have led to the peaceful assimilation of Brittany into the Frankish realm but the prestige of the Carolingian dynasty was about to go into freefall. Louis's greatest problem in his later years was finding an inheritance settlement that would satisfy his three quarrelsome sons and at the same time preserve the unity of the Frankish empire. It was an impossible task. Louis's efforts were continually sabotaged by one son or another and, to nobody's great surprise, civil war broke out soon after his death in 840. The war was ended by the Treaty of Verdun in August 843. This tripartite division of the empire confirmed Brittany as part of the West Frankish kingdom ('France') of Louis's youngest son Charles the Bald (r. 840–77). Nomenoë had always remained loyal to Louis, but the corrosive atmosphere of the civil wars loosened the ties of loyalty between vassals and king throughout the Frankish empire. Nobles increasingly settled disputes by resort to private warfare, and in May 843 fighting broke out between Nomenoë and his neighbour, the count of Nantes. In the autumn, King Charles tried to restore order in the area but failed. When the king made a second attempt to reassert his authority in 845, Nomenoë defeated him soundly at Ballon, near Redon. Four years later Nomenoë expelled the Frankish bishops from the sees of Dol, Alet, St Pol-de-Léon, Quimper and Vannes and installed native Breton speakers in their places. In the Middle Ages, when secular and ecclesiastical authority was symbiotically entwined, such an action amounted to a declaration of independence.

Beset by conflicts with his brothers and a kingdom full of disobedient vassals, Charles would have been hard pushed to bring Nomenoë to heel even had he not also had to face the threat of Viking pirate raids. Vikings first raided the Frankish empire in 799, but it was only when Louis's succession problems began to weaken royal authority in the 830s that the problem became serious. The Vikings were great opportunists, and in 843 they took advantage of the civil war to sack Nantes and set up a base on the island of Noirmoutier, off the Loire estuary and right on Brittany's doorstep. Many Breton monasteries were plundered and in 847 Nomenoë was reduced to buying the Vikings off after they had defeated him in battle three times in quick succession. However, as the Vikings did even more damage to the Franks they were, for the time being, more of a help than a hindrance to the Bretons.

After his successful coup against the Frankish-dominated church, Nomenoë captured Nantes and Rennes, then launched a campaign deep into Charles the Bald's kingdom, only to die suddenly at Vendôme in March 851. Charles immediately invaded Brittany, only to be crushingly defeated later that summer by Nomenoë's son Erispoë in a gruelling three-day battle at Jengland-Beslé on the Vilaine. Charles had to flee ignominiously for his life, leaving his baggage behind for the triumphant Bretons to plunder. In a humiliating peace treaty, Charles was forced to cede to Erispoë all the territory conquered by Nomenoë and – an even greater concession – grant him a royal title. Brittany thus became a kingdom, although Erispoë remained a vassal of the Frankish king. Erispoë was murdered while attending church in 857 by his cousin Salomon, who then seized the throne for himself.

An unscrupulous ruler, Salomon brought the kingdom of Brittany to its greatest territorial extent. At first he professed loyalty to Charles, and was granted further territorial concessions around Angers in 863 as his reward. Three years later, however, Salomon allied with the Vikings and together they inflicted another humiliating defeat on Charles at Brissarthe, near Le Mans. Charles was forced to cede the Cotentin peninsula (in modern Normandy) to Salomon and make him the symbolic gift of a crown.

The new territories conquered by Nomenoë, Erispoë and Salomon were rich but, ironically, they also began the dilution of Brittany's Celtic character. The new territories were culturally, religiously, linguistically and administratively Frankish in character, and the small number of Breton settlers who moved east did little to change that. Brittany became permanently divided into two parts, Bretagne Bretonnante – Breton-speaking Brittany – and Bretagne Gallo – French-speaking Brittany. Bretagne Gallo became an open door for the vigorous and enormously influential culture of medieval France. This is comparable to what happened to Scotland after it acquired English-speaking Lothian in the tenth century. With both countries it was their successes against their neighbours, not defeat by them, which led to the dilution of their Celtic character. Because of their wealth, Breton rulers inevitably began to spend most of their time in the new territories. French-speaking Nantes and Rennes became the main political and cultural centres. However, the flow of ideas was not entirely one way. It was through Brittany that the legends of King Arthur became known in France, where they played a key role in the development of two of the most important manifestations of medieval European civilisation, chivalry and courtly literature.

The Viking onslaught

By the end of the ninth century, the Franks were getting the measure of the Vikings – so too were the English and the Irish. This spelled trouble for Brittany. The Vikings have a reputation for ferocity, but they did not want to fight any harder than they had to to get what they wanted. After the death of King Alain the Great in 907, Brittany began to look more and more like a soft target. When the settlement of Rollo and his followers in Normandy in 911 closed the Seine to raiders, the Vikings turned their full fury on Brittany. As monastery after monastery was sacked, Breton monks fled *en masse* to seek safety in France and England, taking with them whatever books and treasures they could carry. In 919 Breton resistance collapsed completely. The aristocracy followed the monks into exile in France and England and Brittany became a Viking kingdom with its capital at Nantes.

Brittany was liberated by Alain Barbetorte ('twistbeard'), the son of Count Mathuédoi of Cornouaille who had taken his family into exile with him in England. In 936 the English king Athelstan supplied Alain with a fleet to invade Brittany and drive out the Vikings. Landing from the sea,

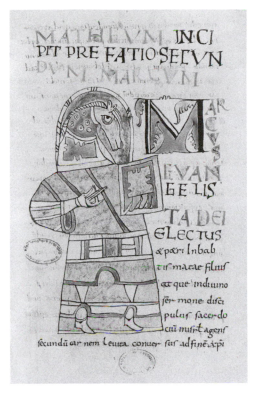

Plate 28 The portrayal of Mark the Evangelist as a horse in this ninth-century
Gospel is a pun on the Old Breton word *marc'h*, 'horse'. Ms 8 f. 42.

Source: Bibliothèque Municipale, Boulogne sur Mer, France/Lauros/Giraudon/Bridgeman
Art Library, www.bridgeman.co.uk

Alain enjoyed complete surprise, capturing and executing a party of Viking
revellers celebrating a wedding. Much hard fighting still lay ahead, but by
939 the last Viking stronghold, at Dol, had been stormed by the Bretons.
Throughout their occupation, the Vikings had lived by plunder. While
York and Dublin prospered as trade centres under the Vikings, Nantes was
semi-derelict when Alain recaptured it in 937 and its cathedral was over-
grown with brambles.

   The Viking occupation dealt a death blow to the kingdom of Brittany.
Although Alain had liberated Brittany, he was unable to assert his authority over the aristocracy and he ruled only as duke, not as king. The Cotentin
and some of the more easterly territories won in the ninth century were
lost to the Normans and Angevins. By the eleventh century Brittany had
become a decentralised feudal principality, dominated by local castellans
who defied the duke almost with impunity. Fortunately for Brittany, the
kingdom of France was in no better a state at this time and posed no immediate threat. France had become a decentralised feudal kingdom. The
king himself controlled little more than the Île de France and his great
vassals, the dukes and counts, could ignore him at their pleasure. Although

Alain and his successors enjoyed some success in reviving monastic life, the dispersal of the learned communities of monks by the Vikings was a permanent blow to Breton culture. The aristocracy gained control over their local churches and bishops ran in family dynasties. In their weakened state, the Breton dukes became vassals of the aggressive dukes of Normandy. When Normandy passed to the counts of Anjou in 1144, Brittany became an Angevin dependency. In practical terms this feudal dependency meant little beyond performing occasional military service, but it did give the overlord the theoretical right to intervene in succession disputes and such like.

From the mid eleventh century, increasing numbers of Bretons opted for emigration, beginning a trend that has continued to the present day. The most popular destination for Bretons was Paris. Poorer Bretons went seeking work in the fast-growing city, and found that their inability to speak French made them figures of fun for the locals. Better-off Bretons went to Paris hoping to enter royal service or to study at its prestigious schools. By far the most famous of these was the controversial philosopher Peter Abelard, better known nowadays for his ill-fated affair with his student Heloise than for his influential works on logic. Many Breton knights and foot soldiers went to England with William the Conqueror in 1066. Some became great landholders there: by the end of William's reign about 20 per cent of England was in Breton hands. Other Bretons joined the Norman advance into Wales, where they found they could understand the language: Geoffrey of Monmouth, who popularised the Arthurian legends in England, was probably a descendant of one of these settlers.

Brittany and the Hundred Years War

The wealth, power and the prestige of the French monarchy increased greatly during the course of the twelfth century. In 1204 King Philip Augustus demonstrated that he ruled as well as reigned when he dispossessed England's King John of most of his French lands. This political earthquake drew Brittany firmly into a French political orbit. Philip consolidated his hold by persuading the pope to abolish the archbishopric of Dol, so ending the independence of the Breton church. The outbreak of the long Anglo-French struggle known as the Hundred Years War in 1337 allowed Brittany to recover some of its independence. As Brittany dominated the sea-lanes between England and its possessions in Gascony, both the English and French kings had an interest in securing influence there. This was a situation the Bretons could benefit from. Brittany was drawn into the conflict in 1341 when Duke Jean III died without legitimate heirs. Philip VI of France proposed his nephew Charles of Blois as duke, a move that would have tied Brittany even more closely to France. However, Charles had a credible rival in Jean de Montfort, the half-brother of Jean III. Civil war was inevitable. Simply because he was not French, Jean enjoyed the support of most Bretons and, not surprisingly, Edward III of England. The important trade links between Brittany and England reinforced the

English alliance. Despite the support of the greatest warrior king of the day, Jean had still not established himself when he died from an infected wound in 1345. The English kept his cause alive on behalf of his young son Jean IV, but it was only after Charles of Blois had been killed in battle at Auray (near Vannes) that the French finally gave up and recognised him as duke in 1365.

Jean IV quickly asserted his independence not only from France but from his English benefactors too. The ongoing Anglo-French conflict made it easy for Jean and his successors to play one party off against the other. The dukes maintained a splendid court, became patrons of scholarship, founded orders of chivalry and were inaugurated to office with regal coronation ceremonies, all in an attempt to demonstrate their equality with the kings of France. Although the culture and language of the elite were now thoroughly French, writers at the ducal court deliberately revived memories of the kingdom of Brittany and emphasised the antiquity and separate identity of the Breton people at a time when both the French and English were developing a recognisably modern sense of national identity. However, the concentration of power in the duke's hands made Brittany vulnerable to a simple dynastic takeover should the opportunity arise.

The end of the Hundred Years War in 1453 decisively altered the balance against Brittany. The notoriously machiavellian King Louis XI (r. 1461–83) understood only too well how 'over mighty' subjects, such as the dukes of Burgundy and Brittany, had exploited the Hundred Years War to their own advantage: cutting them down to size became a major objective of his reign. When it became clear that Duke François II would have no male heirs, he began to prepare the ground for a French takeover of Brittany. The leading nobles were subverted with gifts and favours and Louis encouraged the development of factions at the ducal court. Louis's efforts bore fruit for his successor Charles VIII when, in 1487, a discontented Breton noble, the Marshal Rieux, encouraged a French invasion. Despite receiving help from England, Spain and the Holy Roman Empire, François was crushingly defeated by the French at Saint-Aubin-du-Cormier in July 1488 and was forced to accept humiliating peace terms. All foreign troops were to be sent home, several strategic towns and castles were to be handed over to France and the duke was not to marry his daughters off without the French king's permission. By September, François was dead and the duchy was left in the hands of his astonishingly precocious daughter Anne, aged only 11. The fate of Brittany now hung on Anne's marriage. Anne and her advisers sought a match that would keep Brittany out of French hands, and it seemed that they had succeeded in December 1490 when she underwent a proxy marriage to Maximilian, the son of the Holy Roman Emperor Frederick III (Maximilian was not actually present at the ceremony: afterwards his ambassador symbolically placed his leg in Anne's bed to 'consummate' the marriage). However, a disappointed unsuccessful suitor then handed Nantes over to the French, who went on to lay siege to Rennes in the summer of 1491. With Breton resistance collapsing and the nobility hopelessly divided, Anne reluctantly took the only action that could have secured a lasting peace for Brittany – she married the young French king. Though formal annexation to France did not happen until 1532, the marriage ended Brittany's independence.

Despite its loss of independence in 1491, Brittany remained legally distinct from the rest of France, retaining its thirteenth-century *parlement* and its legislative autonomy. Just as the heir to the English throne took the title 'Prince of Wales', so the dauphin became Duke of Brittany. Breton was still the majority language in fifteenth-century Brittany, but after the loss of independence it gradually began to lose ground to French, especially in the ports, which steadily grew in importance because of France's naval and colonial rivalry with England. However, Breton continued to flourish, in part because the advent of the printing press made literature in Breton widely available for the first time. The Revolution was a turning point in the history of Brittany. Brittany's strong local identity and institutions were seen to be at odds with the new ideology of the indivisible Republic. The Breton *parlement* was abolished and Brittany's administration was brought into line with that of the rest of the French Republic. Five *départements* replaced its medieval seneschalcies. In January 1794 instructions were issued to destroy the Breton language, which was now seen as incompatible with republican unity. Laws established French as the sole language of education. Brittany officially ceased to exist – it remained to be seen whether the Bretons would go the same way.

12

ENGLAND'S CELTIC ULCER

The Duke of Ormond's army was quite dispersed . . . and every person concerned in that interest shifting for their lives; and Cromwell went through as bloodily as victoriously, and many worthy persons being murdered in cold blood, and their families quite ruined. . . . We left that brave kingdom fallen, in six or eight months, into a most miserable sad condition, as it hath been in many kings' reigns, God knows why! For I presume not to say; but the natives seem to me a very loving people to each other, and constantly false to all strangers, the Spaniards only excepted.

Ann, Lady Fanshawe, English Royalist refugee (1650)

The late Middle Ages saw the beginning of a military revolution that would one day allow the Europeans to dominate the world. Key developments were handguns, cannons, artillery forts and ocean-going sailing ships. This new technology was expensive and so was increasingly the preserve of kings, whose coercive power over their subjects was thereby greatly augmented. This set in train a process whereby decentralised feudal kingdoms were turned into centralised national monarchies. The castles of the European nobility, and their status as the elite military class, had enabled them to maintain varying degrees of independence from royal government for centuries. Gunpowder weapons undermined this status. While a knight took years to train, anybody could be trained to use gunpowder weapons in a few weeks. This made the nobility redundant as a military class. Nor were their castles any longer a refuge from royal authority because the king's cannons could knock them down in a day or two. Not only did monarchs acquire greater power to enforce their will, the process of centralisation created its own imperative need to do so. Semi-independent principalities became a politically unacceptable challenge to the absolute power of the monarch. This ultimately spelled the end for the semi-independent Celtic principalities and chiefdoms of Brittany, Ireland and the Scottish Highlands. Brittany was the first to go, conquered by France in 1491 (see p. 153). Ireland, which seemed almost to have shaken free of England in the fifteenth century, was conquered by the beginning of the seventeenth century. The Gaelic chiefdoms of the Scottish Highlands survived the longest, but they too had been subjugated by the middle of the eighteenth century.

In July 1453 at Castillon near Bordeaux, French cannons shattered England's once invincible army of archers and armoured infantry, bringing the Hundred Years War to a decisive end. Almost two centuries of all-round aggression had brought the English scant rewards. True, Wales had been conquered and pacified, but of continental empire, for which so much blood and treasure had been expended, there remained only Calais and the Channel Islands. Scotland had not only been lost but also thoroughly alienated, and in Ireland England controlled only the Pale and a few other lordships in the south-east. The shock of defeat helped throw England into thirty years of dynastic instability and occasional military conflict known as the Wars of the Roses, which were ended only by Henry (Henry VII) Tudor's victory at Bosworth Field in 1485. Ireland had seen little fighting in the wars but, as the great Anglo-Irish families had taken sides, it was important for Henry to establish his authority there.

Henry's initial problem was the governor of Ireland, Gerald Fitzgerald, the earl of Kildare (1456–1513). Kildare had been a supporter of the Yorkist dynasty that Henry had overthrown, but his services could not be dispensed with lightly or easily. He was a most able governor, who commanded the respect of both the Anglo-Irish and the Gaelic lords (who called him Gearóid Mór or the 'Great Earl'). His lands, comprising the counties of Kildare, Wicklow, Offaly and Leix, gave him a strong autonomous power base and all the revenues of Ireland passed through, and often stuck to, his hands. When Kildare supported the unsuccessful Yorkist pretender Lambert Simnel in 1487, Henry was powerless to punish him. When he supported another Yorkist pretender in 1491, Henry decided that extreme measures were necessary. In 1494, he sent Edward Poynings to Ireland with an army to arrest Kildare and replace him as governor. Poynings effectively ended the governor's autonomy by ending his right to call the Irish Parliament without the king's permission and by bringing Ireland's revenues under the supervision of the English Exchequer. His wings satisfactorily clipped, a chastened Kildare was restored to the governorship in 1496: he was still plainly the best man for the job. His son and successor as earl, another Gerald (this one known to the Irish as Gearóid Óg, that is Gerald the Younger), proved just as troublesome to Henry VII's successor Henry VIII (r. 1509–47). Kildare was eventually sent to the Tower in 1533 after being accused of appropriating crown property. When rumours spread that he had been executed, his son 'Silken' Thomas rose in rebellion, but he had little support to begin with and still less after his men murdered the archbishop of Dublin. Thomas surrendered to crown forces in the spring of 1535, and was taken to the Tower, where his father had already died, eventually to be hanged, drawn and quartered. Several other members of the family were also executed and the crown annexed their lands: it was the eighteenth century before the Fitzgeralds recovered any influence. Now

Plate 29 Cloghmore Castle, Co. Mayo, a typical Irish tower house (fifteenth century)

Source: John Haywoood

that Anglo-Ireland was obedient to the crown, it was the turn of the Irish to be brought to heel. However, Henry's religious policy was about to alienate the Irish still further.

The Reformation

The Protestant Reformation was an event that had a more far-reaching impact on the history of the British Isles than that of any since the Norman Conquest, and it greatly complicated Ireland's relations with England. The Reformation came to Britain, not because of a groundswell of popular Protestantism but because Henry VIII wanted a divorce. Soon after his coronation in 1509, Henry married Catherine of Aragon, an attractive and intelligent woman six years his senior and the widow of his elder brother Arthur. By 1526 Henry was a seriously worried man: Catherine would soon be past her childbearing years and she had failed to provide him with a male heir. Henry claimed, and perhaps even believed, that this was a sign that God was displeased with him for marrying his sister-in-law and so he asked Pope Clement VII to grant a divorce. Divorces on the grounds of what was essentially dynastic expediency were not unusual in the Middle Ages, but it was Henry's bad luck that Clement depended for protection on Catherine's nephew, the emperor Charles V, and dared not oblige. Henry had always been a conventionally pious Catholic, but his need for a divorce drove him into the arms of Protestant reformers and a breach with the Roman church in 1533.

In 1534 the English Parliament passed the Act of Supremacy making Henry head of the church in England. Two years later the Irish parliament was easily bullied into passing its own Act of Supremacy, making Henry head of the church in Ireland. Henry was not a natural Protestant and he permitted few doctrinal changes: the most obvious sign of the Reformation was the dissolution of the monasteries in areas under the effective control of the English government (dissolution of the monasteries in autonomous Gaelic areas was not completely accomplished until the early seventeenth century). Irish monasticism was far gone in decline – Ireland's monasteries were no longer centres of learning and they provided little in the way of care for the poor or sick – but the dissolutions still helped provoke a Gaelic rebellion, known as the War of the Geraldine League, which was crushed at the battle of Bellahoe in 1539. A more thoroughgoing Protestantism was introduced – this time without consulting the Irish Parliament – during the reign of Henry's son and successor Edward VI (1547–53), but following his early death Catholicism was restored by his elder sister Mary (1553–8), Henry's daughter by Catherine of Aragon. Henry's last surviving child, Elizabeth I (r. 1558–1603), reintroduced Protestantism, but, despite the introduction of stiff penalties to try to enforce church attendance, by the time of her death the new faith had failed to put down firm roots among either the Gaelic Irish or the Old English (as the established Anglo-Irish were called by this time).

The reasons for the failure of the Protestant Reformation are complex and are only partly to do with a sincere devotion to Catholicism among the Irish people: after all, most of the English were equally attached to their traditional beliefs. The crucial difference was that the English government did not control all of Ireland and so was in no position to enforce Protestant worship, as it was in England. Nor could it prevent priests from being trained in Catholic Europe and returning to Ireland. Even in areas it did control, the government was short of Protestant clergy and there were none who could speak Gaelic, nor were religious texts translated into Gaelic. Worse, most of the Protestant clergy came from England, creating an impression that the Reformation was just another unasked-for English imposition on Ireland, as indeed it was.

Surrender and re-grant

In 1541, Henry abandoned the title Lord of Ireland, which had originally been granted to Henry II by Pope Adrian IV. In view of the continuing breach with Rome, it was no longer expedient, or wise, to rule Ireland using a title granted by the papacy. Henry formally constituted Ireland as a kingdom and adopted the title King of Ireland. Henry's policy towards the Irish could be described as speak softly and carry a big stick. Although he maintained a strong force in Ireland he preferred persuasion to war, which had the disadvantage of being expensive and uncertain. Because of the new constitutional position, Henry sought to regularise the position of the Gaelic lords in their relationship with the crown through the policy of surrender and re-grant. Gaelic lords were induced to submit to the king and surrender their family lands and traditional titles and authority: in return they were promised royal protection and their lands were immediately re-granted under feudal tenure with an English-style title attached. In this way the O'Neill lordship in Ulster became the earldom of Tyrone. Surrender and re-grant gave Gaelic lords an unshakable title to their lands in English law and, although they continued to use their Irish titles and regard them as superior to their new English titles, around 40 took the king up on what looked like a good offer. What none of them seemed to have fully appreciated was that it also gave the king an unshakable legal right to dispossess them of their lands if they proved disloyal – as many of them fully intended to be if it suited them.

The Tudor plantations

From the English point of view, the problem with the Irish was that they perversely preferred savagery (Gaelic culture) to civilisation (English culture). The solution was to impose Anglicisation on Ireland through the introduction of an English-style shire system of local government in which legal, administrative and military authority was held by a royally appointed sheriff. This process had been begun as long ago as *c.* 1200 with the creation of County Dublin, but in the early 1500s it was still confined only to those areas that had been subject to English colonisation. The Reformation made the accomplishment of Anglicisation all the more urgent because England now found itself politically isolated with no major continental ally. Disobedient Ireland was an obvious back door through which the Catholic powers might try to launch an invasion of England, especially now that the Irish might see them as liberators from religious oppression. It was in this context that the English government conceived the idea of plantations. Ireland was about to become a proving ground for English colonialism, as the lessons learned there would be applied in the New World and elsewhere.

Initially plantations were not intended to be a means of ethnic cleansing. Rebellious Irish and Old English lords were despoiled of their lands, which were then handed over to loyal 'New English' and, sometimes, Irish lords. The new English lords would provide islands of authority and be a civilising influence over the peasantry. The first plantation, which took place in Laois and Offaly in 1556, was planned by Edward's government but executed under the Catholic Mary. Later plantations under Elizabeth were intended not only to Anglicise but also to spread Protestantism. Naturally, there was resistance. Because the former owners waged highly successful guerrilla warfare against the planters, the English government committed more and more troops to garrisoning Ireland. The largest of the Tudor plantations took place in Munster in 1584 on more than a quarter of a million acres of land confiscated after the defeat of a rebellion led by James Fitzmaurice. The lands were awarded to thirty-five undertakers (i.e. chief planters), many of whom were happy simply to live off the rents of the existing Irish tenants. Others expelled the Irish from their lands altogether and introduced English agricultural practices and English tenants. By 1592 there were more than 3,000 New English settlers in Munster and the plantation appeared to be prospering. In that year a new plantation, of 'loyal Irish', was made on lands in Monaghan in Ulster which had been confiscated from Hugh Roe MacMahon for breaking his surrender and re-grant agreement.

Except for Carrickfergus and parts of Down, Ulster had never been under effective (or even ineffective) English control. Alarmed by the implications of the Monaghan plantation, Hugh O'Neill, earl of Tyrone and Ireland's most powerful Gaelic lord, secretly plotted a rebellion with his neighbours, the O'Donnells of Tyrconnell and the Maguires of Fermanagh. O'Neill was a canny operator. He had not wasted the time spent in his youth at the English court and he knew how to appear Anglicised even if he was not. While instructing his allies to begin hostilities in 1593, O'Neill made a show of loyalty to the crown that allowed him to sabotage English attempts to suppress the rebellion for two years. O'Neill finally came out into the open when, to prevent its being reinforced, he attacked an English garrison on the river Blackwater in 1595. He was promptly proclaimed a traitor. For the first time, the Irish forces had considerable numbers of firearms, and their numbers were swelled by thousands of redshanks,

Plate 30 Hugh O'Neill
Source: Getty Images/Hulton Archive

lightly armed mercenary infantry recruited in Argyll. What the rebels did lack, however, were cannons and this made it impossible for them to take forts and towns except by surprise, negotiation or starvation after a long siege. O'Neill resorted to guerrilla tactics, attacking the plantations and ambushing English supply columns on their way to isolated garrisons. One such ambush was the memorably named Battle of the Ford of the Biscuits in 1594, where an English column on its way to Enniskillen lost all its supplies at a river crossing. Knowing that Elizabeth was reluctant to commit herself to the huge expense of defeating the rebellion by force, O'Neill spent months in insincere peace negotiations, while he imported arms and trained his troops. By the end of 1595, the rebellion had spread to Connacht and Leinster. After O'Neill destroyed an English army of 4,000 foot and 300 cavalry in another skilful ambush at Yellow Ford near Armagh in August 1598, the Irish of Munster rose too and destroyed the plantation there.

By the beginning of 1599, most of Ireland was once again beyond the control of the English crown. Elizabeth reluctantly accepted that the time for penny pinching and half measures was over and raised the largest English army yet sent to Ireland, over 17,000 strong. To command it, she appointed her favourite, Robert Devereux, earl of Essex, as Lord Lieutenant of Ireland. Essex was a courageous soldier but his dashing appearance had always promised more than he delivered. In Ireland he was utterly out of his depth. Unable to bring the Irish to battle, Essex's poorly supplied army wasted away as he campaigned ineffectively, first in Leinster, and then in Connacht. Ordered by the queen to invade Ulster, Essex met O'Neill face to face near Dundalk in September and agreed to yet another truce. Elizabeth was furious and placed Essex under house arrest when he returned to England, without permission, to try to justify his actions; he was executed for treason early in 1601, after a rather pathetic attempt at a coup.

With the English position now close to complete collapse, the triumphant O'Neill presented the queen with demanding peace terms, amounting to a fully autonomous Ireland. The plantations were to be reversed and land returned to its original owners. Traditional Gaelic laws of landownership were to be restored. There was to be a native Irish judiciary and administration. The Irish would have equal rights to travel and trade in England. Above all, the Catholic church was to be fully restored to its pre-Reformation position in Ireland and a Catholic university was to be founded. Elizabeth could not possibly accept such terms, which her secretary of state, Sir Robert Cecil, described as utopian, and, as she always did when her back was against the wall, she acted decisively. In January 1600 Charles Blount, Lord Mountjoy, was appointed as Essex's successor and given reinforcements, naval forces and a blank cheque. Mountjoy had served in Essex's army and he understood the futility of chasing the more mobile Irish around the countryside. Ignoring O'Neill's attacks on the Pale, which were intended to provoke him into doing just that, Mountjoy concentrated on building and garrisoning a string of forts to cut Ulster off from the rest of Ireland. Meanwhile, two more English armies campaigned in Munster and Connacht. This was an expensive policy but it began to take away O'Neill's freedom of movement and, when the English garrisons began to lay waste the Ulster countryside, it also undermined his popular support.

Mountjoy kept the pressure up right through the winter and spring of 1600–1 but O'Neill's resistance was stiffened by news that Philip III of Spain was sending an army to support him. Unfortunately, when the 3,400-strong Spanish army landed in September it did so at Kinsale in the far south. Having lost many men, and most of his munitions at sea, Don Juan d'Águila, the Spanish commander, did not feel strong enough to take the field, so he stayed put. Mountjoy quickly besieged him with a force of around 7,000 and even risked depleting his garrisons in the north to reinforce it. English ships blockaded Kinsale, cutting off the Spanish army's supplies. O'Neill felt honour bound to go to the aid of the Spanish, but to do this he and his ally Hugh O'Donnell had to leave their northern strongholds and march their armies 300 miles south, evading the English forces which they knew would try to intercept them. Miraculously, they succeeded and by early December Mountjoy found his army trapped, the Spanish on one side, the Irish on the other. The besieger was besieged. The position began to get desperate for Mountjoy as his army began to melt away through disease and desertion, but the Spanish were also suffering and they asked O'Neill to join them in a coordinated attack on the English camp. O'Neill agreed, uncharacteristically risking everything on open battle. Mountjoy had barely 6,000 fit men left to face a combined Irish–Spanish force of over 9,000, so perhaps an Irish victory seemed like a foregone conclusion. Before first light on the morning of Christmas Eve 1601, O'Neill's men began to form up for a surprise attack on the English. They did so clumsily and noisily. Alerted, Mountjoy sent his cavalry to outflank the Irish and attack them from the rear. Thrown into complete confusion by this unexpected pre-emptive attack, the Irish army broke and fled, suffering heavy casualties. It was all over in less than three hours. Throughout, the Spanish never fired a shot – the Irish had not even got close to the agreed rendezvous point. His position now hopeless, Águila negotiated an honourable surrender and withdrew his forces on 2 January 1602.

The flight of the Earls

The battle of Kinsale was decisive. As so often in the history of the Celts a decision to abandon irregular tactics for formal battle had resulted in disaster. The surviving rebel soldiers were scattered and demoralised. Hugh O'Donnell fled to Spain. O'Neill, his support in freefall, was forced onto the run. Old and sick though she now was, Elizabeth knew her strength and she rebuffed his attempts to reopen negotiations – she had had enough of that game. Mountjoy had the coronation stone of the O'Neills at Tullahoge symbolically smashed. Finally, on 23 March 1603, O'Neill made a complete and unconditional submission to Mountjoy. Elizabeth never knew about her victory – she died the next day, before the news could reach her, and the throne of England passed to King James VI of Scotland. James dealt generously with O'Neill, restoring most of his lands and his title as earl of Tyrone. James was similarly generous to Rory O'Donnell (Hugh's brother), who was given the title earl of Tyrconnell. But James did not restore to either their traditional autonomous authority. Ulster was divided into counties and the English judicial system was introduced: the days of Gaelic lordship were over.

O'Neill was never reconciled to his status as a private nobleman. On 4 September 1607 O'Neill, Rory O'Donnell and Cúchonnacht Maguire, lord of Fermanagh, took ship from Rathmullen on Lough Swilly for Spain with some 90 of their followers. They were blown off course to Normandy, and the embarrassed French government packed the fugitives off to Rome as quickly as it decently could, where they spent the remainder of their lives as papal pensioners. Deprived of the patronage of Gaelic lords, Gaelic cultural traditions entered a long decline. The Gaelic language survived, but as the language of an illiterate peasantry it was no longer a vehicle of high culture. The 'Flight of the Earls' has never been satisfactorily explained but it is likely that they feared, wrongly as it happened, that the government had discovered that they were once again conspiring with the Spanish.

Plate 31 Parkes Castle, Co. Leitrim; a seventeenth-century plantation castle

Source: John Haywood

The Jacobean plantations

After the end of the Nine Years War, the Tudor policy of plantation was revived by King James VI and I and applied to Ulster. The first plantations, in 1605, in Antrim and Down, were a private venture by a local Catholic aristocrat, Sir Randall McDonnell, who had been awarded extensive lands for switching sides during the war. As a result of the Flight of the Earls, the English government acquired vast amounts of land in Ulster. After a short-lived uprising in Donegal in 1608, James decided to apply the policy of plantation to the rest of the province. The Articles of Plantation, passed in 1609, provided for most of the Irish population of Donegal, Derry, Tyrone, Armagh, Fermanagh and Cavan to be removed to designated reservations to release the province's best land for plantation with Protestant Lowland Scots and English tenant farmers. The scheme foundered, as all schemes to repopulate Ireland foundered, on its reputation for violence and rebellion. The undertakers (chief planters) who were appointed by the government to oversee the plantation found that it was both necessary and profitable to retain Irish tenants as they were prepared to pay high rents to stay on the land. Although a Protestant majority – mainly of Lowland Scots – was established in Antrim and Down, in the rest of Ulster they were a minority among a resentful Catholic population. The bawns and fortified houses that the settlers built across the countryside are symbolic of their feelings of insecurity.

In 1606 King James established a Commission for the Remedy of Defective Titles. All Irish landowners were required to prove their titles to ownership of their lands. As James knew, the different traditions of landownership in Gaelic Ireland made this impossible in many cases and provided a pretext for another round of land confiscations from the Irish gentry. This made land available for further plantations in the Irish midlands and the south. The sense of tenurial insecurity the commission created was a major cause of the rebellion that broke out in 1641. The wars and plantations had dislocated the Irish economy and caused hard times for many Catholic landowners, many of whom were forced to go into debt or mortgage their estates. A series of poor harvests in the 1630s exacerbated the situation. Sir Phelim O'Neill, the pre-eminent leader of the Ulster rebellion, had debts of over £12,000 in 1640. One of Sir Phelim's creditors, a Mr Fullerton of Loughgall, was, coincidentally, also one of the first to be killed when the rebellion broke out.

The Confederate War (1641–1653)

By the late 1630s both the Irish and the Catholic Old English were seething with discontent. Catholics wished to see their church restored to its pre-Reformation position. Especially in Ulster, many Irish gentry had been dispossessed of their lands to make way for Protestant Scots and English settlers. Charles I had meanwhile promised the Catholic Old

English a measure of religious freedom in return for a sum of £120,000, but the double-dealing monarch had never confirmed their privileges. Yet with all these reasons for dissatisfaction, the king's officials in Ireland were taken completely by surprise when the Irish of Ulster and the Catholic Old English of the Pale finally rose in rebellion in December 1641. One shocked Protestant MP wrote that the rebellion was 'conceived among us, and yet never felt to kick in the womb, nor struggle in the birth'. The Protestant settlers in Ulster were attacked and massacred or driven from their homes. Many of the survivors fled to England and Scotland and spread horrific stories about the rebellion. Their claims that 150,000–200,000 Protestants were slaughtered are certainly gross exaggerations as the settlers probably numbered no more than about 40,000 to begin with. Modern historians estimate the true number of victims of massacres at 'only' around 4,000, with several thousands of subsequent deaths at the hands of 'Colonel Hunger and Major Sickness'. Folk memories of the massacres gave Ulster Protestants a siege mentality that has continued to the present day.

From Ulster, the Catholic rebellion spread throughout Ireland. Soon the English were confined to Dublin and a handful of fortified towns that the rebels, being short of artillery, were unable to take. This gave the government and the settlers a vital breathing space to regroup their forces. James Butler, earl of Ormond, took command of Dublin and pacified the Pale. Richard Boyle, earl of Cork, recovered much of southern Munster while a Scottish army under Robert Monro drove the insurgents out of eastern Ulster. However, this counter-offensive, accompanied by its own crop of massacres, stalled following the outbreak of civil war in England in August 1642. The rebellion in Ireland had led to the final breach between King Charles and the English Parliament.

Meanwhile, the Catholic rebels had met in June at Kilkenny to form a provisional government, the Confederate Catholics of Ireland (often called simply the Confederation of Kilkenny). An assembly of lords, clergy and commoners, chosen partly by election, met for the first time in October. The fact that the assembly of the Confederation debated in English is a sign of the degree to which the prestige of Gaelic had declined since the Flight of the Earls. The main demands of the Confederates were religious – the restoration of the Catholic church and the repeal of all anti-Catholic legislation – but they were couched in terms of loyalty to the crown. This was not a nationalist revolt but an attempt to create a Catholic Ireland within the Stuart triple monarchy.

Following the outbreak of the civil war in England in 1642, Ormond and the remaining English garrisons in Ireland declared for the king. So too did the Confederates, who saw a victory for Charles, rather than the Puritan parliament, as offering the best chance of achieving their aims. A ceasefire was declared in September 1643 and an uneasy three-way alliance developed between the Catholic Irish, Catholic Old English and Protestant Royalists. None really trusted the others and this would fatally hamper their efforts at cooperation against the victorious Parliamentarians after

King Charles's surrender in 1647. The failure to establish a single military command was particularly damaging as it led to leading commanders, such as Ormond in the midlands and Owen Roe O'Neill in Ulster, pursuing different strategies and war aims.

Ormond surrendered Dublin to Parliament in June 1647 and his subsequent attempt to recapture it was decisively defeated at Rathmines on 2 August 1649. Two weeks later Cromwell arrived with 12,000 highly motivated men of the New Model Army that had crushed Royalist hopes in England, and a plentiful supply of stores, money and cannon. Cromwell would have cast a long shadow over Irish history even had English Royalist and Irish Catholic and nationalist historians not (for their own rather different purposes) turned the man into a bloodthirsty monster – the consequences of his campaign for Gaelic Ireland were absolutely devastating. There is in fact no reliable evidence that Cromwell ever committed the massacres of innocent civilians for which he has long been notorious and, indeed, there is some evidence that he sought to spare civilians as much as possible from the rigours of war: he hanged looters in his own army, for instance, and paid for all supplies (unlike the Confederate armies). It is true that Catholic priests were not spared the rigours of war, but to accuse Cromwell of religious bigotry because of this is to judge him by modern, liberal, standards: religious toleration was on no one's agenda in the 1640s, certainly not the Roman Catholic church's. Yet, for all that, Cromwell displayed the familiar English double standard towards Ireland and the Irish. He justified his massacres of the garrisons at Drogheda and Wexford by the rules of war of the day, but he had applied them with a merciless rigour such as had never been applied by either side during the civil wars in England (except where Irish soldiers were involved).

Cromwell's first action was to lay siege to the Old English Protestant town of Drogheda, which had only recently been occupied by a Royalist garrison. The town's governor, Sir Arthur Aston, fatally underestimated the effectiveness of Cromwell's artillery and rejected a call to surrender and avoid bloodshed. Aston would have been well aware that this invited the massacre of the garrison should the town be taken by storm. After only three days' bombardment, the walls were breached on 11 September 1649 and Cromwell's troops poured into the town. The shocked defenders offered little resistance as the parliamentarians cut them down. Altogether around 3,500 of the defenders were slain against parliamentary losses of only about 60. The shock of the rapid fall of Drogheda and its terrible aftermath was such that Cromwell met little resistance until he reached Wexford a month later. Wexford held out for a month before it fell to a sudden assault. As at Drogheda, the defending garrison was massacred. The approach of winter briefly halted Cromwell's campaign, but when he resumed the offensive in spring Protestant Royalists began to give up the fight. There was still fight left in the Confederates and at Clonmel in May 1650 they inflicted a costly defeat on the New Model Army in a brilliantly planned ambush, but having bloodied Cromwell's nose they made good their escape. At this point Cromwell was recalled to England to face a new threat to the republic from Scotland, and it was left to his brother-in-law Henry Ireton to mop up the increasingly disorganised Irish resistance. Galway, the last major town in Confederate hands, was captured in April 1652.

Weak leadership, religious divisions and a lack of resources, especially money, ultimately played as important a role in the failure of the Confederate cause as the superior discipline and firepower of the New Model Army. Perhaps the Confederates' was a lost cause from the outset: would the devious Stuart monarchy ever have delivered on its promises? Much of Ireland had been devastated by the war and it was to be 20 years before the economy returned its pre-war level. Around 600,000 people – a third of Ireland's population – had died, most from hunger and disease rather than in battle or from the atrocities that both sides had perpetrated in equal measure and with equal self-righteousness.

The Cromwellian land settlement

The stage was now set for possibly the greatest dislocation in Irish history – the Cromwellian land settlements, which affected around 50 per cent of Ireland's fertile acreage. Cromwell's conquest of Ireland had cost around £3.5 million: his subsequent land settlement was as much intended to clear this debt as to solve the Irish problem. Royalist and Confederate landowners (Protestants as well as Catholics, but mostly the latter) had their lands confiscated and 105 of the most prominent were executed, exiled or transported to the West Indies. Counties Dublin, Cork, Kildare and Wicklow were reserved for use by the government; ten others – Antrim, Down, Armagh, Meath, West Meath, Laois, Offaly, Waterford, Tipperary and Limerick – were allocated to some 1,500 adventurers (investors who had funded the Irish campaign) and nearly 35,000 veterans of the parliamentary army, who were given debentures (bonds) in lieu of back pay. It was intended that the new landowners would expel their Catholic Irish tenantry, who would be transplanted to Counties Mayo, Galway, Roscommon and Clare, and replace them with English Protestant tenants. Although the settlement resulted in a revolution in land ownership, it did not work out as planned. Ireland's well-earned reputation for rebellion meant there was no influx of English settlers – England's new colonies in North America and the West Indies were much more attractive prospects – and less than a third of the army veterans actually took possession of their lands: most sold out to the adventurers or Old Protestant landowners and went home. First and foremost, landowners wanted a return on their investments, so very few Catholic Irish tenants were actually expelled and most of those that were soon drifted back. Cromwell's settlement certainly destroyed what was left of the native landowning class, but everywhere outside Ulster there remained a majority of Catholic Gaelic speakers.

Some Catholics did have their lands restored to them by Charles II after the Restoration but the Protestant ascendancy was confirmed by the

Williamite War (1689–91), which saw the Protestant William of Orange defeat the Catholic King James VII/II. The pattern of landownership that was to prevail until the later nineteenth century had been established – large estates owned by an English-speaking Protestant elite, tenanted (except in Ulster and the Pale) by a mainly Gaelic-speaking, Catholic peasantry. United, and equally disadvantaged, by their Catholicism, the old division, based on language, between the Gaels and the Old English began to blur and was replaced by a new division based on religion.

13

THE END OF THE CLAN SYSTEM

That the disaffected and savage Highlanders need to be bridled and kept in awe by garrisons and standing forces, 'till the present generation wears out is evident to all men of common understanding, and that those unhappy and infatuated people will still continue savages if nothing is done to recover them from their ignorance and barbarity; but as the rest of the people of Britain who are now civilized were once as wild and barbarous as the Highlanders, I think it is not to be doubted but that proper measures would civilize them also.

Edmund Bruce (1750)

The suppression of the Lordship of the Isles in 1493 ended any real possibility that a Gaelic polity would arise that could challenge the political dominance of the Kings of the Scots in their Lowland heartlands. Despite this, Scottish kings continued to find it very difficult to impose their authority north of the Highland line. The rugged terrain and undeveloped economy had much to do with this state of affairs, but the Highlands also contained a much higher proportion of Scotland's population in early modern times than they do today, after the Clearances, and much of this population was armed and willing to fight. Although the Scottish crown had shown that it was more than a match for even the most powerful Highland magnate, the fall of the Lordship of the Isles left a power vacuum in the Highlands that the royal government was only partially able to fill. This left space for Gaelic clans to rise to political prominence. The crown exercised its authority indirectly by using loyal clans as its agents and enforcers by giving them commissions to use fire and sword against disobedient clans. The reward for the chiefs of these clans was wealth, land, status and prestige. Three clans in particular came to dominate the Highlands through their allegiance to the crown: the Campbells in the west Highlands, the Mackenzies in the northern Highlands and Hebrides, and the Gordons in the north-east. There were dangers to the crown in its dependence on these clans, whose chiefs, especially the Campbell dukes of Argyll, proved adept at manipulating government policy to their own advantage.

Origins of the Highland clans

The word 'clan' derives from Gaelic *clann*, whose primary meaning is 'children' but which acquired a new meaning as 'kindred' in the eleventh or twelfth centuries. In theory a clan can be defined biologically as a patrilinear descent group deriving from a common ancestor for whom the clan is named. In reality, for many clan members this kinship link was purely fictive as clans actively recruited outsiders (or 'broken men' as they were called) to augment their strength. A well-known fictional example of this, from Walter Scott's *Waverley* (1814), is the Jacobite chief Fergus MacIvor, who is prepared to recruit anyone 'willing to call himself a son of Ivor' to maximise his clan's fighting strength. By the late Middle Ages, the appearance of kinship could be maintained by new recruits adopting the clan name as a surname, but this was by no means universal. Because clans were not closed societies, personal loyalty to the chief was as important to clan unity as a sense of common kinship. Successful clans could expand their territories by subjugating weaker clans and forcing them into a client relationship or even expelling them from their lands altogether, as the Campbells did to the MacGregors of Glen Orchy. It was also possible for a large clan to split up into smaller clans. This happened to the Clann Shomhairle, founded by Somerled in the twelfth century, which split up into three kindreds, the MacDougals, the MacRuairies and, the most successful of the three, the MacDonalds. The MacDonalds themselves broke up into several subdivisions during the declining years of the Lordship of the Isles. Questions of loyalties, inheritance, jurisdiction and landholding in clan society could be very complex because of the hierarchy of senior and junior kindreds within clans and the different degrees of clientage of the subordinate clans in clan lordships. Highland clans arose from the merging of feudal institutions of landholding, private jurisdiction and primogeniture with traditional Gaelic kinship ties in the twelfth century. The system was adopted by the Norse settlers in the Hebrides (for example, MacLeod from the Norse name *Liotr*, and Lamont from *lagman*, 'lawman') and Lowland and Anglo-Norman families who were granted lordships in the Highlands (such as the Chisholms, Frasers, Sinclairs, Stewarts and so on). The turbulent families who dominated the Borders in the later Middle Ages are also often described as clans, but these were not, and never had been, Gaelic societies and are more accurately described, as they described themselves, as 'surnames'.

In an age of centralising monarchies, the multi-layered loyalties and power relationships among the Highland clans could only be seen as an anomaly, while the chieftain's right of private jurisdiction over his clan's people was a real obstacle to the crown's goal of subjecting the entire kingdom to direct royal government. The duty of clansmen to perform military service was another serious problem as it gave clan chiefs private armies, answerable only to them. Clan armies could be substantial forces. Around 1600 the Gordons, for example, could raise 3,000 armed men. Scotland in the sixteenth century suffered a succession of regencies and minorities and it was only towards the end of the century that, encouraged by a misleadingly optimistic report on the wealth of the Hebrides, James VI (r. 1567–1625) began a serious attempt to subdue and pacify the Highlands. After James became king of England in 1603, his efforts were redoubled because of his ambition, unfulfilled in his lifetime, to create a unitary kingdom of Great Britain. Lowland opinion had by this time become quite viciously antagonistic towards the Gaels on account of the clan warfare of the Highlands, and the opinion of one anonymous author, who claimed that God had created the first Highlander from a horse turd, was probably widely shared. James's measures were generally coercive, extending even to attempted ethnic cleansing and genocide. In 1597, James required all chieftains in the Highlands and Islands to produce their titles to their lands, knowing full well that the traditions of Gaelic landholding would make this impossible in many cases. Failure to produce title then became a pretext for dispossession and transfer of the lands to a loyal Lowlander or clan chief who, James was confident, would be willing to pay a handsome rent to the crown (a similar campaign preceded the Jacobean plantations in Ulster). In this way, James was able to order the dispossession of almost all the Gaelic chiefs of the Hebrides, except the MacLeans of Mull. However, few of the dispossession orders were actually carried out. In part this was due to James's unrealistic expectations for rents. For example, an arrangement with the Earl of Huntly to take over lands in the Outer Hebrides on the condition that he extirpated the resident population broke down over negotiation of the rent. In the case of Lewis, which James had granted to the Fife Adventurers Company, it was successful resistance by the displaced MacLeods that led to failure. James's most ruthless act was the outlawing and virtual extermination of the MacGregors after they had defeated a rival clan in battle in 1603. Most of the leading MacGregors were hunted down and killed and the survivors were forced to change their names. Thanks to the protection of other clans, Clan Gregor was able to re-establish itself later in the century (though it was also soon outlawed again). Like most Lowlanders, James equated Gaelic culture and language with barbarism. In the Statutes of Iona, promulgated in 1609, he sought to detach the clan chiefs from their traditional culture and turn them into agents of Lowland civilisation. The statute included measures to help the Reformed church get established in the still largely Catholic Highlands, banned patronage of bards and required clan chiefs to send their sons to be educated in the Lowlands. A few years later, a knowledge of English was made a condition of succession to a clan chieftaincy. Charles I (r. 1625–49) began by continuing his father's policies but his reign soon became mired in religious controversy. Charles's advocacy of an Episcopalian church alienated Scotland's Presbyterian majority, whose opposition to royal interference found powerful expression in the popular Covenanting movement, which was named after the National Covenant, a defence of Presbyterianism published in 1638. Charles's unsuccessful attempt to destroy the Covenanters in the Bishops' Wars (1639–40) began the series of civil wars that wracked Britain and Ireland until 1652 and ended with the creation of the first unitary state of Great Britain and Ireland under the Lord Protector Oliver Cromwell.

The clans and the civil wars

When war broke out between King Charles and the English Parliament in 1642, the sympathies of Presbyterian Scots lay naturally with the Puritan-dominated Parliament. They also saw that if the king defeated Parliament, he would be able to turn the full resources of England against them and their Presbyterian church would be doomed. Therefore, in January 1644, the Covenanters allied with the English Parliament against the king. In the process, they probably wrecked any chance that the Highlands could be peacefully incorporated fully into the Scottish state. Although Low-landers overwhelmingly supported the Covenant, there was considerable sympathy for the king in the Catholic Highlands. For over 18 months an army of Royalist Highlanders, reinforced by Irish Catholics, under the brilliant leadership of James Graham, marquis of Montrose, ran rings around Covenanter forces until it was defeated at Philiphaugh in the Borders in September 1645. This armed intervention greatly increased the animosity of Lowlanders towards Highlanders. In future Highlanders would not only be thought of as barbarian cattle thieves but as rebels and supporters of Popery.

The alliance between the Covenanters and the English Parliament broke down in 1648. After the English Parliament parted Charles I from his head in 1649, the Scots proclaimed his son Charles II king. This presented a clear danger to the new English republic and in 1650 Oliver Cromwell, fresh from his victory in Ireland, invaded and conquered Scotland. For the first time, all of Britain and Ireland was under the control of a single government. Scotland was given back its independence by Charles II at the Restoration in 1663 but Cromwell had shown that the balance of power in the British Isles had swung decisively in favour of England. Developments in tactics, weapons and logistics meant that even remote inhospitable regions like the Highlands could be brought under the control of a central government, providing it had the will and the money to pay for it. But Scotland after the Restoration was wracked by religious conflicts as the government began a persecution of the Covenanters, known as the 'Killing Times', in which Highland levies played a prominent part. The Highlands were allowed to go their own way until after the so-called Glorious Revolution in England in 1688 which saw the Catholic King James VII and II deposed and replaced by the joint rule of his Protestant sister Mary and her Dutch husband William of Orange. James's supporters, known as Jacobites (from the Latin *Iacobus*, 'James'), actively sought his restoration to the throne.

Jacobites and Highlanders

Although the Jacobite cause had supporters in all parts of Britain and Ireland, it has become particularly associated with the Highlands. Because the Stuarts were a Scottish dynasty there was always more support for Jacobitism in Scotland than in England. This was especially true after the Act of Union abolished the Scottish parliament in 1707, when Jacobitism became a convenient vehicle for anti-English sentiment. However, Jacobitism was indelibly tainted with Catholicism and this ensured that it had little appeal for most Lowland Scots. Even the Highlands were by no means united in the Jacobite cause. The Jacobites could count on the MacDonalds, MacLeans, MacGregors, Stewarts, Gordons, Farquharsons and others, but some clans, like the Campbells and the Rosses, always supported the government, while others, like the Mackintoshes, tried to remain neutral. The real importance of the Highlands to the Jacobite cause was not so much the strength of feeling there, but that, because of the clan system, it was the only region of Britain where its supporters could raise large bands of fighting men easily. Some 70 per cent of the earl of Mar's army in the 1715 Jacobite rising was made up of clan levies, as was 90 per cent of Charles Edward Stuart's army in 1745.

The Scottish parliament quickly confirmed England's deposition of James VII and II and reinstated Presbyterianism, but once again there was a Highland intervention. An army of Highland Jacobites defeated a larger but inexperienced Williamite force at the Pass of Killiecrankie, near Pitlochry, in July 1689, but its leader, the Viscount of Dundee, was fatally wounded in the fighting. The death of their leader took the wind out of the Jacobites and they advanced no further than Dunkeld on the edge of the Highlands. The Jacobites were finally defeated at the battle of Cromdale on Speyside in May 1690. A little over a month later King William routed James's army of Irish Jacobites on the river Boyne, effectively ending his hopes of regaining his throne. The fall of Limerick to Williamite forces in 1691 finished Jacobitism as a political force in Ireland, but in Britain the plotting continued. As part of the pacification of the Highlands, clan chiefs were ordered to swear loyalty to William and Mary before 1 January 1692. The chief of the Jacobite MacDonalds of Glencoe turned up late, so in February the Scottish government sent a force to obtain their submission. The officers of the government troops were Campbells, whose lands the MacDonalds had recently raided and who were out for revenge. After being treated to traditional Highland hospitality, the troops turned on the unsuspecting MacDonalds and massacred around 40 of them. Many others of the clan who escaped later died of exposure during the cold winter night. Neither the government in Edinburgh nor King William had intended the massacre, but no one was punished for it either. It was a propaganda gift for the Jacobites and the resentment lingers on: the appointment in March 2002 of a Campbell to run a new visitor centre in Glencoe drew protests from some of the more atavistic MacDonalds.

Though other risings were planned, the next Jacobite rising to get off the ground took place in 1715, the year after George I of the German Hanoverian dynasty was brought to the throne of Great Britain to ensure a Protestant succession after the death of the last, childless, Stuart monarch, Queen Anne. The Jacobites received considerable help from France, which was at war with Great Britain. The Jacobites ambitiously planned three simultaneous risings: in south-west England, in the north of England and the Scottish borders, and in the Highlands. In the event the rising in the south-west was pre-empted by the government. The earl of Mar rallied the Jacobite clans at Braemar in September and quickly won control of the Highlands and Perth. Mar's advance on the Lowlands was, however, blocked by a smaller government force at the battle of Sherrifmuir, near Stirling, on 13 November. The next day another government force defeated the northern English and Border Jacobites at Preston in Lancashire. A spate of public executions to all intents and purposes finished off English Jacobitism. When news of this defeat spread north, Mar's forces began to disperse and the rebellion collapsed. Another rising was attempted in the Highlands in 1719, this time with the support of Spanish troops, but this was defeated at Glenshiel. The final Jacobite rising in 1745–6 took place against the background of the War of the Austrian Succession (1740–8), which once again pitted Britain and France against one another. By now the great white hope of the Jacobites was James VII and II's grandson Charles Edward Stuart, known variously as 'the young pretender' or 'Bonnie Prince Charlie'. Charles had confidence, good looks and charm but he had neither military nor political acumen. Despite his lack of ability, his ultimate failure was not inevitable. The best government troops were fighting abroad and neither the Scots nor the English felt much love for the dour Hanoverians. Apart from a few hundred Irish 'Wild Geese', supplied by his French backers, Charles was almost entirely dependent on clan levies for his army. He optimistically hoped volunteers would rally to his cause as he marched south. The small Jacobite army (it was never more than about 6,000 strong) performed surprisingly well against the more numerous and better-equipped Hanoverian forces. Using the favoured tactic of Celtic armies since ancient times, the reckless, terrifying headlong charge, the Highlanders routed nervous and inexperienced government armies at Prestonpans (1745) and Falkirk (1746). But though Charles marched as far south as Derby, there was no popular rising in either the Lowlands or England. Dissatisfaction with the Hanoverians did not translate into enthusiasm for a Stuart restoration. A dash on London, where panic reigned, might have persuaded the French to invade England and so have won the day for Charles, but he was unable to persuade his followers to continue. He retreated to the Highlands and to crushing defeat by the Duke of Cumberland's army at Culloden on 16 April 1746. The Highlanders relied on their tried and tested charge but this time they were facing well-drilled opponents, who had also the advantage of a strong position on rising ground. As Caesar's legionaries had done long before, Cumberland's redcoats confidently stood their ground and drove the Highlanders off with heavy losses. Many wounded Jacobites who could not flee were bayoneted or clubbed to death where they lay. Hanoverian dragoons roamed the countryside hanging anyone caught in Highland dress, including many innocent people who had taken no part in the battle. Charles became a hunted fugitive but he was not betrayed, despite the offer of a considerable reward, and he escaped the retribution that the government now meted out to his loyal followers. Like their leader, most of the Jacobite clan chiefs escaped abroad and were forfeited of their lands in their absence; three only were caught and, as befitted their rank, sent to the block. Some 3,400 Jacobite rank-and-file prisoners were taken to England for trial and imprisonment, transportation to the colonies or the gallows. The '45 has come to be popularly regarded as the last Anglo-Scottish war but this is a long way from the truth. Charles had the support of only about half the clans, while the Hanoverian army at Culloden included more Scots in its ranks than did the prince's. The absolute subjugation of the Highlands that followed was an end long desired by Lowlanders and they supported it fully. The Jacobite Highlanders who lay wounded in the heather at Culloden were as likely to be dispatched by their fellow countrymen as by an English redcoat.

The subjugation of the Highlands

French and Spanish support for the Jacobites meant that it no longer mattered that subjugating the Highlands would not pay for itself: it was now politically imperative, and the cost, compared with the resources of the British state, was easily affordable. In 1724 General Wade was commissioned to build a network of all-weather roads through the Highlands to facilitate troop movements, and garrisons were established in forts at Ruthven, Inverness, Fort Augustus, Fort William and other strategic points. These proved ineffective during the '45 – in fact the roads were more used by the Jacobites than by government troops, while the isolated garrisons were easily neutralised. In the aftermath of the '45, the system of military roads was greatly extended and new forts were built, the most impressive of which was Fort George, near Inverness, a huge artillery fort that could be supplied by sea. The Highlands remained garrisoned until after the end of the Napoleonic Wars in 1815, long after any real Jacobite threat had ended. By this time, the main duty of the garrisons was trying, without any great success, to suppress illegal whisky stills. The military occupation was backed up by a raft of oppressive legislation (the Disarming and Heritable Jurisdiction Acts of 1746–7), which abolished the clan chiefs' heritable private jurisdictions and their private armies. Other measures included bans on playing bagpipes, speaking Gaelic and wearing Highland

Plate 32 Corgarff Castle, a sixteenth-century tower house converted into a barracks for Hanoverian troops in 1748

Source: John Haywood

dress, but these proved unenforceable and were soon abandoned. Far more destructive of Gaelic culture than government legislation were the economic changes and clearances (see pp. 194ff) that followed the '45 and depopulated vast areas of the Highlands. Quite apart from their human impact, these changes completely altered the Highland landscape. Before the clearances moved the population to crofts and villages on the coast (if not out of the Highlands altogether) to make way for sheep, every glen had its hamlets, tilled fields and hay meadows. The deserted 'natural' wilderness that the visitor to the Highlands sees today has been denuded of its native trees by lumbering and overstocking and is, therefore, as much the product of human economic activity as any other in the British Isles.

Would it have made any difference to the fate of the Highland clans if Charles Edward Stuart had been victorious in 1745, or if the Act of Union had never happened? The answer is probably no. The economic depression that followed the civil wars in Scotland had already begun to change the attitude of clan chiefs to their lands, which they began to manage more commercially. This was the period when cattle droving to the Lowlands really took off. The agricultural and industrial 'revolutions' of the eighteenth century would sooner or later have provided an Edinburgh-based government with the resources to impose its authority throughout the Highlands. Once this had happened, clan chiefs would have taken a long hard look at their estates and asked themselves if they really needed so many tenants. As for a Stuart restoration, the Stuarts were at heart royal absolutists and, though gratitude may perhaps have stayed Charles Edward's hand, they would surely have found the autonomy of the Highlands as unacceptable as their predecessors had done. As kings of Great Britain – for a dissolution of the union was never on the cards – the restored Stuarts would have had ample means, as the Hanoverians had, to subjugate the Highlands. Whatever happened, by 1700 the essentially medieval society of the Highland clans was living on borrowed time. Yet even while the last embers of independent Celtdom were being stamped out, new cultural forces were being born that would give the Celts a second lease of life.

14

THE CELTIC REVIVAL

I am sensible Mr. Camden, Boxhornius and others have long since taken notice of the affinity of our British [i.e. Welsh and Cornish] with the Celtic: but there being no vocabulary extant of the Irish (or ancient Scottish) they could not collate that language therewith, which the curious in these studies, will now find to agree rather more than ours, with the Gaulish. . . . And we are further to consider that as the Gauls were a people that consisted of three several nations, of so many different languages, some of those words attributed to them in general, might have been Celtic properly so called, some Aquitanian and others Belgic.

Edward Lhuyd, *Archaeologia Britannica* (1707)

By the end of the seventeenth century the Celts were heading for extinction. Some would even argue that they were extinct. Certainly whatever self-conscious degree of Celtic identity had existed in the Iron Age did not survive the Roman Empire. Although there were still peoples who spoke Celtic languages, they themselves did not know this as the term had yet to be coined. They were, in any case, the descendents of insular peoples who had never shared in the Celtic identity, or, indeed, any other sense of common identity. It was well over a thousand years since anyone had described him- or herself as a 'Celt'. That there are today millions of people in all corners of the globe who do identify themselves as Celts is largely the achievement of one man, an impoverished Welsh scholar called Edward Lhuyd, whose book *Archaeologia Britannica* did more than any other single work to define modern ideas about the identity of the Celts. However, Lhuyd's scholarship did not resurrect the Celts by itself. His ideas struck a chord with the Celtic-speaking peoples of his day and provided a solution to particular problems that then confronted them.

Born in 1660 in Glan Ffraid in South Wales, Lhuyd was a native Welsh speaker. He remained committed to his Welsh identity and language throughout his life. Lhuyd's childhood cannot have been easy, for he was the illegitimate child of a poor man, but he got a good schooling and in 1682 he became a student at St John's College at Oxford University.

Lhuyd's ambition had been to become a lawyer but at Oxford he began to study natural history under Dr Robert Plot, the keeper of the Ashmolean museum. Though he was an able student, Lhuyd struggled to support himself financially and he never completed his degree. In 1684 he took a job as assistant to Dr Plot at the Ashmolean and succeeded him as head keeper when he retired in 1690. Lhuyd's work at the Ashmolean made him a respected academic. His studies of the flora of the Welsh mountains and the marine fossils of Oxfordshire attracted the attention of the leading scientists of the day: Sir Isaac Newton even paid for the publication of one of his books. Lhuyd brought a critical and open mind to his studies. At a time when most Europeans still believed the Bible to be literally true, he boldly questioned the commonly held belief that fossils were the remains of creatures that had perished in the Deluge.

Lhuyd published *Archaeologia Britannica* in 1707, a year of great significance in British history for other reasons too. One of Lhuyd's main purposes in writing was to demonstrate that the Welsh had a separate, and older, historical identity than the English. Lhuyd had trekked round London trying to find a publisher who would finance his project, which would involve him in extensive travels in Britain, Ireland and Brittany, but no one would touch it unless he agreed to pay for publication himself. There was a stigma attached to vanity publishing even in the eighteenth century and Lhuyd knew that this would wreck any chance of his ideas being taken seriously. Instead, Lhuyd published his work with the support of subscribers, who included a fair cross-section of the great and good of his native Wales. In the event, the subscribers were rather disappointed with what they got for their money. They had expected a work of romantic antiquarianism, which was then popular. Instead, they were presented with a dry work of philology, comparing the Welsh, Cornish, Breton and Gaelic languages. Lhuyd had been warned that his work would not be well received: one bookseller had told him that not half a score people in the whole country would want to read it. In his introduction, Lhuyd justified himself, explaining that acquiring an understanding of the ancient languages of Britain was an essential preparation for the historical study that would follow in subsequent volumes. But there were to be no subsequent volumes: none had been completed before he died in June 1709, aged 49. Most of his unpublished manuscripts were bought for a private library where they were later destroyed in an accidental fire.

Rediscovering the Celts

Lhuyd's interest in antiquarianism began in the early 1690s when he was commissioned to tour Wales to collect material for a revised edition of William Camden's *Britannia*. Originally published in 1586, this had been the first serious study of British prehistory. In the Middle Ages, history was understood in theological terms, as the working out of God's plan for the world. The European view of the past was dominated by stories from the Bible and the Greek and Roman classics, and popular myths and legends, such as the tales of King Arthur. There was little attempt to distinguish fact from fiction. Virgil's epic *Aeneid* and Caesar's *Gallic War* were treated as being equally historical. Such was the residual prestige of the Roman Empire that there was little interest in Europe's pre-Roman past. Many European peoples, including even the Welsh, constructed legendary histories giving themselves a common origin with the Romans.

As was the case with so many other disciplines, the sixteenth and seventeenth centuries saw the beginning of a recognisably modern, rationalistic approach to history in Europe. Pioneering antiquarians like Camden and John Aubrey (1626–97), who is sometimes described as the first English archaeologist, studied and surveyed the surviving ancient monuments of the European countryside. A more critical attitude was taken to legendary traditions, and Classical literature was studied anew for what Greek and Roman writers had to say about the barbarian peoples of Europe. European contacts with less developed peoples in the New World gave antiquarians plenty of food for thought about what prehistoric Europeans might have been like. John Aubrey, for example, imagined the ancient Britons to have been 'two or three degrees . . . less savage than the Americans'. Gradually antiquarians began to break free of the medieval view of the past and construct a prehistory of Europe. From a modern perspective, it is easy to underestimate the difficulty of this task. There were no scientific techniques for archaeological excavation and, before the development of modern geology and scientific dating methods, the true antiquity both of the Earth and of humankind was simply not conceived of. Well into the nineteenth century, historians had to work within an established chronology in which the Creation in 4004 BC and the Deluge in 2348 BC were regarded as fixed points. All of European prehistory had somehow to be telescoped into the 2,000 years between the beaching of Noah's Ark on Mount Ararat and the rise of Rome.

In the process, the ancient Celts were rediscovered. One of the first scholars to write about the Celts was the sixteenth-century Scot George Buchanan. Buchanan believed the Celts to have been a people of southern Gaul, some of whom had migrated, via Spain, to Ireland. It was from their language that Gaelic had developed, he argued. Buchanan also recognised similarities between the surviving fragments of the ancient Gaulish language and modern Welsh, Cornish and Breton, which he described collectively as the 'Gallic' languages. Thus for Buchanan the Irish, and their Scots descendants, were Celts but the Gauls, Britons and Picts, and their modern descendants, were not. For others, such as the decidedly eccentric Breton scholar Jacques-Yves Pezron, Celt was simply another name for the Gauls. Lhuyd's achievement in *Archaeologia Britannica* was to unite these different schools of thought by conclusively demonstrating the close relationship between Gaelic and what Buchanan had called the Gallic languages. Given the evidence, Lhuyd would have been quite justified in sticking with Buchanan's terminology and calling the language family he had defined the Gaulish or Gallic languages. There were good reasons why he did not. By

1707, 'Gallic' had become closely associated with the French, who, of course, speak a Romance language, and in 1707, too, England and France were at war with one another. Instead Lhuyd chose to call his language family the 'Celtique' or 'Celtic' languages.

Although Lhuyd believed that Britain had been colonised from Gaul and had, elsewhere, described the ancient Britons as Celts, he did not call the modern Celtic-speaking peoples 'Celts' – but the implication was clear enough. The link between language and identity is a close one and what Lhuyd had failed to say explicitly, others soon did. On 1 May 1707, just three weeks after the publication of *Archaeologia Britannica*, the Act of Union united England and Scotland to create a united Kingdom of Great Britain. The earl of Cromarty expressed the hope that in future, 'may we be Brittains and down goe old ignominious names of Scotland and England.' While this prospect may have pleased at least some of the English and Scots, it had unwelcome implications for the Welsh. The Welsh had always regarded themselves, justifiably, as the descendants of the ancient Britons, that is the original inhabitants of Britain. Even after they had been conquered and formally incorporated into England, this prior claim to the land remained important for the Welsh in maintaining a non-English identity. Little wonder, then, that the new British identity was problematic for them. The English-dominated kingdom of Great Britain had usurped an important part of their identity. By the nineteenth century 'British' and 'English' had become almost synonymous. The Welsh needed a new way to emphasise their non-English identity and their prior claim to Great Britain. The Celts fitted the bill in a way that the Gauls, being already associated with another colonialist state, never could have. Within a few years of the publication of *Archaeologia Britannica*, educated Welsh people were describing themselves as Celts and were showing a revived interest in their own language. What began with the Welsh spread in the course of the nineteenth century to the rest of Lhuyd's 'Celtique' speakers, the Gaelic-speaking Irish and Highland Scots, the Manx, the Cornish and the Bretons. The modern concept of Celtic identity had arrived.

Romanticism and Celtomania

The Celts suddenly gave form and definition to what had until then still been rather vague notions about the peoples of prehistoric Europe. The mysterious beliefs and practices of the Druids exercised a particular fascination. John Aubrey had proposed that the megalithic circles at Stonehenge and Avebury, now known to be Neolithic in date, were Druidical temples. These ideas were taken up and popularised in England by William Stukeley and in France by Malo de la Tour-d'Auvergne and Jacques Cambry. By the end of the eighteenth century the association between Druids and megaliths was firmly established in the popular imagination: despite the best efforts of archaeologists, it has still not been entirely dislodged. There was indeed something about the Celts that later eighteenth-century Europeans simply found irresistible, and they went down with a bad case of what came to be known as 'Celtomania'. Though Celtomania burned itself out before the middle of the nineteenth century, the Celts themselves have loomed large in the European historical imagination ever since.

Celtomania was a manifestation of the Romantic movement, a cultural rebellion against the rationalism and materialism of the Enlightenment. Romanticism exalted imagination, irrationalism, individualism and rebellion, and love of wild nature, the mysterious and the exotic. The aesthetic sensibilities of Europeans were radically altered as a result, leaving no aspect of the arts unaffected. These aesthetic changes had a great impact on attitudes to the Celts. Everything that was then known about the ancient Celts came from the works of hostile Classical Greek and Roman writers, who had regarded them as dangerous barbarians. These writers constructed what in their eyes was an unflattering stereotype of the Celts as violent, proud, undisciplined and superstitious barbarians. Treated uncritically, this originally hostile and inaccurate stereotype seemed to embody to the Romantics everything that their movement stood for. The Celts were transformed from dangerous savages into noble savages, unspoiled by decadent civilisation. Although almost nothing was known about their beliefs, the Druids became examples of spirituality to be emulated by intellectuals who were disillusioned by the impersonal nature of organised religion and repelled by the ugliness created by the industrial revolution. Druids began to appear in poetry, paintings and even operas. Landowners, like William Danby of Swinton Hall in Yorkshire, adorned their estates with megalithic Druidic temples and oak groves. Beginning with the foundation of the Order of Bards, Ovates and Druids in London in 1717, several attempts were made to revive Druidism. Imagination made up for the dearth of knowledge, and the neo-Druids decked themselves out in fanciful costumes and invented solemn rituals, such as the Maen Gorsedd bardic ceremony, which was first performed in 1792. This famous ritual was the invention of Edward Williams (better known by his assumed bardic name of Iolo Morgannwg), who even forged documents to prove its authentic antiquity: it has become part of the ceremonies of the National Eisteddfod. Fortunately, there was no attempt to revive the profoundly unromantic (but authentic) Druidic practices of animal and human sacrifice.

One of the first and most influential works of the period of Celtomania was the Ossianic poems of James Macpherson (1736–96). Macpherson was born at Ruthven near Inverness and grew up with a good knowledge of both Gaelic language and poetry. In 1760 he published *Fragments of Ancient Poetry*, which he later claimed were translations from ancient manuscripts of epic poems by the semi-legendary Gaelic bard Ossian, who perhaps lived in the early Christian period. The book was a bestseller and two more volumes of Ossianic poems, *Fingal* (1762) and *Temora* (1763), soon followed. Partly due to residual prejudice against the Gaels (how could such a primitive people have a tradition of epic poetry?), many in the literary establishment were openly sceptical about the authenticity of the poems. Macpherson's failure, when challenged, to show his manuscripts to the

public, seemed to justify these doubts. The truth is, as Dr Johnson sur-
mised at the time, that Macpherson had taken names, stories, phrases and
passages from old Gaelic songs and blended them into a composition
that was largely of his own invention. The controversy over the poems'
authenticity did not affect their popularity and they inspired romantics,
nationalists, revolutionaries, poets and artists across Europe. Macpherson's
admirers included Goethe, Napoleon, Wordsworth, Walter Scott and
Mendelssohn. Macpherson's poems are little read today and their lasting
value is that they stimulated interest in collecting and preserving genuine
Celtic literature and oral traditions at a time when far-reaching social and
economic changes threatened their survival. Among the more important of these works were *Poetry of the Ancient Welsh Bards* by Evan Evans
(1764), the Gaelic folklore collections of John Francis Campbell of Islay
(1860–2), and *Barzaz-Breiz* ('Songs of Brittany') by Vicomte Hersart de la
Villemarqué (1838).

Celtic identity and the Welsh 'renaissance'

The most important long-term consequence of Celtomania was that it
reawakened a sense of pride in the modern Celtic-speaking peoples in their
culture, language and identity by increasing its status. Romantic is better
than backward. This did not happen overnight. Because of the relatively
high levels of illiteracy in Celtic-speaking areas, and a lack of institutions to
disseminate ideas, this new awareness of Celtic identity spread only slowly
and until the middle of the nineteenth century it was confined largely to an
educated elite. Celtomania also changed the way the modern Celts were
viewed by others. This was a highly selective process, and it was the twentieth century before the Celtic-speaking peoples saw much in the way of
material or political benefits from it. Being thought to be romantic rather
than savage did not protect the Highlanders from the Clearances, and
Celtomania was at its height when France's revolutionary government
introduced legislation intended to undermine Breton identity in its drive to
create a unitary French state.

The revival of Celtic identity began with the Welsh. At the beginning of
the eighteenth century Welsh culture was at a very low ebb. Little was
being written in Welsh, there was not a single printing press in the whole
country and the language itself was in decline. It seemed to many as if the
Welsh were being inexorably assimilated by the English and might eventually lose their identity altogether. Lhuyd's *Archaeologia Britannica* had
been an attempt to bolster the non-English identity of the Welsh and, as he
had hoped, it did lead to a revival of interest in the Welsh language. The
first definitive grammar of the Welsh language was published in 1725 and
the first dictionary three years later. Literacy in Welsh gradually increased,
in large part through the efforts of SPCK (Society for Promoting Christian
Knowledge) and the system of travelling schools set up by Gruffydd Jones
in the 1730s. Growing demand for books in Welsh led to the establishment

of the first printing presses in Wales at Newcastle Emlyn in 1717 and Carmarthen in 1721.

The bardic traditions of medieval Wales were long dead by the eighteenth century, but the publication of collections of early Welsh literature, such as Evans's *Poetry of the Ancient Welsh Bards*, inspired a new generation of poets to revive the art. They found that there was a real popular demand for poetry and song in the Welsh language. Informal, and sometimes riotously drunken, meetings of poets led to the staging of the first formal *eisteddfod* (assembly of poets) since the Middle Ages at Corwen in 1789. Wales was still a land of hamlets and small market towns in the early eighteenth century and the largest, and best-educated, urban Welsh community was in London. These expatriates founded learned societies, such as the Society of Ancient Britons (1715) and the Honourable Society of Cymmrodorion (1751), to promote Welsh language and culture, not only among the Welsh but among English intellectuals too. This was aimed at increasing English recognition that the Welsh were a distinct and separate people in their own right. By the early nineteenth century, the Methodist Revival had absorbed much of the energy that had driven the Welsh 'renaissance' and cultural renewal did not develop into political nationalism. Although the decline in the Welsh language had been only temporarily arrested, the Celtic revival had given the Welsh a new confidence in their identity and their assimilation by the English no longer seemed inevitable.

The Celtification of Scotland

The difficult relationship between the English-speaking Lowland Scots and the Gaelic-speaking Highlanders reached a nadir after the '45. Lowlanders had always regarded the Highlanders as savages and thieves – now they were rebels too. The use of the Gaelic word 'Sassenach' (Saxon), now used by Scots solely as a slightly insulting name for the English, symbolises the internal division of Scotland: in the eighteenth century it was still used by Highlanders to describe all English-speakers, including those in the Scottish Lowlands. At the same time, some Lowlanders, such as the philosopher David Hume, could even describe themselves as being English. Thanks in large part to the Celtic revival, this division had all but disappeared by the end of the nineteenth century.

The rehabilitation of the reputation of the Gaelic Highlanders after the '45 was begun by tourism. The spirit of romanticism changed attitudes to the environment in eighteenth-century Europe. Now that humankind increasingly had the upper hand over untamed nature, wild landscapes, that had been thought dreary and frightful, came to be seen as beautiful and spiritually uplifting. Publicised in part by Macpherson's Ossianic poems, the spectacular scenery of the Highlands drew increasing numbers of tourists, whose experiences cast an aura of romance over the region and its inhabitants. The image of the Gael was further enhanced by the performance of Highland regiments in the wars with France. Though initially wary of recruiting Highlanders, doubting their loyalty, by the end of the eighteenth century the British army regarded them as its finest infantry and preferred shock troops. The tradition of the wild Highland charge survived, though with bayonets rather than claymores. To help foster regimental *esprit de corps*, the army adopted bagpiping, tartans and uniforms based, somewhat loosely, on traditional Highland dress, aiding their survival and raising their prestige.

With the days of cattle raids and Jacobite rebellions safely in the past, Lowlanders could allow themselves the luxury of romanticising the Gael. Most influential in this respect was Sir Walter Scott's enduringly popular novel *Rob Roy* (1818) in which Rob Roy MacGregor, a real-life eighteenth-century cattle thief and protection racketeer, was turned into a Celtic Robin Hood. Scott's prestige as a historical novelist allowed him to stage-manage King George IV's visit to Edinburgh in 1822. This was the first time a reigning monarch had visited Scotland for over 150 years and it generated great excitement. Scott dressed the main participants, including the king himself, in tartan, kilts, sporrans and bonnets, in the process single-handedly inventing the idea that the kilt is the traditional dress of Scotland. In fact the pleated kilt, or philibeg, had been invented as recently as 1727 by Thomas Rawlinson, an English ironmaster, for his employees at a Highland ironworks, when he found that their then traditional dress, the belted plaid, hindered their work. Lowlanders did not wear tartan, traditional plaids or new-fangled kilts, and most of them at the time saw through the charade and many agreed (as a great many still do) with James Stuart of Dunearn, that 'Sir Walter has ridiculously made us appear a nation of Highlanders'. However, the clan chiefs cooperated willingly – they were eager to deflect public attention away from the Clearances, then in full swing – and the image has stuck. Queen Victoria's love affair with the Highlands and the 'Balmoralisation' of the royal family only reinforced it. Canny Lowland textile manufacturers soon cashed in, inventing clan tartans as a clever marketing device – although particular tartans had traditionally been associated with particular areas, tartan was never a badge of clan identity – and even extending the system to Lowland family names. The truth was, Lowland Scots were beginning to find the Highlanders' Celtic identity increasingly attractive, not simply because it was romantic but because, by adopting many of its trappings (real or invented), they could use it to accentuate the differences between themselves and the English. This reflected a very real fear among nineteenth-century Lowland Scots of cultural assimilation by the English. The Celtification of Scotland was further aided by the migration of tens of thousands of Highlanders to the industrial towns of the Lowlands in search of work. This, and the steady spread of the English language into the Highlands, has led to the blurring of Scotland's ancient divisions and the emergence of a more homogeneous national identity in which the Celts play an important part. However, the modern Scottish National Party (though by no means all its supporters) has officially rejected ethnic nationalism in favour of a more inclusive civic nationalism.

Plate 33 Romantic statue of Vercingetorix (d.46 BC), Gallic chief of the Arverni, 1865

Source: Alise-Sainte-Reine, Côte d'Or, France/Peter Willi/Bridgeman Art Library, www.bridgeman.co.uk

The Celts and Irish nationalism

Scotland was not the only country where the Celts were pressed into the service of nationalism. Belgium, which became independent from the Netherlands in 1830, took its name from the Belgae and promoted Ambiorix as a national hero. Viriathus became a national hero in Spain and Portugal. The French emperor Napoleon III sponsored excavations of the *oppida* at Alesia and Bibracte, the sites of fierce Gallic resistance to the Romans, as part of a campaign to inspire a spirit of national resistance at a time when France was threatened by the rise of Prussian power. A heroic statue of Vercingetorix, which Napoleon erected at Alesia, is thought by some to have more than a passing resemblance to the emperor. It would not be inappropriate if it did as, just like Vercingetorix, Napoleon turned out to be a loser and he ended his life in exile in England two years after France's humiliating defeat by Prussia in 1871.

Nowhere did the Celtic revival play a more important role in the development of the modern national identity than in Ireland. While in Scotland the Celtic revival helped create a national identity that the vast majority of Scots could subscribe to, in Ireland it helped to divide still further an already deeply divided society. Modern Irish nationalism and republicanism began to develop at the end of the eighteenth century with support from Catholics and Protestants alike. The man often credited with founding the republican movement, Wolfe Tone, was a Protestant, and the Society of United Irishmen, which he and others founded in 1791, drew its support equally from Catholics, Anglicans and Presbyterians. Opposition to the Act of Union, which abolished the Irish Parliament and incorporated Ireland into the United Kingdom in 1801, was actually strongest among Protestants. These early nationalists were inspired by the non-sectarian ideals of the American and French revolutions, rather than romantic visions of the Celtic past, but as the movement developed this was to change. The Celtic revival stimulated an interest in Ireland's prehistory and in Gaelic language and literature, which was shared across religious divides. The first society for the preservation of the Gaelic language was even founded by a group of Ulster Protestants in 1795. Yet within a hundred years most Irish Protestants had come to see the Gaelic language as a threat to their identity. Many still do. One of the many difficulties in reaching the 1998 Good Friday Agreement on the future of Northern Ireland was the Nationalist demand that Gaelic be given equal status with English. Gaelic was already extinct as an everyday spoken language in the Six Counties at the time of the partition of Ireland in 1921, and neither Unionists nor Nationalists believed that giving it equal status was going to produce a sudden revival: it was what the language had come to symbolise that made its status so controversial.

It was perhaps inevitable that as Irish nationalism developed in the course of the nineteenth century it would increasingly come to be defined by the country's Catholic majority. As England was held to be responsible for all of Ireland's problems, nationalists rejected eight centuries of English influence on Ireland and the Irish as having no part of true Irishness. Instead they looked for the roots of Irishness in an idealised Catholic-Celtic past of saints, scholars and legendary kings and warriors. Before the twentieth century, nationalism expressed itself mainly through peaceful activities. Political action, aimed at achieving home rule rather than outright independence, is the most obvious, but there were also many recreational and cultural organisations with a nationalist agenda, such as the Gaelic Athletic Association that promoted traditional Irish games, like hurling and Gaelic football, and the Gaelic League, which promoted the Gaelic language. Through the League's activities, Gaelic became closely associated with nationalism, though this did not halt the language's decline in everyday use.

Unfortunately, with the notable exception of Gladstone, most British politicians were either indifferent or hostile to nationalist demands for land reform and home rule. Inevitably, frustration with the lack of progress led to sporadic outbreaks of violence, as in the Fenian risings in 1867 and the Land War of the 1880s. None of these remotely threatened British rule but they were often followed by concessions to head off full-scale rebellions. Tragically, by acting only under threat, the British government undermined constitutional nationalism and, by demonstrating that it was the only way to get results, encouraged the growth of the tradition of political violence that still blights Ireland. Those who chose the path of violent nationalism cast a romantic aura over their terrorist activities by closely identifying themselves with the legendary Celtic past. The popular name of the Irish Republican Brotherhood (IRB), the Fenians, derives from legendary Irish warriors, while a statue of the dying hero Cúchulainn was chosen to commemorate those Republicans who fell in the 1916 Easter Rising, which was led by the IRB.

By the late nineteenth century it was getting very difficult for a Protestant to be accepted as a real Irishman. Immersion in the mythical pre-Christian past was one way, exemplified by the poet W.B. Yeats, whose influential collection of Irish folklore *The Celtic Twilight* was published in 1893. Most Protestants, however, felt threatened and alienated by the rise of a nationalism that was intolerant of their cultural identity, and their support for Unionism grew rapidly in the later nineteenth century. Increasingly Protestants began to identify themselves as British rather than Irish. By the early twentieth century Protestants were even stockpiling weapons in order to resist home rule by force. Sinn Féin's sweeping victories in the 1918 elections on a ticket of complete independence and the Anglo-Irish war (1919–21) that followed made the continuance of British rule untenable. To avert the threat of armed Unionist resistance to a settlement with the nationalists, the British government decided upon the partition of Ireland. The greater part of Ireland achieved independence as the Irish Free State (now the Republic of Ireland) in 1922 while six counties of Ulster, which had Unionist majorities, formed the province of Northern Ireland and remained part of the United Kingdom. Northern Ireland preserved a fragile stability until Protestant attempts to stifle the Catholic Civil Rights movement led to the outbreak of the inter-communal violence of the 'Troubles' in 1969 from which the province is only now emerging. As the ruling power, the British government must bear the largest share of the responsibility for the outbreak of the Troubles, but it also deserves to be recognised that it was the failure of nationalism to develop an inclusive Irish identity that set Ireland on the road to partition and that has stood in the way of rapprochement between the country's two traditions ever since.

The Pan-Celtic movement

Recognition by the Celtic-speaking peoples of their linguistic and cultural kinship led in the nineteenth century to the development of the Pan-Celtic movement. Like other similar movements of the period, such as Pan-Slavism and Pan-Scandinavianism, Pan-Celticism promised more than it delivered. The movement grew from the natural desire of Celtic speakers to feel that they had allies in their struggles to maintain their cultures, languages and identities, but it never developed into a successful international political movement. Symptomatic of this failure was the lack of interest shown in the movement by the government of the Irish Free State after its creation in 1922. Nor did the professions by idealistic activists of pan-Celtic friendship mean that Irish emigrants to Scotland and Wales met with a warm welcome from their fellow Celts. They did not.

The beginnings of Pan-Celticism may be discerned in the 1820s in the cooperation between the Welsh scholar Thomas Price and the Breton Jean-François le Gonidec to produce a translation of the Bible into Breton. From 1834 the annual eisteddfod at Abergavenny became a favoured meeting place for scholars from Wales, Brittany and other Celtic countries. From this grew the first Pan-Celtic Congress, held at Abergavenny in 1838. In 1864 Charles de Gaulle (the uncle of the French president Charles de Gaulle) published a work calling for the establishment of an annual Celtic Congress, the development of a common Celtic language and, ultimately, a federation of independent Celtic countries. After some false starts, de Gaulle's call for an annual Celtic Congress was fulfilled in 1899 but the rest of his vision remains as far away as ever.

The Bretons have been the most enthusiastic pan-Celticists. As the most isolated of the Celtic-speaking peoples, and the ones facing the greatest degree of government hostility, their need to feel that they have allies in the struggle to preserve their culture and identity is understandable. The discriminatory laws passed by the Directory in 1794 remained in force as late as the 1950s and the government is still hostile to any kind of special status for Brittany. The indivisibility of the republic remains a potent ideology in French government circles. Even the very limited devolution granted to Corsica in 2000 led to ministerial resignations. Pan-Celtic links were, perhaps, most important for Brittany in the immediate aftermath of the Second World War. During the German occupation of France, small numbers of Breton nationalists collaborated with the enemy in the hopes of winning self-government. Minor though it was compared with that which went on in the rest of France, this collaboration provided the excuse for the post-war French government to attempt to suppress the Breton movement as a whole. Pan-Celtic links provided observers for the trials of activists, a refuge for exiles in Ireland, and support for the re-establishment of the Breton movement in the 1960s. The Bretons' quest for a measure of self-government continues.

15

THE CELTIC DIASPORA

We performed, with much activity, a dance which, I suppose, the emigration from Sky has occasioned. They call it America. *Each of the couples, after the common involutions and evolutions, successively whirls round in a circle, till all are in motion; and the dance seems intended to shew how emigration catches, till a whole neighbourhood is set afloat.*

James Boswell, *Journal of a Tour to the Hebrides with Samuel Johnson* (1785)

There are today on every continent people who regard themselves as Celts or who at the very least are proud to claim a Celtic ancestry. The Celtic identity has been globalised as a result of the worldwide emigration of millions of Irish, Scottish Highlanders, Welsh, Bretons, Cornish and Manx over the last four centuries. Although it is convenient to call this remarkable mass movement the Celtic diaspora it is a moot point how many of these emigrants actually consciously regarded themselves as Celts – probably, before the later nineteenth century at any rate, very few of them indeed because the revival of Celtic identity was still confined largely to an educated elite. However, the emigrant communities formed by this movement, to a greater or lesser extent, resisted complete assimilation by their host communities and maintained family and cultural ties with their homelands. These ties ensured that as consciousness of Celtic identity was popularised in the Celtic countries in the later nineteenth and twentieth centuries it would also spread widely abroad.

Although most emigrants eventually achieved significantly higher standards of living than they would have enjoyed had they stayed at home, emigration from the Celtic countries is nearly always portrayed in a negative light as enforced exile from the homeland with emigrants playing the role of victims of hunger or oppression. Although many emigrants from the Celtic countries had little choice in the matter, in reality most were not desperate refugees but modestly ambitious people who saw an opportunity to make a better life for themselves and their families. The negative image of the Celtic diaspora has come about mainly because of the prominent place that events such as the Irish Famine and the Highland Clearances have achieved in folk history. Traumatic events provide comfortably simple explanations for far from simple phenomena. The Celtic diaspora is often thought of as a largely nineteenth-century phenomenon, but it continued for much of the twentieth century. Emigration from Scotland actually reached its peak as late as the 1920s and it is only in the last few years, with the development of the booming 'Celtic Tiger' economy, that Ireland has ceased to be an exporter of population.

The worldwide diaspora of Celtic peoples was a by-product of English and, to a lesser extent, French colonial expansion. In the sixteenth century the French and English watched the growth of the Spanish and Portuguese New World empires with undisguised envy and determined to emulate them if they could. Both countries made more or less disastrous attempts to found colonies in the New World in the sixteenth century, but it was not until the early seventeenth century that either enjoyed any success, the French in Canada and the Caribbean, the English in New England, Virginia and the Caribbean. By 1700 England and France had laid the foundations of global empires and the rivalry between them had become intense. Between 1689 and 1815 England (Great Britain from 1707) and France fought their 'Second Hundred Years War'. Though it lost its 13 most populous American colonies along the way, Britain emerged victorious to enjoy a century of global dominance. Commerce and sea power contributed greatly to this success, but the key factor was England's success as an exporter of population. In 1700 England had a colonial population approaching half a million compared with a home population of 5,000,000; France, with a home population of 20,000,000, had only 70,000 colonial subjects. This disparity became steadily greater in the course of the eighteenth century. When France ceded Canada to Britain in 1763 it had a population of only 60,000 Europeans – by this time Britain's North American colonies had a population of 2,000,000 Europeans, fully one quarter of the home population. Emigration surged in the nineteenth century: around 17,000,000 people left the British Isles, a little over half of whom came from Ireland, Scotland and Wales.

Welsh and Breton pioneers

The Welsh and the Bretons were active in the European colonisation of North America from the outset. The Catholic church's prohibition against eating meat on Fridays ensured that medieval Europe supported a thriving trade in salted and dried fish. By the fifteenth century ships from Brittany, the Basque country and the English West Country port of Bristol were pushing further and further out into the Atlantic in search of new fishing grounds. These seafarers regarded their discoveries as commercially sensitive information and did not publicise them, but there are hints in contemporary documents that ships from Bristol had already sighted the North American coast by the 1480s: certainly something was in the air. Bristol was a convenient base for many Welsh ship owners, the most prominent of whom was John Thloyde (Lloyd), who was described as the 'most expert shipmaster of all England'. In 1466 Thloyde made a mysterious voyage to 'exterior parts' and in 1480 he spent nine weeks on the open sea searching unsuccessfully for 'the island of Brasil to the west of Ireland'. Another Welshman who sponsored voyages of exploration from Bristol was the merchant and customs officer Richard Amerike (i.e. ap Meurig). Amerike was a patron of the Italian navigator John Cabot's voyages to Newfoundland and it is just possible that it was for him, rather than the better-known Amerigo Vespucci, that America was named. John Dee, Elizabeth I's Welsh astrologer and latter-day Merlin, later popularised stories of even earlier Welsh voyages to the New World, by the legendary Prince Madog *c*. 1180 and earlier still by King Arthur, as a way of legitimising his queen's territorial claims there. It was also Dee who first coined the term 'British Empire', though he was of course thinking of the ancient Britons. There was also an unsuccessful attempt to found a 'New Wales' in Newfoundland by Robert Vaughan of Llangyndeyrn between 1616 and 1632.

Soon after John Cabot discovered the Grand Banks in 1496, fishermen from St Malo in Brittany, as well as from England, Spain and Portugal, began to cross the Atlantic to exploit their astonishingly abundant stocks of cod. The shoals were so vast that it was said that the tightly packed cod could be caught simply by lowering a basket into the sea. Those medieval fishermen would find it hard to believe that their modern descendants had fished the Grand Banks' cod to extinction. Though the Bretons preferred to fish well offshore, like fishermen from other countries, they sometimes set up temporary summer camps on the coast of Newfoundland for ship repairs or for drying and salting fish to preserve it for the long trip home. The Breton navigator Jacques Cartier was undoubtedly exploiting the geographical knowledge of Breton fishermen when he discovered and explored the Gulf of St Lawrence in 1534–6. Cartier led the first French attempt to found a permanent colony in the New World in 1541–3 and, though it failed, Breton ships continued to sail to the St Lawrence to fish and trade for furs with the Iroquois Indians for the rest of the century. After the settlement of 'New France' began with the foundation of Quebec in 1608, Bretons became the first emigrants from the Celtic countries to live permanently in the New World. Bretons even continued to emigrate to Quebec after the British conquered it in 1759, but in the nineteenth century it was the USA that became the favoured destination of Breton emigrants. The Industrial Revolution led to a collapse of the rural textile industry in Brittany and emigration increased dramatically in the nineteenth century. In the century between 1851 and 1951 over a million Bretons left, equivalent to a third of the population.

Scots and Irish already numbered among England's colonial subjects by the end of the seventeenth century. Some of them were the descendants of Scots and Irish prisoners of war transported to the West Indies and Virginia by Parliament during the civil wars. Others were Catholic Irish displaced by the Jacobean plantations who had settled in the West Indies as indentured servants of English planters – many of them later left for Maryland after it introduced toleration for Catholic worship in 1649. Scots merchants and planters were settled on Barbados and Scottish courts often transported criminals to English colonies, which welcomed the cheap labour. Scottish Presbyterians emigrated to South Carolina and New Jersey, to escape the religious oppression of their own government. However, before the Act of Union in 1707, Scots who wished to emigrate had tended to favour the Baltic, for its commercial opportunities, or Ulster, for land. Scotland's two attempts at founding colonies of its own were failures. An early seventeenth-century settlement in Nova Scotia fell foul of Anglo-French rivalry in the region, while an attempt to found a colony at Darien in Panama in 1698–9 was a disaster that almost bankrupted the country and paved the way for the union with England. However ambiguous Scots felt about the union, it did at least give them equal access to the British Empire. Proportionate to their numbers, the Scots proved to be even more enthusiastic imperialists than the English. Throughout the eighteenth and nineteenth centuries, Scots wholeheartedly participated in the British Empire, whether as settlers, merchants, colonial administrators, missionaries, engineers or soldiers.

It would be simplistic to present all Scottish emigration as Celtic emigration. It is not the case that even today all Scots would regard themselves as Celts, and before the mid nineteenth century the cultural divide between the Anglophone Lowlands and Gaelic-speaking Highlands was a sharp one. And before the nineteenth century it was from the Lowlands that most Scottish emigrants came. Given the cultural differences, it is not surprising that Lowland and Highland emigration differed in nature. Lowlanders were more individualistic and were generally seeking improved personal career opportunities, much like English emigrants in fact. Highlanders were much more likely to emigrate in family or community based groups, often trying to transplant their communal way of life to a new country. The unique character of Highland emigration was a result of the Clearances, which uprooted entire communities in the name of agricultural modernisation.

The Highland Clearances

The Clearances were part of the wider process of the commercialisation of agriculture throughout western Europe in the early modern period, which saw millions of peasants forced off the land. This process had begun in England in the sixteenth century with the enclosure of common land and the consolidation of scattered holdings into larger units. Those displaced from the land drifted to the towns, where they became the cheap labour of the Industrial Revolution, or they emigrated to the colonies. Highland landowners were not ignorant of developments in England but the particular social and political circumstances of the Highlands did not favour their adoption before the '45. Clan chiefs needed tenants for their private armies. Tenants owed military service, hence the more tenants a chief had, the bigger his private army and the more powerful and influential he was. When Duke John II of Argyll began to reduce the number of tenants on his estates in the 1730s he was held to have weakened the military and political influence of his clan, the Campbells, and he found few imitators.

The traditional system of tenure was rendered obsolete when the Highlands were finally brought firmly under central government control in the aftermath of the '45. Deprived of their private jurisdictions and feudal rights, clan chiefs began to reject their traditional responsibilities to junior clan members and became simply ordinary landowners, determined to raise the maximum possible income from their estates. The first tenants to go were the tacksmen. Tacksmen were clan gentry who acted as the chieftain's military lieutenants, leasing land (tacks) from the chief and subletting it at a higher rate to peasant farmers who served under him in wartime. The days of private warfare being over, they could be dispensed with as unnecessary and expensive middlemen and they were forced out by steep rent increases. Many decided to emigrate to the North American colonies and were often able to persuade their communities to go with them with the promise of freehold land for all. North Carolina, which had a Scots governor, was probably the most popular destination for Highlanders before the American War of Independence broke out in 1776. It was emigration of this sort that the Lowlander James Boswell recorded in his journal of his Highland tour with Dr Johnson in 1773. During their tour Boswell and Johnson met Flora MacDonald, already a romantic heroine, who emigrated to North Carolina with her husband in 1774. Both, surprisingly perhaps, were Loyalists during the War of Independence. Flora returned to Scotland in 1779, her husband two years later after a period of imprisonment by the revolutionaries. This wholesale emigration was neither encouraged nor welcomed either by landowners, who resented the loss of tenants, or by the government, which resented the loss of highly valued Highland recruits for the army. After American independence, the government changed its tune and began to encourage emigration to Canada, whose sparse population made it vulnerable to American attack.

The introduction of the Cheviot sheep to Perthshire from the Borders in 1765 provided a further stimulus to emigration. In the later years of the eighteenth century it became more and more common for landowners to restructure their estates to create large single-tenant sheep farms. This led to the large-scale eviction of farming tenants and their resettlement in planned villages – most of them on the coast – where they were expected to make a living from crofting, fishing and kelping (making fertiliser from potassium-rich seaweed). The most reviled figure of the Clearances is without doubt George Granville Leveson-Gower, the duke of Sutherland, who cleared almost the entire population of eastern Sutherland, some 10,000 people, to villages on the coast between 1812 and 1820, leaving the interior of the county a depopulated wilderness for sheep. The cynical treatment of the cleared tenants, who were given crofts that were too small

Plate 34 Farewell messages from evicted crofters, Croik church, Glencalvie, Easter Ross (1845)

Source: John Haywood

for subsistence, so forcing them also to labour on the duke's estates, only added to their bitterness. Landlords frequently faced resistance from tenants. In one of the most serious incidents, in 'the Year of the Sheep' (1792), troops were called in to Kildermorie in Easter Ross after tenants repeatedly drove the landowner's sheep off the hills. Widespread discontent with the new arrangements meant that the flow of emigrants continued. Landlords continued to do their best to discourage emigration and successfully lobbied for the introduction of the Passenger Act in 1803, which forced up the cost of emigration by imposing new regulations on shipping lines. Despite emigration the overall Highland population was rising rapidly, in large part because of the introduction of the potato and of health care improvements, such as inoculation for smallpox.

The landlord-driven emigration that has become so notorious in Highland folk memory began only after the end of the Napoleonic Wars in 1815. Imports of cheaper fertilisers, such as guano, made kelping uneconomic. Soon after, wool prices began to decline because of competition from Australia and, later, New Zealand. The economy suffered a further blow in the 1840s when potato blight brought famine to the Highlands. Fortunately, Highland crofters had not become so absolutely dependent on the potato as the Irish peasantry, and government aid was more forthcoming, so, though there was much hardship and hunger, there were few deaths. Faced with rapidly declining income from rents, Highland landowners decided that emigration was not such a bad thing after all. Landlords and colonial organisations introduced various schemes to assist surplus and impoverished tenants to emigrate. Varying degrees of compulsion were used. John Gordon of Cluny was one landowner who became notorious for the violence used against his Hebridean tenants to force them to emigrate. From the late 1830s land sales in Australia were used to fund the emigration of 5,000 Highlanders to New South Wales. The passage of another 5,000 to South Australia, Victoria and Tasmania was funded by the Highland and Island Emigration Society in the 1850s. New Zealand was also a popular destination for Scots emigrants but relatively few of them were Highlanders. Emigration schemes usually allowed families and communities to emigrate together – persuading Highlanders to emigrate would have been difficult otherwise – but when they arrived in Australia settlement agencies made no attempts to keep communities together by making collective land grants. Highland settlers were dispersed among the wider population, and without supportive communities Gaelic culture and language did not long survive.

Because it was relatively accessible and cheap to reach, Canada was the most important destination for Highland emigrants after the American colonies became independent. The most important settlements were in southern Ontario, especially Glengarry County, Prince Edward Island, and on Cape Breton Island and around Pictou and Antigonish in Nova Scotia. Whether they organised emigration themselves, or were funded by a landowner, because Highlanders emigrated and settled in community groups and subsequently helped finance the emigration of family members who

Plate 35 Abandoned crofts at Lonbain, Wester Ross

Source: John Haywood

had been left behind (this is known as chain migration), they formed distinctive and enduring Gaelic-speaking communities in Canada, and even today it is claimed that there are more speakers of Gaelic in Canada than there are in Scotland itself. Though Gaelic was in decline in Ontario by the 1880s and Cape Breton by the 1930s, Gaelic musical traditions remain strong as do other manifestations of the modern Scottish Highland identity. A Gaelic college at St Anns, Cape Breton, promotes Highland culture and traditions.

The Wild Geese

In contrast to Scotland, early emigration from Ireland was motivated mainly by political and religious reasons. Beginning with the defeat of the Desmond rebellion in 1583, Irish refugees fled to Spain and Portugal. Some served in the Spanish Armada of 1588. Thousands fought for Spain in Flanders during the Thirty Years War. Owen Roe O'Neill and many who fought for the Confederate Catholics in the civil wars of the 1640s gained their military experience this way. By 1649 Tyrone's regiment, formed in 1605, claimed to have suffered over 12,000 casualties in the service of Spain, most of them in battle. Throughout the seventeenth century a steady stream of exiles had made their way to the continent to serve in the Spanish, French and Austrian armies. Smaller numbers went to Bavaria and Russia. The flow increased after the Cromwellian conquest and again after the Irish Jacobites were defeated in the Williamite War (1689–91). The English government did nothing to impede the flow of battle-hardened malcontents out of Ireland: it was glad to be rid of them and helped them on their way, allowing passage through England or even providing ships, as the Williamites did. Jacobite sympathisers, many of them from Munster, headed south to join *Na Géanna Fiáine* (the 'Wild Geese'), as the Irish brigades in the service of Spain and France had become known. Motivated by the desire to fight the English and restore the Stuart dynasty, the Wild Geese distinguished themselves in many battles. Their most notable action was at Fontenoy (near Tournai in modern Belgium) in 1745, when a dramatic charge by the Irish brigades defeated British and Hanoverian troops under the duke of Cumberland. Ironically, the victory helped persuade Charles Edward Stuart to launch his ill-fated attempt to overthrow the Hanoverian dynasty later that year. It was 400 men of France's Irish Brigade who provided the most professional unit of Charles Edward's army and it was the one that fought hardest at Culloden.

Some Irish exiles rose high in foreign service: The Jacobite Charles Wogan became governor of La Mancha, and Alexander O'Reilly, who joined Spain's Hibernia regiment as a teenager, became the military governor of New Castile (Venezuela). Sometimes, changing political circumstances allowed military exiles to return – as happened after the restoration of Charles II – while those who settled overseas permanently did not form long-lasting Irish communities but integrated into local society (it did not help that most emigrants were male). Cambrai, Graz and Prague were known as popular retirement places for Irish officers. Later in the eighteenth century the British government began to discourage foreign recruitment in Ireland, since it needed the manpower for its own forces, and this together with a relaxing of discrimination against Catholics (after 1793 Catholics were allowed to hold commissions), and the availability of British colonies and the USA for emigration, led to the decline (but not the end) of the tradition of military emigration.

Emigration from Ireland increased steadily in the eighteenth century as around 250,000 Presbyterian Ulster Scots, disillusioned with the Anglican establishment and high rents, chose to leave for Britain's North American colonies. With their ideals of self-reliance and hard work and their ready-made frontier mentality, the contribution of Ulster Scots to the founding values of the United States was immense, yet today the Irish-American identity is overwhelmingly a Catholic one. Partly this has to do with numbers: Catholic Irish emigrants eventually greatly outnumbered Protestant ones. Mainly it has to do with alienation: Catholic Irish emigrants met the same discrimination in Protestant America that they had experienced at home. While Protestant Irish immigrants integrated easily into a society they had helped shape, Catholic Irish immigrants could not and, eventually, did not want to.

The impact of the Great Famine

Despite their economic and political marginalisation, there were by the beginning of the nineteenth century more Gaelic speakers in Ireland than at any time in its history. The rapid spread of potato cultivation in the eighteenth century led to a population explosion. In the 50 years before 1841 Ireland's population more than doubled, from around four million to 8.2 million. The potato's high nutritional content and ability to thrive even in wet infertile soils made it an ideal staple crop for poor peasant farmers. A family could be supported on the produce of tiny plots. Visitors noticed how healthy and well nourished even the poorest Irish peasant families appeared despite otherwise living in conditions of extreme material poverty. These impressions are confirmed by British military records of the period, which show that Irish recruits to the army were on average taller than their more urbanised English counterparts, who lived in unhealthy slums and whose food was often adulterated by profiteering merchants. While landowners ensured that the best land continued to be devoted to grain production and stock rearing, most of it destined for export to Britain, they were happy to encourage peasant farmers to take out tenancies on more and more marginal land. Lazy beds (artificial raised ridges of soil used for cultivation in Ireland since the Neolithic) spread onto the edges of bogs and up mountainsides. Maintaining the lazy beds was labour intensive, but this was not a problem with a rapidly growing population and the yield, by area, was three times higher than that of ploughed land.

Ireland developed a bizarre population distribution whereby it was the less fertile areas, especially in the west in Connacht and Munster, which were the most densely populated ones.

A long agricultural depression followed the end of the Napoleonic Wars in 1815. Declining prices forced poor tenants further into dependence on the potato as they needed to sell all of their more valuable cash crops such as oats to pay their rents. Cattle were simply beyond the means of most of the peasantry and milk, butter and cheese vanished from their diet. The decline of stock rearing contributed to an increasing reliance on a single strain of potato, the Lumper, which flourished in poor soils and needed little manuring but was watery and nutritionally inferior. One observer noted that the 'Lumper is not indeed human food at all. Mix them with any other kind of potato and lay them before a pig, and she will not eat one of them until all the good kind are devoured.' By the 1830s over 3,000,000 people, one third of Ireland's population, relied on potatoes for 90 per cent of their calorie intake. The growing dependence on the potato was watched with concern by the government, which saw quite clearly that failure of the crop would lead to famine – potatoes can be stored for about nine months at most, so farmers were unable to build up stocks in the good years against years of shortages.

In June 1845 potato blight broke out in Belgium where it is thought to have been introduced in a cargo of fertiliser from South America. The disease quickly spread across Europe: it reached Ireland in September of that year. The disease – a fungal infection that rots tubers in the ground – took Europe by surprise. Perhaps it ought not to have done, as it had been raging in North America since 1843. Potatoes were an important crop for peasant farmers in many areas of Europe and the blight brought hunger to thousands in the Low Countries, Germany, Switzerland and Scotland but nowhere was the dependence as absolute as it was in Ireland. Initial assessments suggested that 80 per cent of the Irish crop would be lost in 1845. When the loss turned out to be only half that, most people thought that the worst was already over. When the crop failed again the next year, hunger turned to starvation for millions. Exactly how many people died in the six years before the potato crop recovered is not known; most estimates are in the range of 500,000 to one million with the higher figure being perhaps the more likely. Mortality was highest in those areas dominated by clachans (nucleated groups of farmhouses where landholding was organised communally): contagious diseases spread more quickly through their densely packed inhabitants, already weakened by starvation. In some areas of Connacht and Munster an estimated 25 per cent of the population died during the famine.

It might be thought that the government of the United Kingdom, then the world's wealthiest country, could have intervened to mitigate the effects of the potato blight, but it was wedded to the ideologies of Malthusianism and *laissez-faire* capitalism. The British government believed that overpopulation was the root cause of Ireland's problems so the outbreak of potato blight and the resulting famine was seen as a necessary, even a welcome,

Plate 36 Starving Irish peasants clamour at the gates of a workhouse
Source: Getty Images/Hulton Archive

corrective which would in due course lead to a more prosperous, economically modern country as soon as the population had fallen to a level deemed to be in balance with the available resources. Food aid and a ban on food exports were also opposed on free trade grounds, as it was feared that these would undermine prices and put Irish farmers unaffected by the blight out of business, so reducing the country's food production even more. Apologists for the British government argue that it lacked the resources and expertise to have provided effective famine relief, even had it wanted to, but the sad fact is that it had both. On the one occasion that the government did intervene on a large scale, in the summer of 1847, it set up a system of soup kitchens that fed over three million people daily. Though the nutritional quality of the meals was often poor, the rate of mortality was considerably reduced. Had even this parsimonious system been set up in 1846 and maintained until potato crops recovered in 1852, most of the mortality of the famine could surely have been prevented, as it was in Scotland. Amazingly, in 1846 Ireland was even denied grain imports until Scotland had been supplied. Mass starvation was unacceptable in Britain but it was in Ireland. Although Ireland had been a part of the United Kingdom since 1801, the British government still regarded it as a colony, not an equal partner entitled to a share of the national wealth in time of need. Even though Ireland contained over a quarter of the United Kingdom's population, government spending on famine relief never exceeded a derisory 0.3 per cent of the gross national product. No wonder, then, that the memory of the famine brought a new and lasting bitterness to Anglo-Irish relations. However, that was for the future: the immediate reaction of its victims was to interpret the famine in religious terms. There had been such good harvests in the preceding years that large quantities of surplus potatoes had simply been dumped and left to rot. The blight was God's punishment on a wasteful people.

The tradition of exile

In Irish and, especially, Irish-American tradition the famine has come to be seen as the main cause of the mass emigration and depopulation which Ireland experienced in the nineteenth century. But does the famine, traumatic though it was, really deserve this reputation? Certainly, between the censuses of 1841 and 1851 the Irish population dropped by about 20 per cent and in the seven years that the potato blight continued (1845–52) some one and a half million people emigrated from Ireland. There can be no doubt that the immediate impact of the famine was dramatic. Yet mass emigration continued until the outbreak of the First World War in 1914, by which time the Irish population was only 4.4 million. Clearly, the famine cannot be the sole, or even the major cause of *sustained* Irish emigration.

In fact emigration was already increasing in the 1820s and 1830s. This can be linked to the collapse of Irish rural industries (especially woollen textiles) in the face of competition from the fast-growing textile manufacturing centres of northern England and Ulster. It is estimated that, in a third of Irish counties in 1821, more people were engaged in manufacturing, trade and crafts than in farming: the impact of de-industrialisation in terms of lost employment opportunities was therefore enormous. It is also significant that, while Ireland's population as a whole declined, that of the poorest west coast districts, where smallholders were most dependent on the potato crop, actually increased in the 30 years after the famine. Only in the 1880s, after another succession of bad harvests, did mass emigration from these areas begin. It is therefore apparent that changing patterns of land-holding also influenced emigration. Emigration was higher from the fertile and intensively farmed east because land was scarce. In the west, because of the thousands of evictions of destitute tenants that had happened during the famine, land – poor land – was available in abundance. Once land became more difficult to obtain in the west, emigration increased. It would seem, then, that lack of opportunities in industry and agriculture were the real reasons for sustained emigration in the nineteenth century.

There is also the question why such a high proportion of Irish emigrants went to the USA. At first sight it appears obvious that there was a strong and sustained desire to escape British oppression, a belief which nineteenth-century US government and Irish nationalist propaganda deliberately encouraged. Again things were not so simple. The overriding importance of a desire for liberty seems dubious in view of the fact that both before the famine and throughout the twentieth century Britain was the most popular destination for Irish emigrants, and even in the second half of the nineteenth century it was the second most popular destination after the USA. The fact that the Catholic Irish were not exactly welcomed with open arms in Protestant America also argues against the primacy of this motive. More important than this, 1840s Britain was suffering from a serious industrial recession, encouraging emigrants to take the more expensive option of going to America where employment opportunities were better. Money sent back home by migrants to their relatives subsequently funded a self-sustaining chain of emigration that continued for the rest of the nineteenth century.

A key part of the Irish attitude to the experience of emigration has been to treat it as exile, rather than as a search for better opportunities. This is why the famine is so central to the Irish-American identity. Why is this when it is clear that neither the famine nor British rule was the main cause of Irish emigration? Emigration is for most people a great emotional wrench: it involves severing close relationships, abandoning parents and other elderly relatives, sometimes never to see them again, engendering intense feelings of guilt. By seeing their experience as a continuation of the seventeenth- and eighteenth-century tradition of going into exile for political reasons and blaming the British for forcing their decisions on them, Irish emigrants were more easily able to come to terms with actions that might otherwise have seemed rather selfish.

Saving Welsh

Wales did not experience the same degree of emigration and depopulation as Ireland and Scotland. Quantifying emigration from Wales is difficult as, after the Acts of Union, it ceased to have any separate legal identity from England and no separate statistics were kept. However, it was certainly much lower per head of population than either Scotland or Ireland. Economic change in the Welsh countryside was a gradual process, without the cataclysmic discontinuities of plantations, clearances and famine. As was happening in England at the same time, the enclosure of common lands was driving small farmers off the land, but the losses of rural opportunities were more than compensated for by the rapid industrialisation of the coalfield areas of south and north-east Wales which began in the eighteenth century. Wales became a land of opportunity that attracted hundreds of thousands of English immigrants in the nineteenth century. The South Wales coalfield area experienced an economic boom (as to a lesser extent did the smaller North Wales coalfield) and rapid urban growth, fuelled by a rapidly increasing birth rate, inward migration from the English Midlands, Cornwall and Ireland, and English financial investment. The population of Wales more than doubled between 1770 and 1851, increasing from around 500,000 to 1,163,000, and it had more than doubled again by 1914. Despite the abundance of opportunities at home, there were those who emigrated because they thought they could do better abroad. The skills of Welsh miners and iron workers were especially in demand in the USA as it began to industrialise in the second half of the nineteenth century. A period of aggressive enclosure of common lands, which mainly benefited major landowners, displaced many peasant farmers from the land during the period of the Napoleonic Wars, fuelling emigration.

The rapid increase in the numbers of English speakers in nineteenth-century Wales began to be seen as a threat to Welsh language, culture and identity. This inspired the most self-consciously Celtic element of the Celtic diaspora – attempts to found Welsh-speaking colonies abroad where Welsh culture could be preserved from Anglicising influences. The first overseas Welsh language communities were founded in North America, such as at Cambria in Pennsylvania and Bangor in Saskatchewan. These settlements proved too successful for their own good because they attracted English-speaking settlers in such large numbers that they soon began to swamp the Welsh speakers. This led to attempts to found colonies outside the English-speaking world, in Russia, Brazil and Argentina. The most successful of these was founded in 1865 in the Chubut valley in Argentinean Patagonia. Of the original 163 settlers only two had any experience of farming and for several years the colony struggled to survive. But survive it did. Beginning in the mid 1870s the colony began to attract new waves of Welsh settlers until by 1914 its population reached about 3,000. Y Wladfa was a completely self-contained Welsh-speaking community, with Welsh the language of chapel, school, business, law and local government. The Argentinean government had promised that it would recognise Y Wladfa ('The Colony') as one of the states of Argentina but this promise was never fulfilled: it was worried that the presence of the Welsh would provide a pretext for British territorial claims in the area. In 1880 the Argentinean government began to assert control over the rather too independent colony, imposing conscription and, in 1896, Spanish as the language of education. At the same time Spanish and Italian settlers flooded into the valley, quickly outnumbering the Welsh. The Welsh language entered a long decline, but there has been a modest revival in the last 20 years. Welsh heritage is celebrated with *eisteddfodau* and the old colony has become something of a tourist attraction. While the Patagonian Welsh may be secure for the immediate future, Y Wladfa is not the New Wales its founders hoped for.

16

THE CELTS TODAY

To many, perhaps to most people outside the company of the great scholars, past and present, 'Celtic' of any sort is . . . a magic bag, into which anything may be put, and out of which anything may come. . . . Anything is possible in the fabulous Celtic twilight, which is not so much a twilight of the gods as of the reason.

J.R.R. Tolkien (1963)

The foundation of the Celtic Congress in 1899 made it necessary formally to ask, who are the Celts and what is a Celtic country? For many, to be a Celt it is necessary to speak a Celtic language, but such a narrow definition would have excluded the Cornish, whose language had become extinct in the eighteenth century. The definition finally settled on, that the Celts are the inhabitants of those countries in which people speak Celtic languages, or have spoken them in recent historic times, is not one that is universally accepted in the countries so defined. By no means all the inhabitants of Scotland, Wales, the Isle of Man, Cornwall, Brittany and Ireland would accept that they are Celts, though it has certainly been part of the agenda of the Pan-Celtic movement to persuade them that they are. The definition also raises the issue of how important language really is to the modern Celtic identity.

The Celtic languages today

Four Celtic languages – Welsh, Breton, and Irish and Scottish Gaelic – are still spoken on an everyday basis today. Two others – Manx and Cornish – which died out in (in terms of Celtic history) relatively recent times, are the subjects of language revival campaigns. The exact number of Celtic speakers is uncertain. Around two and a half million people claim to be able to speak a Celtic language but the number of habitual speakers is certainly very much lower, probably less than 500,000. It is a well-established misconception, deliberately encouraged by nationalists, that the decline of the Celtic languages is due to official persecution by British and French governments. This may have been a factor in the decline of Breton but British governments are guilty mainly of indifference. The real reasons for the decline of the Celtic languages are more complex: emigration, immigration of non-Celtic speakers, lack of social, economic and educational opportunities are all more important than calculated governmental malice. Speaking Welsh in Welsh schools, for example, was punished not by government diktat: it was punished (if it was punished – the practice was not universal) by Welsh-speaking teachers with the support of Welsh-speaking parents who believed, rightly, that fluency in English would give their children better opportunities in life. Similarly, the decline in Gaelic language teaching in the Highlands in the nineteenth century was the result of parental pressure, not government policy.

A key role for persecution as a factor in the decline of the Celtic languages is disproved by the experience of Irish Gaelic. Around 1800 there were probably about four million Gaelic speakers in Ireland but the Famine of the 1840s and the mass emigration that followed began a rapid decline in the second half of the nineteenth century until there were only 55,000 at the time of independence. An important factor in the decline of Gaelic was the reluctance of the Catholic church to sanction the translation of the scriptures into the vernacular: thus Gaelic was never able to become the language of religion in Ireland as Welsh had in Protestant Wales. Many early nationalists, such as Daniel O'Connell (1775–1847), were contemptuous of Gaelic and encouraged Gaelic speakers to learn English, the better to compete with their colonial masters. Following independence, Gaelic became, with English, the official language of the Irish state. *Gaeltachts* (Gaelic-speaking areas) received special status and government subsidy, while Gaelic became a compulsory subject in all schools. The result of this is that, superficially, Irish Gaelic is the most flourishing of the Celtic languages – over 1,400,000 people claim to be able to speak it. The reality is very different. Despite 80 years of government support, Gaelic has experienced an unremitting decline as an everyday spoken language. In 1991 only 22,000 people claimed to be habitual speakers of Gaelic and, according to the most pessimistic estimates, the real figure may be as low as 10,000 (less than 0.3 per cent of the Republic's population). Even in many *Gaeltachts*, habitual Gaelic speakers now make up less than 50 per cent of the population. It is quite possible these days to visit a *Gaeltacht* and not hear Gaelic spoken at all. In surveys, the Irish show a consistently high level of support for Gaelic, and it is clearly an important element of Irish identity, yet this does not translate into a willingness to speak the language. The truth is that, in practice, the Irish are unwilling to forgo the advantages of the English language, which has allowed them very successfully to present their culture to an appreciative worldwide audience.

Scottish Gaelic also continues to decline. The 66,000 speakers in Scotland in 1991 had fallen to 58,000 by 2001, but with nearly 30,000 habitual speakers Scottish Gaelic is in a better state than its Irish counterpart. Despite considerable state support for Gaelic language education, broadcasting and publishing, equivalent to a subsidy of over £500 a year for every Gaelic

Plate 37 'Say no to the language bill!' Welsh language protest at the Welsh Office in 1993

Source: PA Photos

speaker, Gaelic is probably past saving on the Scottish mainland. There remain self-contained Gaelic-speaking communities in the Hebrides where the language may have a viable future. One hopeful sign for the future is the high level of support for Gaelic language education among incomers to the Hebrides, who want their children to be able to integrate into the local community. Gaelic has never been the language of all of Scotland, and enthusiasts for Scots (i.e. the form of English spoken in the Lowlands, the language of Burns' songs and poems) have argued that their language should also receive state recognition and support.

Welsh is undoubtedly the healthiest of the Celtic languages. In absolute terms the numbers of Welsh speakers peaked around 1851, but as a proportion of the total population of Wales they were already in decline. By 1900 only half of the people of Wales were Welsh speakers and by 1991 it was down to around 19 per cent (total speakers 591,000, habitual speakers 326,000). Even so, it is still the dominant language over large areas of rural north, mid and south-west Wales. In the last decade, there have been signs that the decline has been turned around, with a considerable overall increase in numbers of people able to speak some Welsh registered in the 2001 census, up to 797,000 (28 per cent of the population). Much of the credit for this goes to the Welsh nationalist party Plaid Cymru (The Party of Wales), which was founded to campaign on language issues in 1925. The party's campaigning won equal status for Welsh with English in 1967 and many measures supportive of the language have followed, including a Welsh language TV channel and compulsory instruction in the Welsh language in schools in Wales. Bearing in mind the plight of Gaelic in Ireland, however, it remains to be seen whether these achievements will lead to a sustained increase in the use of Welsh as an everyday language. Welsh language teaching has not been universally welcomed. In English-speaking areas, many parents regard Welsh lessons as a politically motivated waste of their children's time.

The state of Breton is the hardest to judge because of the lack of official statistics (a deliberate policy of successive French governments). Because of the demands of Brittany's flourishing tourist industry and the growing monoglot French-speaking population, Breton speakers habitually only use their language privately, when among family and friends. Visitors, especially to the towns and the beautiful coastal areas, now rarely hear Breton spoken in public. While it is believed that a majority of adults living in rural areas west of Vannes and St Brieuc have some knowledge of Breton, the language is spoken habitually only in six or seven isolated pockets. In the early 1990s there were an estimated 660,000 Breton speakers but perhaps as few as 100,000 of these were habitual speakers. While there are now greater opportunities for education in Breton, there is no sign of the language's decline being arrested.

Cornish and Manx Gaelic became extinct only in recent historical times, the last native Cornish speaker dying in 1891, the last native Manx speaker as recently as 1974. Both languages are the subjects of ongoing revival campaigns but the number of people who have attained proficiency in them is very small, perhaps less than a hundred. Cornish never became a true literary language and knowledge of its grammar, syntax and vocabulary is incomplete. 'Revived Cornish' is actually a synthetic language, containing elements borrowed from Breton and Welsh. The majority of the populations of the Isle of Man and Cornwall are now of English extraction and the idea that Manx and Cornish can be restored as everyday languages is surely a romantic fantasy. Realistically, their future is probably as 'hobby languages' for enthusiasts. Although Cornish did receive government recognition in 2002, its use on road signs and such like will be little more than a gimmick intended to appeal to tourists.

The long-term future for the Celtic languages must be at best uncertain; only Welsh seems really secure. Language campaigners persist in believing that the decline of the Celtic languages can not only be halted but also reversed, even that they may become truly national languages again. To support their belief, they point to the successful revival of Hebrew in modern Israel after it had been extinct as a spoken language for over 2,000 years. But the circumstances are hardly comparable. Israel was a nation of immigrants from many different countries who did not share a common language. Everybody, therefore, had an interest in learning Hebrew. Modern Celts, however, have no such incentive as they all, whether they speak a Celtic language or not, also speak English or French. People will certainly continue to learn the Celtic languages as a way to better understand and to express their commitment to their cultural identity but, in practice, how many of them will invest the considerable effort required to attain true fluency in a language for which they will have little everyday use?

For some, a Celt is essentially someone who speaks a Celtic language. For them, the future survival of the Celts depends upon the survival of their languages: if the languages become extinct, then so will the Celts. Such a view seems overly pessimistic. It is increasingly clear that most modern Celts attach as much or greater importance to other cultural, political and historical aspects of identity as they do to language. The Celtic identity is developing independently of its linguistic roots and is still spreading and winning new converts. A case in point is the remarkable example of the growth of Celtic identity in Galicia in north-west Spain, which owes nothing to the Celtic languages. Modern Galician Celts argue that folklore, building traditions, costumes, folk music and social values are just as valid a basis for a Celtic identity as language. Although the Celtic Congress turned down Galicia's application for membership, on the grounds that Celtic languages have been extinct there for nearly 2,000 years (Galego, the modern Galician language, is a form of Portuguese), some Galicians claim that their culture is actually more Celtic than that of the recognised Celtic countries.

It is also clear that language issues play little part in the revival of Celtic identity in Cornwall. Despite the very small numbers of people attaining proficiency in Revived Cornish, a recent survey of schoolchildren in the county showed that a third saw themselves as being Cornish rather than English, while a tenth of the population of the county has signed a petition calling for the setting up of a Cornish assembly. Economic grievances, such as high unemployment caused by the decline of traditional industries such as tin mining and fishing, low wages and house prices inflated to unaffordable levels by well-off Londoners looking for holiday homes, are the root cause of this nascent separatism. The revival in 1998 of Cornwall's medieval Stannary parliament, which once governed tin mining in the county, was essentially a publicity stunt to draw attention to the decline of that industry. It is not a truly representative body as only members of the stannary (tin mining district) community can vote and eligibility is based on Cornish descent. Despite this the parliament is claiming a wider campaigning role for itself. In 2001 three stannators (members of the Stannary parliament) stole English Heritage notices from ancient monuments around Cornwall, branding them as evidence of 'English cultural aggression'. When the stannators were eventually caught by a security guard and arrested, the parliament issued a statement describing the thieves as political prisoners. There is also a Cornish nationalist party, Mebyon Kernow: though it was founded in 1951, it has yet to make an electoral breakthrough, suggesting that, while devolution may be an important issue for many Cornish people, nationalism is not.

The growth of Celtic identity in Galicia also highlights one of the main reasons for the wider success of the modern Celtic identity. For Galicians, adopting a Celtic identity is part of their wider struggle to maintain a non-Spanish identity. The Celtic revival of the eighteenth and nineteenth centuries occurred for very similar reasons – the need of marginalised peoples to maintain a separate identity and avoid assimilation by powerful neighbours. The reason that the Celts remain such a potent part of the Welsh, Irish, Scots, Cornish, Manx and Breton identities is that those needs have not gone away. In fact they have intensified. While in 1800 the English made up only half of the population of the British Isles, by 2000 they made up 75 per cent. The Bretons are similarly increasingly outnumbered by the French, even in Brittany. In addition there is the powerful lure of globalised culture which even large nations like the English and French cannot resist. It has been said that what Ireland needs to worry about now is not so much Anglicisation as 'Los Angelisation'. When cultures start to become homogenised, the importance of small differences is magnified. Celtic identity is also being strengthened by wider political developments, such as devolution in the United Kingdom, which saw the opening of a Welsh assembly and a Scottish parliament in 1999, and European Union regional policies, which have allowed minorities in member states to appeal over the heads of central governments for recognition, cultural funding, language support and economic aid. In fact a Celtic past is something that is shared by almost all the countries of the European Union. Could the idea that Europeans are all Celts under the skin one day be promoted as a basis for a common identity? The idea is not so far fetched: it was probably not by accident that a major European Union-sponsored exhibition of Celtic art and archaeology in the early 1990s was subtitled 'The Fathers of Europe'.

New Age Celtomania

Just as the Celtic identity continues to spread, so too does Celtomania. Modern Celtomania is inextricably linked to the growth of the environmental movement, which can be said to have begun with the publication of Rachel Carson's *Silent Spring* in 1962. Carson argued for the protection of the natural environment not only on scientific grounds but on moral grounds also. Drawing on a tradition of American thought going back to Ralph Waldo Emerson, she argued that humanity needed to show more humility before the forces of nature and abandon attitudes that 'supposed that nature exists for the convenience of man'. Carson's scientific arguments convinced governments worldwide to regulate the use of pesticides but her moral arguments had an even wider influence, striking a chord with those who were dismayed by the destruction of the natural environment for gain and the alienation of humanity from nature in the industrial world.

In doing this, she helped give the modern environmental movement its quasi-religious belief that salvation for humanity lies in a harmonious relationship with nature. Allied to other aspects of the social revolution of the 1960s – disaffection of (usually affluent) youth from materialism, rebellion against traditional attitudes to the family, gender relationships, nationalism, militarism and imperialism – this created fertile ground for a resurgence of Celtomania by renewing the appeal of the noble savage (although, unlike in the eighteenth century, the Celts now had to share the role with the American Indian). The positive image of the Celts has also been aided by changes in European values. Since the mass destruction of the world wars of the twentieth century, conquest and empire-building are no longer seen as praiseworthy activities. As 'Europe's beautiful losers' this has given the Celts a certain (and certainly undeserved) aura of moral superiority. It is for these reasons that, despite great advances in the academic study of Celtic history and archaeology, modern Celtomania focuses not so much on the historical Celts as on the romanticised Celts created by the first period of Celtomania.

The most important manifestation of modern Celtomania is an increase in interest in neo-Druidism, Wicca and other pantheistic 'New Age' paganisms, which have a strong emphasis on the need to live in harmony with nature. Though the first neo-Druids of the eighteenth century probably believed that they were reviving an ancient religion, most modern Druids are more realistic about their religion and freely acknowledge its synthetic nature. They would claim no more than that they believe that they are re-creating the spirit of Druidism and, in particular, its respect for nature. Even this requires some large assumptions about ancient sensibilities though. Modern Druidism has no organised theology and no narrowly defined creed to which its followers must subscribe; they may mix and match. Therein lies the appeal of neo-Druidism for those who are at odds with modern materialism but who find organised religion impersonal, unacceptable or simply unbelievable. Such was the popularity of the neo-Druidic solstice celebrations at Stonehenge among the so-called 'New Age Travellers' by the 1990s that the Conservative government of the day, which regarded them as the great unwashed on wheels, somewhat vindictively restricted access to the stones, the justification being to protect them (the restrictions have since been relaxed). It is very easy to be cynical about New Age Celtomania – it has, after all produced some pretty bizarre offshoots, including Celtic tarot, Celtic shamanism, Celtic sex magic and even Celtic tea bag folding – yet its results have been mainly benign, boosting tourism in the Celtic countries and raising awareness of Celtic culture, especially its music and art. Celtomania has, however, also bred an uncritical attitude to Celtic history, so that the enemies of the Celts, be they Romans, Normans, English or whatever, are always 'ruthless' and the Celts are always the innocent victims. This one-dimensional image of the Celts as victims, their own days of aggressive expansionism conveniently forgotten, has often been exploited by nationalists in Wales, Scotland and Ireland, not to mention Hollywood film makers. An extreme example of

Plate 38 The Goddess and the Green Man, a shop in Glastonbury, Somerset, specialising in *wicca* and paganism

Source: John Haywood

this is the way that, during the Troubles, Irish republican terrorist groups, like the Provisional IRA, successfully presented their activities before world opinion as a simple continuation of an age-old struggle of the Celts against English oppression. They gave apparent substance to this claim by not conducting terrorist activities in Wales and Scotland. The political (and financial) benefits to the Republican movement of doing this were considerable. It might be said in passing that the adoption of a decentralised cell structure by the IRA enabled it to maintain a terrorist campaign for 30 years in the face of the vastly superior resources of the British state and it remained, to what we must hope is the end, unbroken. The Celts have also been appropriated by white supremacist groups in the southern states of the USA, such as the League of the South, which claims that the white settlement of the south was essentially Celtic, while that of New England was English. In this scenario the American Civil War becomes an extension of the Anglo-Celtic struggle and the battle of Gettysburg a re-run of Culloden where the dashing freedom-loving Confederate Celts are mown down by the grim Anglo-Yankees. Not all uses of the past are good uses.

Have the Celts got a future?

Despite the decline of the Celtic languages, it might seem that the long-term survival of the Celts is certain. Yet this might not be so. The revival of Celtic identity that began in the eighteenth century was a self-conscious response by the surviving Celtic-speaking peoples to particular circumstances of economic, social and political marginalisation. But identities that are self-consciously adopted can be just as self-consciously abandoned if they are deemed to have become irrelevant or unattractive in changed circumstances. Ireland has been transformed in the last 30 years from one of Europe's most economically backward countries into the prosperous hi-tech 'Celtic Tiger'. Spoken Gaelic is almost extinct, the most popular music is country and western, the Catholic church is steadily losing influence and the country has ceased to be an exporter of population: instead it is having to come to terms with the problems of integrating immigrants from the Third World into what is still a very homogeneous society. Despite its long history of economic migration, Ireland has not proved to be very welcoming to modern-day economic migrants. The other Celtic countries are changing too as they gradually achieve greater political empowerment and economic prosperity and as they become more integrated into the wider European community. Will these changes confirm people in their Celtic identity? Or will they lead people to re-evaluate it? It is not impossible that an identity that is rooted in the Iron Age may one day come to be seen as inappropriate to self-consciously modern, multi-cultural societies. The Celts could, therefore, find themselves relegated to the role of honoured ancestors, as they have been in France. Perhaps the future of the Celtic identity will be more as a personal or cultural identity rather than a national or ethnic identity. This would be singularly appropriate for an identity that has already transcended national boundaries. And what of Celtomania? On the one hand, there seems little prospect that the environmental and social problems that fired modern Celtomania will be resolved soon, but the future will have concerns of its own and they may not be the same as ours. Celtomania is an important prop for the Celtic identity because it creates the popular perception that it is attractive and desirable. Will it diminish the commitment of Celts to their identity if non-Celts become indifferent to it? This may be of particular significance in the Celtic diaspora as a high proportion of those currently acknowledging Celtic roots are actually of mixed descent and could with equal justification claim English, or other European, roots if they wished. The continuing survival of the Celtic identity must therefore be uncertain as it enters its fourth millennium.

Select Bibliography

This is a selective bibliography, limited exclusively to works in English, most of which have been published recently and should be readily available to the non-academic reader. I would like to take the opportunity here to acknowledge, in a general way, my debt to the archaeologists and historians upon whose research this book has been based, and to thank the Department of History at Lancaster University for supporting my work with an honorary research fellowship.

Alcock, L., *Arthur's Britain* (Harmondsworth, 1971)

Arnold, B. and Gibson, D.B. (eds), *Celtic Chiefdom, Celtic State* (Cambridge, 1995)

Audouze, F. and Büschsenschütz, O., *Towns, Villages and Countryside of Celtic Europe* (London, 1991)

Ball, M.J. (ed.), *The Celtic Languages* (London and New York, 1993)

Barber, E.W., *The Mummies of Ürümchi* (London, 1999)

Berresford-Ellis, P., *The Celtic Revolution* (Talybont, 1985)

Black, R., Gillies, G. and Ó Maolalaigh, R., *Celtic Connections, Vol. 1: Language, Literature, Culture, History* (East Linton, 1999)

Broun, D. and Clancy, T.O. (eds), *Spes Scottorum: Hope of Scots* (Edinburgh, 1999)

Carr, G. and Stoddart, S. (eds), *Celts from Antiquity* (Cambridge, 2002)

Chapman, M., *The Celts: The Construction of a Myth* (Basingstoke and London, 1992)

Clyde, R., *From Rebel Hero: The Image of the Highlander 1745–1830* (East Linton, 1995)

Coffey, M. and Golway, T. (eds), *The Irish in America* (London and New York, 2000)

Collis, J., *The European Iron Age* (London, 1984)

Cowan, E.J. and McDonald, R.A. (eds), *Alba: Celtic Scotland in the Medieval Era* (East Linton, 2000)

Craig, D., *On the Crofters' Trail: In Search of the Clearance Highlanders* (London, 1990)

Cunliffe, B., *The Ancient Celts* (London, 1999)

Cunliffe, B., *Facing the Ocean: The Atlantic and its Peoples* (Oxford, 2001)

Cunliffe, B., *Iron Age Communities in Britain* (3rd edn, London and New York, 1991)

Cunliffe, B., *The Oxford Illustrated Prehistory of Europe* (Oxford, 1994)

Curchin, L.A., *Roman Spain: Conquest and Assimilation* (London, 1991)

Davies, J., *The Celts: Prehistory to the Present Day* (London, 2000)

Davies, J., *A History of Wales* (London, 1993)

Davies, R.R., *The First English Empire: Power and Identities in the British Isles 1093–1343* (Oxford, 2000)

Davies, R.R., *The Revolt of Owain Glyn Dwr* (Oxford, 1995)

Davies, W., *Wales in the Early Middle Ages* (London and New York, 1982)

De Paor, M. and L., *Early Christian Ireland* (London, 1965)

Drinkwater, J.F., *Roman Gaul* (London, 1983)

Duffy, S. (ed.), *Atlas of Irish History* (Dublin, 1997)

Dumville, D.N. (ed.), *Saint Patrick* (Woodbridge, 1993)

Durkacz, V.E., *The Decline of the Celtic Languages* (Edinburgh, 1983)

Ellis, S.G., *Ireland in the Age of the Tudors* (London, 1998)

Eluère, C., *The Celts: First Masters of Europe* (London, 1993)

Filip, J., *Celtic Civilisation and its Heritage* (Prague, 1962)

Frere, S., *Britannia* (3rd edn, London, 1987)

Galliou, P. and Jones, M., *The Bretons* (Oxford, 1991)

Grant, A., *Independence and Nationhood: Scotland 1306–1469* (London, 1984)

Green, M.J. (ed.), *The Celtic World* (London and New York, 1995)

Green, M.J., *Exploring the World of the Druids* (London, 1997)

Harvey, D.C. *et al.* (eds), *Celtic Geographies: Old Culture, New Times* (London and New York, 2002)

Haywood, J., *The Historical Atlas of the Celtic World* (London, 2001)

Henig, M., *The Heirs of King Verica: Culture and Politics in Roman Britain* (Stroud, 2002)

James, S., *The Atlantic Celts: Ancient People or Modern Invention?* (London, 1999)

James, S., *Exploring the World of the Celts* (London, 1993)

Jones, M., *The Creation of Brittany* (London, 1988)

Jones, M., *Ducal Brittany* (Oxford, 1970)

King, A., *Roman Gaul and Germany* (London, 1990)

Laing, L., *The Archaeology of Late Celtic Britain and Ireland c. 400–1200 AD* (London, 1975)

Laing, L. and J., *The Picts and the Scots* (Stroud, 1994)

Macinnes, A., *Clanship, Commerce and the House of Stuart* (East Linton, 1996)

McDonald, R.A., *The Kingdom of the Isles: Scotland's Western Seaboard, c. 1100–c. 1336* (East Linton, 1997)

McLynn, F., *The Jacobites* (London and New York, 1985)

Mallory, J.P., *In Search of the Indo-Europeans* (London, 1989)

Maund, K., *The Welsh Kings* (Stroud, 2000)

Megaw, V. and R., *Celtic Art from its Beginnings to the Book of Kells* (rev. edn, London, 2001)

Morris, J., *The Age of Arthur* (London, 1973)

Morris, J.E., *The Welsh Wars of Edward I* (Oxford, 1901, reprint Stroud, 1996)

Ó Cróinín, D., *Early Medieval Ireland 400–1200* (London and New York, 1995)

O'Sullivan, P., *The Meaning of the Famine* (Leicester, 1997)

Otway-Ruthven, A.J., *A History of Medieval Ireland* (2nd edn, London, 1980)

Piggott, S., *The Druids* (rev. edn, London, 1975)

Pittock, M.G.H., *Celtic Identity and the British Image* (Manchester and New York, 1999)

Raftery, B., *Pagan Celtic Ireland: The Enigma of the Irish Iron Age* (London and New York, 1994)

Rankin, D., *Celts and the Classical World* (London, 1987)

Reilly, T., *Cromwell: An Honourable Enemy* (London, 1999)

Renfrew, C., *Archaeology and Language* (London, 1987)

Salway, P., *Roman Britain* (Oxford, 1981)

Simms, K., *From Kings to Warlords* (Woodbridge, 1987)

Smyth, A.P., *Warlords and Holy Men: Scotland AD 80–1000* (London, 1984)

Snyder, A.P., *The Britons* (Oxford, 2003)

Snyder, C.A., *An Age of Tyrants: Britain and the Britons AD 400–600* (Stroud, 1998)

Todd, M., *The Southwest to AD 1000* (London, 1987)

Turvey, R., *The Welsh Princes 1063–1283* (Harlow, 2002)

Walker, D., *Medieval Wales* (Cambridge, 1990)

Webster, B., *Medieval Scotland, The Making of an Identity* (London and Basingstoke, 1997)

Webster, G., *Boudica: The British Revolt against Rome AD 60* (London, 1978)

Wells, P.S., *The Barbarians Speak: How the Conquered Peoples Shaped Roman Europe* (Princeton and Oxford, 1999)

Wells, P.S., *Beyond Celts, Germans and Scythians* (London, 2001)

Whyte, I. and K., *On the Trail of the Jacobites* (London and New York, 1990)

Williams, G., *The Welsh in Patagonia* (Cardiff, 1991)

Williams, R., *The Lords of the Isles* (London, 1984)

Withers, C.W.J., *Gaelic Scotland* (London and New York, 1988)

Index

N.B. *The index lists 'Christianity, Christians' up to the Reformation; after that the index is by denomination (e.g. 'Catholicism, Catholics', 'Nonconformity' etc.).*